ROMANESQUE CHURCHES OF FRANCE

Peter Strafford is a distinguished journalist who worked on *The Times* for more than three decades, including in Paris and Brussels, and was, among other things, the *Times* correspondent in New York for five years and a leader-writer in London commenting on international affairs. His last position was editor of the *Times*'s special reports on foreign countries, many of which he visited himself.

ROMANESQUE CHURCHES OF FRANCE

A Traveller's Guide

by

Peter Strafford

WITH PHOTOGRAPHS BY THE AUTHOR

dlm

First published in 2005
by Giles de la Mare Publishers Limited
53 Dartmouth Park Hill, London NW5 1JD

Reprinted 2010

Typeset by Tom Knott
Maps by John Flower
Printed and bound by CPI Group (UK) Ltd, Croydon, CR0 4YY

A CIP record of this book is available
from the British Library

ISBN 9781900357241 paperback original

for Jackie

*who has given constant support
and encouragement*

Acknowledgements

The photographs are all by Peter Strafford, except for the following, which are by
Joest Martinius, who has kindly given his permission to reproduce them: the tympanum of Neuilly-en-Donjon (page 48), the tympanum of Charlieu priory church
(page 58) and a capital in the abbey church of Vézelay (page 99).

I should also like to make an acknowledgement to the following authors and
publishers for the use of extracts that I have reproduced in my book:

David Watkin, *A History of Western Architecture*, Laurence King, 1986: on Speyer
Cathedral, page 18

Richard Barber, *The Penguin Guide to Medieval Europe*, Penguin Books, 1984:
translation of remarks by St Bernard of Clairvaux, page 33

Annie Shaver-Crandell and Paula Gerson, *The Pilgrim's Guide to Santiago de
Compostela*, Harvey Miller Publishers, 1995: translation on page 40

John Beckwith, *Early Medieval Art*, Thames and Hudson, 1969: on Islamic
influence at Moissac, page 264

Contents

Warning to readers. The bigger churches in this book are usually open every day but are closed for a time at midday. Some of the smaller ones are closed for one or more days a week, depending on the season. Tickets are sometimes required to visit the cloister and other peripheral areas of a church. The necessary information is normally available from the local tourist office.

Glossary

Abacus: strip running along the top edge of a column capital, sometimes carved

Ambulatory: semi-circular walkway round the outside of the choir and behind the altar

Apse: semi-circular extension to a church; usually at the east end

Arcade: continuous line of arches

Arch:

Blind arch: arch without windows

Relieving arch: broad arch that encompasses two or more smaller ones

Transverse arch: arch that supports the main vault, running across the nave

Archivolt: arch set immediately inside another, larger arch; often one of several such internal arches and sometimes carved

Bay: section of the nave consisting of the square or rectangular space formed by four columns or pillars, two on each side

Capital: decorative feature placed at the top of a column and often carved

Chevet: east end of the church as seen from outside, often with an apse and radiating chapels

Choir: part of the central body of the church that lies beyond the nave, or the transept crossing if there is one, and before the altar

Clerestory: uppermost level of the nave walls, usually containing windows

Cornice: overhanging edge of a sloping roof

Crypt: part of the church that is wholly or partly below ground level

Cupola: dome

Engaged column: half-column set into a flat or flattish surface

Flying screen: line of arches that runs above a principal arch of the crossing below the main vault

Gallery: raised section of the church running along the nave and divided from it by arches

Lombard bands: decorative feature consisting of rows of small blind arches divided by vertical pilasters

Mandorla: almond shape within which Christ is often seated in painting or sculpture

Narthex: more or less enclosed area at the western end of some churches

Oculus: circular opening enclosing a window

Pendentive: concave triangle that provides support at each corner for a circular dome built over a square space

Pilaster: column with a square or rectangular cross-section

Squinch: small arched vault that provides support at each corner for a circular dome built over a square space

Transept: transverse part of many churches, built at a right angle to the nave, which it crosses

Transept crossing: space formed by the transept as it crosses the nave

Tribune: raised section in the nave or transept of a church

Triforium: section of nave wall above the main columns and usually marked by arcades

Trumeau: central pier that divides a doorway in two

Tympanum: semi-circular space above a doorway, often filled by sculpture

Vault:

    Barrel vault: round or pointed vault that runs the length of the nave, supporting the roof

    Groin vault: support system for the roof of a bay formed by the intersection of two barrel vaults

    Rib vault: support system for the roof of a bay formed by diagonal weight-bearing ribs

General Introduction

In Britain, the style is known as 'Norman'. But in France, where the Normans came from, it is called *roman*, or 'Romanesque', and it is an architectural style which, while it is found all over western and central Europe, showed French builders to be some of the most innovative of their time.

There are Romanesque buildings – mainly churches – from Scotland to Sicily, and from Ireland to the Czech Republic. One of the greatest of them all, Durham cathedral, is in England. But many of the best are in France. In this book I have set out to describe some of the masterpieces that were built in the various French regions in the course of the eleventh and twelfth centuries, when Romanesque was in its heyday.

It is a particularly attractive style that does not always receive the attention it deserves, partly because it is overshadowed by Gothic, which replaced it in the later Middle Ages. But though Gothic derived directly from Romanesque, being based on technical innovations made by Romanesque architects, the two styles are quite different in spirit, and Romanesque can stand proudly on its own achievements.

It is appealing for the way in which the various parts of the building – the nave, aisles, transept, apse and bell-tower – are combined to form a harmonious whole, both outside and in, and for its use of decoration – sculpture, painting and even mosaics – which is often an integral part. Romanesque draws the eye upward with its naves, transepts and towers; but it does not soar in the way Gothic tends to because the upward movement is balanced by the other parts of the building, all of them clearly presented, and by the relationship between them.

This harmony and balance is found in all Romanesque churches, from tiny chapels to large cathedrals and basilicas. At times the style looks ahead to Gothic, but sometimes, because it draws on the architecture of ancient Rome, it anticipates the Renaissance.

One of its main features is that it invites you not just to look at the building as a whole, but to linger over carefully worked points of detail. It is mostly the

Notre-Dame-la-Grande, Poitiers: the west front (see page 223)

sculpture that survives, but a number of churches still have outstanding Romanesque paintings, and there are a few with mosaics. Such decoration is one of the main attractions of the style for visitors today.

Church building in the Romanesque period coincided with, and was largely responsible for, the re-emergence in western Europe of monumental sculpture, which had been largely forgotten as an art since classical times. Sculpture was created, often on a small scale, for the capitals of columns in churches and cloisters, for doorways and the tympana above them, and for the vast expanses of some western façades.

A list of sculptural masterpieces would include the capitals of Autun, Vézelay and Serrabone, a small church in the Pyrenees, the ornate west fronts of Notre-Dame-la-Grande in Poitiers and St-Gilles-du-Gard, the cloisters of Moissac, Arles and Le Puy-en-Velay, and, above all, the superb tympana of Moissac, Beaulieu-sur-Dordogne, Conques, Vézelay and Autun.

Less painting has survived because it is more vulnerable, but the frescoes that can still be seen in such churches as St-Savin-sur-Gartempe, near Poitiers, and Tavant, near Tours, or in tiny chapels such as Berzé-la-Ville in Burgundy and St-Martin-de-Fenollar in Roussillon, demonstrate the talent of Romanesque artists. There are even fewer mosaics, but those at Ganagobie in Provence and Lescar in the foothills of the Pyrenees show that the skills passed down from Roman times had not been lost.

Of course France as such barely existed in those days. There were more or less autonomous entities such as Normandy, Burgundy, Aquitaine and the county of Toulouse, where the rulers paid scant attention to the kings of the Capetian dynasty, whose power-base was the Ile-de-France. The Capetians had nominal sovereignty over most of what is now France, but at that time they had little real control over what happened outside Paris and the surrounding areas; and some regions, such as Provence, were not even nominally under their authority.

However, this political diversity, coupled with the difficulties of travel, encouraged local originality, so that the main regions produced their own variants of Romanesque; and this is one of the most entrancing aspects of the style. There are big differences between, for instance, the great basilica of St-Sernin in Toulouse, designed to accommodate pilgrims, with its round barrel vault over the nave, Autun cathedral in Burgundy, which was built under the influence of the powerful monastery of Cluny and has a pointed barrel vault, and Angoulême cathedral in south-western France, which has a system of domes over its nave.

The basilica of Vézelay, one of the most beautiful of all Romanesque churches, is also in Burgundy, and it has an unusual arrangement in its nave, with a groin

France

0 miles 100

0 kilometres 160

Jumièges
St-Martin-de-Boscherville
Lessay • Bayeux • Caen • St-Martin-de
Rheims
Morienval

NORMANDY
Mont-St-Michel
PARIS
Marne
Seine
Seine

Chartres •
Vignory

Montoire-sur-le-Loir
Orléans
St-Benoît-sur-Loire

Tours
LOIRE VALLEY
Vézelay
Dijon

Cunault
La Charité-sur-Loire
BURGUNDY
Loire
Autun

St-Jouin-de-Marnes •
Nevers
Tournus

Poitiers •
St-Savin-sur-Gartempe
Paray-le-Monial
Cluny

Aulnay-de-Saintonge
WESTERN FRANCE

Atlantic Ocean

Saintes
Angoulême
Clermont-Ferrand
Lyon

Talmont-sur-Gironde •
St-Nectaire

Périgueux

Bordeaux
Souillac
Dordogne
MASSIF CENTRAL
Le Puy-en-Velay

N
SOUTH-WEST FRANCE
Cahors
Garonne
Lot
Conques

Moissac
Tarn
Ganagobie

St-Guilhem-le-Désert
St-Gilles-du-Gard
Sénanque

Toulouse
PROVENCE
Le Thoronet

Lescar •
CENTRAL PYRENEES
ROUSSILLON & LANGUEDOC
Stes-Maries-de-la-Mer
Arles
Marseille

St-Bertrand-de-Comminges
St-Michel-de-Cuxa
Elne
Rhône

SPAIN
St-Martin-du-Canigou
Mediterranean Sea

ANDORRA

vault over each bay, and round transverse arches that are coloured alternately reddish-brown and white between them. By contrast, the former cathedral of St-Trophime in Arles, in Provence, has an elaborate, classically-influenced western portal but a plain, narrow nave inside, topped by a pointed barrel vault.

What these churches have in common, in the sections that were constructed in the Romanesque period, is a more or less distant link with the architecture of ancient Rome, and a sense of balance and harmony. It is also significant that each one of them has some outstanding sculpture.

The differences between them show how far Romanesque architects had diverged from Roman originals. Romanesque emerged gradually about a thousand years ago at a time when people were finally recovering from the turbulence and poverty of the Dark Ages, and when relatively peaceful conditions enabled them to create the first architectural style to make a lasting impact since the collapse of the Roman Empire.

The architects based themselves on certain features of ancient Roman architecture, and in particular on the Roman basilica with its system of parallel aisles divided by columns. Hence 'Romanesque', a term invented in the early nineteenth century. But so many modifications were made to the basilica form over the centuries, first by the early Christians, and later by the Carolingian architects in the eighth and ninth centuries, that although the Roman architects would have recognized certain elements in Romanesque buildings, they would have been astonished by the scale and sophistication of many of them, and their rich decoration.

The Romanesque builders also drew on a wide range of other cultures – Germanic, Celtic, Byzantine and even Islamic – and these influences can be seen, not merely in the structure of the churches, but in their often prominent sculptural decoration. The tiny chapel of St-Michel-d'Aiguilhe, for instance, which is perched on an outcrop of rock on the outskirts of Le Puy-en-Velay, has a façade that is clearly influenced by the Islamic architecture of southern Spain.

This gives the style a certain exotic appeal. And there are other characteristics that account for the continuing appeal of Romanesque today. Not the least is the fact that Romanesque churches, even the largest of them, achieve a sense of intimacy, of being on a human scale.

Sometimes they are quite dark. The churches and cathedrals of that time often had to be massively built, with thick, solid walls, so that there were not many windows and the ones they had were not big. But even when the churches were dark, which was not always the case, the lighting was subtly contrived; and the impression of solidity was softened partly by the proportions of the buildings and partly by the use of decorative design, both inside and out.

My book is confined to Romanesque churches in France, but it does in fact include many of the best buildings of the period to be found anywhere, and my aim in writing it is to show that although they were created by a very different society from our own, they are readily accessible to us now. They are the products of an age when religion played an enormously important part, and these churches, and the works of art they contain, convey a strong Christian message.

But their appeal is also aesthetic. There are the forms and proportions of the churches, great and small. There is the breathtaking power of the great sculptural ensembles; the mastery of sculpture on a small scale in the column capitals; the haunting quality of the surviving paintings; and, not least, the quirkiness and humour that enliven much of the sculpture.

It was a time when there was widespread illiteracy and most people had little chance to see books, paintings or images of any sort. So the use of sculpture and wall-painting as an integral part of an architectural design must have been not only visually striking but educational, too. Biblical stories were told from both the Old and the New Testament, the lives of saints were recounted, and the terrors of Hell for those who had led a sinful life were vividly depicted.

Not all the subject-matter is of such an improving character, however. The masons seem often to have been given a free hand, and there is extraordinary variety in their work, making this one of the most remarkable features of Romanesque architecture. The subjects of their sculptures range from religious and morally inspiring scenes to horrific monsters and elaborately stylized plant designs and abstract patterns, some of them inspired by Arab or Persian art. There are even erotic scenes.

St Bernard of Clairvaux, the most prominent leader of the Cistercian Order, which believed in an austere form of monastic life, complained in the twelfth century about the irreligious character of much Romanesque sculpture, not least the monsters, and he was critical of Cluny for encouraging it. But today one can enjoy the vigour of the carving and the touches of humour which are an integral part of its appeal, in addition to the sheer beauty of much of it.

It is true that Romanesque art can often seem simple or naive, particularly when compared with the more polished art of the classical period or the Renaissance, or the Gothic art which followed it. But apparent naivety can conceal sophistication, and the masterpieces of the Romanesque period, like the Vision of the Apocalypse carved on the tympanum of the abbey church at Moissac, on the river Tarn in south-western France, are milestones in the history of western art.

Much of the church-building was carried out by the monasteries, such as Cluny and Moissac, which were often wealthy and influential institutions that played a leading role in the life of those times. Another significant development, which the monasteries encouraged, was the great popularity during the Romanesque period of going on pilgrimage, whether to the shrine of a local saint or, increasingly often, to Santiago de Compostela in north-western Spain.

Compostela owed its fame to the announcement, made in about 813, that the tomb of the Apostle St James the Greater, son of Zebedee and brother of St John, had been discovered there, and this remote shrine came to rank only after Jerusalem and Rome as a pilgrimage centre.

One early, prominent pilgrim was Godescalc, bishop of Le Puy-en-Velay, who travelled to Compostela in 950 or 951 accompanied by a huge entourage of clergy, local aristocrats, troubadours and others. And he was the first of many. By the twelfth century four main pilgrim routes led through France to the Pyrenees – they began in Paris (or St-Denis, just outside), Vézelay, Le Puy-en-Velay and Arles respectively – and there was also a network of smaller ones. Churches had to be built, and specially designed, to meet the pilgrims' needs.

There is a point that should be made clear. One of the features most often identified with Romanesque is the round arch, derived from the Romans. It is frequently seen as distinguishing the style from Gothic, which used pointed arches, and it is true that round arches are one of the distinctive characteristics of Romanesque architecture. They are found in such outstanding buildings as the abbey church in Vézelay, the basilica of St-Sernin in Toulouse, and the cathedral in Santiago de Compostela itself.

But pointed arches are also widely to be seen in Romanesque buildings, particularly in churches built under the influence of Cluny and its later rival, Cîteaux, also in Burgundy and home of the Cistercian Order. They are a central feature in what is left of the last church at Cluny, known as Cluny III, for instance, the building of which began in the closing years of the eleventh century, and also in the smaller Cluniac church at Paray-le-Monial, a few miles away, as well as in Autun cathedral.

The Cistercians used the pointed arch even in their earliest churches, that were constructed in the first half of the twelfth century. Their abbeys, such as Fontenay in Burgundy, were largely built to a common pattern, and in the early days that included a minimum of decoration because of their belief that Cluny's love of decoration was a sinful aberration. But in spite of that, their churches were very elegant, and their earliest ones were Romanesque in spirit.

It is thought that the pointed arch came to Europe from the Arab world, and one theory is that the builders at Cluny were influenced by arches they had seen at Monte Cassino, the monastery south-east of Rome that was originally founded by St Benedict of Nursia in the sixth century. In any case, the use of pointed arches spread from Burgundy, and they are an important feature of, for example, the magnificent Romanesque church of Aulnay-de-Saintonge, in the west of France, as well as of others in that region.

Those churches used the pointed arch in a barrel vault, where it replaced the earlier round arch. The evolution to Gothic came with the development of the more complex rib vault, principally in the Ile-de-France, where it was combined with flying buttresses and could be used to support a taller and heavier structure, and the large window spaces that that made possible.

But even the rib vault had first been used in Romanesque churches, above all in Durham cathedral, built under Norman inspiration, and in the abbey church of Lessay (see page 132) in Normandy itself. If the technique there foreshadowed Gothic, the spirit of Romanesque, with its emphasis on harmony and balance, was still present.

Romanesque flourished for the best part of two centuries and gave birth to many outstanding buildings, as this book aims to show. They range from the grandeur of Vézelay and St-Sernin in Toulouse to the moving simplicity of the early abbey church of St-Philibert in Tournus, in Burgundy, and the unsophisticated charm of thousands of smaller churches and chapels in towns and villages across Europe.

Romanesque style

STONE VAULTING

Just when Romanesque began is impossible to pinpoint, and any attempt to fix a precise date is bound to be arbitrary. Architectural styles evolve gradually, and Romanesque was the product of centuries of often violent history. The name itself was only invented in the early nineteenth century, as I have mentioned – by a Norman art historian, Charles Duhérissier de Gerville, who wanted to distinguish this style of architecture from Gothic.

But one innovation was so important for the evolution of church-building that it can be taken as marking a new chapter. It was the practice of building stone vaulting over the nave. This began around the turn of the tenth and eleventh centuries, and it radically affected the way churches were built. It can be taken as marking the beginning of Romanesque.

Stone vaulting of the nave begins to be found in small churches that were built in the style known as the First Romanesque, particularly in the eastern Pyrenees, where some early churches have round barrel vaults. In time, stone vaults gradually replaced the timber ceilings that had generally been used until then in western Europe.

Barrel vaulting was not a new technique, since it had been developed many centuries before by the Romans – though they did not always use it. There are some small pre-Romanesque churches with vaulted naves in northern Spain which date back to the remote kingdom of Asturias that flourished in the ninth century. But in most of western Europe Roman skills had tended to be forgotten, or discarded, during the first wave of barbarian invasions and the political and economic dislocation that followed the collapse of the western Roman Empire in the fifth century. So unlike the practice in the eastern Roman, Byzantine Empire, timber ceilings had become the norm.

The advantage of stone vaulting was that, quite apart from aesthetic considerations, it was much safer than wood, which was liable to catch fire. Too many churches had gone up in smoke during the raids by Vikings, Magyars and Saracens in the ninth and tenth centuries. So although timber ceilings continued to be used in the eleventh century – and, being much less heavy, they did not present the same structural challenges – stone barrel vaults became increasingly common.

In some churches, support was given to the barrel vaults by transverse arches, which spanned the nave at intervals, marking off the bays. Such arches were used in round vaults in the early pilgrimage churches of St-Sernin in Toulouse (see page 274) and Conques (see page 174), for instance, and also later on in pointed vaults when these came to be used.

But barrel vaulting presented structural difficulties because, as a result of its weight, and the way it was constructed, the vault pushed the walls of the nave outwards. It meant that ways had to be found of countering this pressure, and that was one of the biggest challenges confronting Romanesque architects. They exercised all their ingenuity in meeting it.

The simplest solution was just to thicken the walls of the nave in order to make them stronger, or to build buttresses. But more sophisticated methods were soon devised.

The most widespread was to use the outer walls of the aisles, or the galleries above the aisles, or sometimes a combination of the two, to absorb the sideways stresses from the vault. In order to achieve this, different structures were developed. While some churches had galleries built over their aisles, others did not. Whichever method was used, it was always a delicate business to balance the various thrusts, and it was not usually possible to have many windows, or very large ones.

The use of the pointed arch, with pointed barrel vaults that were supported by pointed transverse arches, was a big step forward – and one that led eventually to the Gothic style. Pointed vaults had the advantage that more of the weight was directed downwards rather than sideways, and they became increasingly common, initially in churches erected under the influence of the abbey of Cluny (see page 61), and in due course more extensively.

It was not merely for structural reasons that such vaulting appealed to the Cluny monks. It also had good acoustic effects, and singing played an important part in their services. So they used pointed barrel vaulting at the great church of Cluny, known as Cluny III, as I have said, and it spread to other churches elsewhere, both Cluniac and non-Cluniac.

Another method of reducing sideways pressures was the use of groin vaulting. It was achieved by having two barrel vaults that intersected at right angles to each other, so that they formed diagonal groins across the bay where they met. This directed the weight of the vault downwards to the corners of the bay. It was frequently used in the aisles of Romanesque churches, but although it was occasionally used to cover the nave – at Vézelay (see page 93), for instance, and in a few other churches – it was not well suited to such a wide span.

The most unorthodox method of spanning the nave is that found at the abbey church of Tournus in Burgundy (see page 86), but almost nowhere else. This consists of a sequence of round barrel vaults which, instead of running the length of the nave, cross it in parallel from north to south, and provide support for each other. It was an arrangement that allowed for good-sized windows, and Tournus is one of the most enchanting Romanesque churches. But it was not taken up elsewhere, perhaps because it ran counter to the line of movement within the church from west to east.

Then there were the domed churches, which are only found in south-western France, and are thought to have been influenced by the Byzantine churches that were seen by the Crusaders as they marched east. These churches, such as Souillac (see page 270) and Angoulême (see page 200), are impressive in their own distinctive way. They solve the vault problem by having a sequence of domes whose weight is borne entirely by massive pillars at the four corners of each of them, so that they do not need side-aisles.

The longest-lasting innovation of the Romanesque period was rib vaulting, where a weight-bearing rib crossed diagonally from one corner of the bay to the opposite one, and provided a robust system of support, even for the wide spaces of the nave. It later became one of the key features of Gothic style when it was combined with flying buttresses to provide the structural framework that was needed for height and for large windows. But Durham and Lessay (see page 132) show that it was first developed by Romanesque architects.

Abbey church of Vézelay: the nave (see page 93)

THE AMBULATORY

Another of the distinctive features of the Romanesque style was the ambulatory, a walkway which circled round the outside of the sanctuary within the church and often had chapels radiating outwards from it. This arrangement had its beginnings in France and, strictly speaking, during the Carolingian period, since the crypt of Chartres cathedral (see page 102), for example, has an ambulatory of that sort, and parts of it date back to the ninth century.

In time ambulatories came to be built above ground. The first of those appears to have been constructed early in the tenth century in Tours, at the important pilgrimage church of St-Martin.

It was only later, however, that the possibilities of the ambulatory were fully developed, and it then became a prominent feature of many Romanesque churches, particularly those handling large numbers of pilgrims. It was both practical and aesthetically appealing. Over the years the chevet, or east end, became one of the main features of Romanesque – and, later, Gothic – churches.

The basic requirement was to accommodate the crowds that poured in to venerate the relics of saints that were the pride of churches and monasteries – and to do so without disturbing the religious services being held by monks or canons around the altar in the centre of the church.

The solution was to make the pilgrims circulate round the ambulatory. This enabled them to stop and pray at the various chapels that radiated outwards, and that often contained the relics they had come to see, and also to look inwards to the sanctuary.

There were five churches, all built in a similar style in the years after 1050, that are generally taken as having exemplified this design, and having been pilgrimage churches *par excellence* – St-Martin in Tours, St-Martial in Limoges, Ste-Foy in Conques (see page 174), St-Sernin in Toulouse (see page 274) and the cathedral in Santiago de Compostela itself. Each of the first four was on one of the main pilgrim routes, the *chemins de St Jacques*, which led through France to Santiago.

Sadly, St-Martin and St-Martial have both been pulled down, but the other three are among the outstanding churches that survive from the Romanesque period. And there are many other Romanesque churches, not least the distinctive group of Auvergne churches (see page 162), that have the ambulatory arrangement they pioneered.

Abbey church of Issoire: the 'chevet' (see page 180)

Origins: from the days of the ancient Greeks

As I have indicated, the origins of Romanesque can be traced back to the days of the Romans and the use made by the early Christians of certain features of Roman architecture, in particular the basilica. But the Roman architects had themselves drawn on a model that had first been devised by the ancient Greeks, so that the roots of the style go far back to the earliest days of European history.

What happened was that in the fourth century, after years of persecution, the Christians were finally recognized by the Emperor Constantine, and from then on were free to put up churches. Not surprisingly, they rejected the Greek or Roman temple as a model. This was partly because of its pagan associations, but also for a more practical reason: it was always a relatively small building which had never been intended to accommodate a congregation.

Instead, therefore, the early Christians chose the basilica, a much larger building that usually stood beside the forum and was used both as a meeting place and a law-court. It was suitable for large gatherings, and it was also associated with the notions of authority and judgment. So the Christians took this basic structure and adapted it over the years for their own purposes. As a result, the term is used to describe many of the churches of the Romanesque period.

The word 'basilica', however, has a Greek root, and the story can be taken back to ancient Athens. There, in around 500 BC, a portico known as the *stoa basileios* was erected on the edge of the *agora*, or forum. This simple building was the distant ancestor of the medieval church. It was rectangular, with a flat roof, three walls, and a row of columns along its long, fourth side which opened it to the forum. Significantly, it also had another line of columns running the length of the building, down the middle, which divided it into two aisles.

Basileios or, sometimes, *basilike* meant 'royal', and the portico took its name from the *archon basileus*, an official who had taken over some of the religious functions of the ancient kings of Athens after they were overthrown, including the judging of charges of impiety and murder. The *archon* had his court in the portico, and gave it its name. But it was also used for the everyday activities of the forum, and had shops and places for people to meet (the Stoic philosophers took their name from a neighbouring *stoa*).

When the Romans arrived, they took over the concept of the *stoa basileios*, or *basilike*, along with much else, from the Greeks, and called it a basilica. The Roman version came to be widely used across the empire, and it became increasingly large and elaborate, with a nave and aisles, colonnades running between them, and even a semi-circular apse that provided a suitably imposing setting for the magistrate to sit in.

Abbey church of St-Savin-sur-Gartempe, from the east (see page 241)

The early Christians adopted all these features, but proceeded to modify them. Most important, they reorientated the building, so that instead of being open on the long side, it had its entrance on one of the short ones, with the sanctuary at the far end – and eventually, usually in the east. And whereas in the Roman basilica the apse, too, was more often on one of the long sides, the Christians ensured that it was always behind the altar and used it as the seat, or *cathedra*, of the bishop.

Another important innovation was the addition of a transept, which gave the worshippers more space on either side of the sanctuary, and at the same time provided extra wall space for doors and windows. It also became common to have an open courtyard, or atrium, at the western end of the church – something that can still be seen in the Romanesque church of Sant' Ambrogio in Milan – and that was eventually replaced by the narthex, the entrance hall at the western end of a church.

Finally, at some point in the early centuries, the church authorities also began to build bell-towers, partly for summoning the faithful and partly as observation points to give warning of danger.

Things developed differently in the east, in what became the Byzantine Empire, because Christian builders there continued to use the cupola, which became the central point of their churches. But in what was left of the western Roman Empire they concentrated on developing the basilica form with its long nave, and its symbolism of the cross, and for a long time they retained the practice, commonly used by the Romans, of covering the nave and aisles of their churches with timber structures.

The next significant stage of development came under the Carolingian dynasty, and particularly Charlemagne, the greatest of them, who was King of the Franks from 768 to his death in 814 – and was crowned Holy Roman Emperor in 800. It was a time when a certain stability returned to western Europe after the long period of disruption caused by the barbarian invasions, and Charlemagne was keen to re-create the glory of the Roman Empire.

So church-building began again across his huge empire, which stretched across much of France, the Low Countries and Germany, and reached down into Italy and Spain.

The Carolingian architects used the architectural features that had been developed by earlier builders and that were later central to the Romanesque style – the apse, the transept and the bell-tower, for instance. They also invented certain features themselves, including the *Westwerk*, or 'westwork', a tower-like structure that eventually evolved into the western façade of Romanesque and Gothic churches.

Not many churches of the period survive but it is known that some of them were complex and sophisticated buildings. One small, but attractive example is in France: the little church of Germigny-des-Prés (see page 156), on the Loire a few miles upstream from Orléans, which was built by Theodulf, one of Charlemagne's chief advisers, and completed in 805. It has a square plan, with a central lantern tower, and originally had apses on all four sides, including three on the east.

But the flowering of the arts that took place under the Carolingians faded as their power disintegrated in the later ninth century, partly as a result of the raids by Vikings, Magyars and Saracens that I have already mentioned. Continuity was lost in the disorder, and conditions only improved towards the end of the tenth century, when the stage was set for the emergence of Romanesque.

Exchanges with neighbouring countries

Many of the most interesting developments in Romanesque architecture took place in France. But they did not happen in isolation. France received influences from neighbouring countries, and transmitted its own ideas to some of them.

The region which is often taken as having been the birthplace of Romanesque is **Lombardy**, in northern Italy, because it was there that the style now known as the First Romanesque was created in the course of the ninth century. The style subsequently spread to nearby regions, including southern France and Burgundy, as well as Catalonia, Dalmatia, Switzerland, the Rhineland and further east.

There are still churches of the First Romanesque to be seen in Burgundy, and also on both sides of the eastern Pyrenees, in the French region of Roussillon and in Spanish Catalonia beyond the Pyrenees. The two regions were closely linked at that time, both politically and culturally, and some of the best surviving examples of the First Romanesque are in that 'greater Catalonia'.

It is there that some of the earliest churches with stone-vaulted naves are found. There are examples on both sides of the Pyrenees dating back to the tenth century, including St-Martin-du-Canigou (see page 335), which was built around 1000 on a remote and spectacular mountain site in Roussillon.

The Lombards were skilled stone-masons as well as builders, and teams of Lombard masons, known as *magistri comacini*, travelled widely, to France and elsewhere. *Lombardus* was for a long time a synonym for mason, and the *magistri comacini* may have derived their name from Como, though that is not certain.

The Lombards had become part of the Carolingian empire after being defeated by the Franks in the second half of the eighth century. Their masons had inherited much of their expertise from Roman times, and were influenced by the buildings that could still be seen in Ravenna, with its Roman traditions and its sixth-century basilicas. Ravenna had been the last capital of the Western Roman Empire, and later came under the rule of Byzantium.

The churches and monasteries of the First Romanesque are accomplished, well-proportioned buildings, many of them quite small, with a variety of the characteristic Romanesque features: elegant bell-towers, semi-circular apses, often in triplicate, transepts and, sometimes, round barrel-vaulted naves instead of flat wooden ones.

One of the most distinctive features of the First Romanesque style is a decorative pattern that was applied to the outside of churches and is often known as 'Lombard bands'. These consist of pilaster strips that run up the wall and have, in between them, a string of small blind arches under a cornice. It is a device found on churches throughout the world of the First Romanesque and, interestingly, it is clearly derived from Ravenna because it is first found on the outside of the Orthodox baptistery there, that was constructed during the Byzantine period.

Germany also has churches built in an early Romanesque style, although they are very different from those in France. The Carolingian empire had broken up in the ninth century, and in 919 a new Saxon dynasty came to power in the German-speaking parts which established internal control, defeated the Slavs and Magyars in the east, and took the place of the Carolingians as the most powerful force in Europe.

The dynasty was named 'Ottonian' after Otto I, the Great, who reigned from 936 to 973 and was crowned Western Emperor in Rome in 962. So was its architectural style. The Ottonians integrated the Church closely into their power structure, giving bishops a militant, almost princely role, and from the tenth century on they were responsible for some large and imposing churches and cathedrals, as well as building castles and raising armies.

With their multiple towers, double transepts and powerful westworks, the Ottonian architects based themselves on Carolingian work, which they developed. They also incorporated some aspects of the First Romanesque style, in particular the Lombard bands, and their buildings were influential over a wide area, particularly in the north of Italy and northern Europe, including Normandy.

David Watkin writes in *A History of Western Architecture* of Speyer cathedral, which was built between 1030 and 1106, that it is 'a classic example of what we mean by Romanesque, with its surging rhythm uniting all the architectural parts into an overall system dominated by the endlessly repeated round arches of arcades, corbel tables, windows, apses and vaults'.

France, by contrast, recovered slowly from the disintegration of the Carolingian empire and the devastation that accompanied it. The situation improved in the course of the tenth century when stability returned, but unlike what happened in the Germanic parts of the empire, no strong central ruler emerged for a long time.

So in the eleventh and twelfth centuries, when Romanesque architecture was being created, powerful local rulers became virtually masters in their own regions, whatever nominal loyalty they might profess to the Capetian rulers who had formally succeeded the Carolingians.

This did not stifle creativity, however, and French influence was strong, therefore, even though it was diffused. It spread to the Holy Land, for instance, as a result of the Crusades. Jerusalem was captured in 1099 in the First Crusade, and that led to an important French presence there. At the same time, it is thought that the domed churches in south-western France were built in imitation of the Byzantine churches that the Crusaders had seen in the east.

French influence also extended to **England**, but specifically in its Norman form, and particularly after the Conquest in 1066. Romanesque had already reached England before 1066 because Edward the Confessor, who had spent much of his early life in Normandy, used its techniques when rebuilding Westminster Abbey. But the real transformation came after the Conquest when the Normans asserted their presence by building churches and cathedrals across the country – all in the Romanesque, or 'Norman', style.

Another country in which the influence of France was strong, and which also influenced it, was **Spain**. By the early eleventh century the *reconquista*, the long process of reconquest by which the Muslims were gradually expelled from Spain, was well under way, at least in the north of the country, and there was considerable French involvement in it.

French knights fought alongside the Spanish Christians, and French clerics and monks played an active part in the religious life of north-western Spain. Abbeys such as Cluny encouraged people to go on a pilgrimage to Santiago de Compostela, and French masons and sculptors, coming mainly from Languedoc and Aquitaine, helped to build the churches and cathedrals.

The cathedral of Santiago, for instance, is similar in style to the pilgrim church

Le Puy-en-Velay: doorway of chapel of St-Michel-d'Aiguilhe (see page 185)

of St-Sernin in Toulouse (see page 274) and to others built along the pilgrim routes that crossed France.

But, again, the influence was by no means all in one direction. There were many contacts, and Islamic Spain had a developed culture with much to offer, not least such magnificent buildings as the great mosque in Córdoba, which were widely admired. So Islamic building techniques and decorative motifs were introduced into France, usually by Mozarabs, the Christians who had lived in the Islamic part of the peninsula and migrated north.

One of the most striking examples of Islamic influence is the cathedral in Le Puy-en-Velay (see page 185), where the elaborate patterns on the west façade, and the alternation of dark and pale-coloured stones in the arches, are of Moorish origin. There is even an inscription in *kufic* script on one of the doors. Moorish influence is also very evident in the façade of the tiny church of St-Michel-d'Aiguilhe, built on a rock on the outskirts of Le Puy.

The abbey church of Moissac (see page 262), on the river Tarn, is another building that shows Islamic influence – in the cusped form of its magnificent doorway on the south side of the church, and in the pattern of radiating ribs in the upper chapel of the narthex. And there are many other examples of such influence.

Romanesque was always an international style, and a diverse one. The pilgrims who spent long months on the road, stopping from time to time in towns and cities on the way, will have had the time to appreciate not just its beauties but its range, too.

France in the Romanesque period

France as such barely existed in the eleventh and twelfth centuries when the Romanesque style was at its height, as I have said. There was a royal dynasty in the north of the country, the Capetians, who claimed to rule most of the lands between the English Channel and the Pyrenees, but even those territories were much smaller than those of modern France, and for many years the Capetians had little real power outside the small royal demesne centred on Paris, Orléans and the Ile-de-France.

Elsewhere, there was a shifting pattern of power centres in which great nobles like the dukes of Normandy, Aquitaine and Burgundy, and the counts of Anjou, Toulouse and Flanders, were virtually independent of royal power.

Most people had strong local loyalties, and felt little affinity with the inhabitants of other regions – who might not even speak the same language. Basques, Bretons and Flemings all had languages of their own, and even among speakers of a Latin-derived language there was the difference between the dialects of the north, which became the *langue d'oïl* and, eventually, French, and those of the south, known collectively as the *langue d'oc*.

Not surprisingly, these differences were reflected in their patterns of life, including the style of their architecture. In Provence, for instance, there was a greater sense of continuity from the closing days of the Roman Empire, while in regions such as Languedoc, Aquitaine, Burgundy or Normandy builders developed their own styles.

Bishops and abbots were an important part of this complex power structure. The Church had played a leading secular role in Europe since the days of the later Roman Empire, and this continued after the Western Empire had collapsed in the fifth century. So the heads of episcopal dioceses and monastic institutions were significant figures. The bishop of Cahors, for instance, was given the ex-officio titles of count and baron in the eleventh century, and the bishops of Le Puy-en-Velay and Poitiers were political and military figures as well as religious ones.

This pattern, or lack of it, in what eventually became France was the outcome of those centuries of invasions and chaos which had begun in the fourth century

Cathedral of Le Puy-en-Velay: the west front (see page 185)

when Germanic tribes first infiltrated, and then took over, vast swathes of the Roman Empire. In Gaul, which had been an important part of the empire, the south was initially occupied by the Visigoths. But they were defeated by the Franks, who emerged as the rulers not only of Gaul but of much of the rest of western and central Europe.

That included what are now Germany and northern Italy, and even parts of northern Spain, as well as France.

Charlemagne was a man of many talents, a tough fighting man and a skilful administrator who also took an active interest in the promotion of learning and the arts. Much of his long reign was spent in warfare, but he set up an institutional framework for the vast Carolingian empire, in close alliance with the Church, and much of the system that he created survived him. His aim was a political, religious and cultural revival, with the defunct Roman Empire as a model; and as part of that process he appointed counts to administer counties as well as bishops for dioceses.

He gave a prominent role to the Church, and particularly to the monasteries, which he saw as a force for both economic and cultural improvement. Monasteries were established throughout the empire, often in remote or backward areas, and were seen simultaneously as centres of learning and the focus for agricultural development.

The Carolingian empire fell apart under Charlemagne's successors, however, and its two main component parts, known as West and East Francia, formed the cores of what eventually became France and Germany.

One of the main factors in the disintegration of the empire was the second wave of invasions from outside, which reached a peak in the ninth century and continued well into the tenth. Vikings from Scandinavia raided the coastal areas, making their way up the rivers and sacking towns and monasteries. Saracens from North Africa launched attacks from bases they had established on the Mediterranean coast, particularly at Fraxinetum – modern Frainet, near Cannes. Magyars stormed in on horseback from the east.

East Francia recovered in the tenth century, as we have seen, when the German Empire was established, and it became the strongest power in Europe. But the invasions hit West Francia particularly hard. They had caught the people of the time unprepared, and caused enormous damage. Normal life was largely disrupted, particularly in the exposed coastal areas. In many places monks gathered up their saintly relics and headed inland, sometimes spending years on the road. Economic life was badly set back.

In due course more peaceful conditions returned and reconstruction began. The

Vikings were bought off in 911 by Charles the Simple, the Carolingian King of the West Franks, who granted them land on the lower Seine, which was expanded to become Normandy, and a powerful duchy. The Magyars did not appear again after their defeat by Otto I, the German Emperor, at Lechfeld in southern Germany in 955. The Saracen base at Fraxinetum was destroyed in 972.

But the damage had been done, and it was not just economic.

The counties and dioceses of Carolingian times remained, however, and because of the weakness of the king, in West Francia the counts succeeded in making what had originally been just an office into a hereditary position. The counties tended to be grouped together under the rule of an even more powerful, princely figure, sometimes a count and sometimes a duke.

One of the consequences of the raids was the militarization of society. Fortifications had been built for protection, understandably enough, around towns and even private residences, and in due course, when the external threat had passed, the owners of castles were able to use their position to dominate the surrounding areas. Might was right in an essentially lawless society.

The Capetian dynasty which eventually came to rule France, as we saw, had had distinctly unpromising beginnings. Hugh Capet succeeded to the throne of West Francia in 987 after many years of rivalry between his family and the last Carolingian kings, and of struggles for power among the nobles. Because, unlike Germany, France was far from united, the result was that Hugh and his immediate successors in the eleventh century had little say in most of the lands they claimed to rule.

Those lands included parts of what is now Belgium, reaching as far north as Bruges and Ghent, and northern Catalonia, in what is now Spain, but they excluded most of what is now eastern France. Lorraine, Alsace, Franche-Comté, Dauphiné and most of Provence all came under the German Emperor.

Even within the 'French' lands, Normandy was a special case because after 1066 the Duke of Normandy was also King of England and as such unwilling to regard the King of France as his superior. During the twelfth century these Anglo-Norman lands grew as a result of dynastic marriages, and in particular that of Henry Plantagenet, later to become Henry II, King of England, to Eleanor of Aquitaine in 1152. They came to include most of western France, all the way to the Pyrenees in the south, and for a time they were larger than those ruled by the French king.

But the other great lords were also resistant to any royal intervention in their territories, and only accepted the nominal suzerainty of the Capetians when, for one reason or another, it suited them – over jurisdictional disputes, for instance.

For their part, the Capetians trod carefully, and they only intervened on the rare occasions when they had the military power to do so.

They were, however, formally recognized as the successors of the Carolingians, and this gave them a nominal authority that they were able to exploit. They also had the backing of the Church. So they were occasionally able to intervene when there were disputes within the various principalities, or between them. In 1047, Henry I helped Duke William of Normandy, later William the Conqueror, to defeat Norman rebels. But generally they confined themselves to keeping the affairs of the royal demesne, and their own authority there, in good order.

The power of the dukes and the counts was based not so much on control of territory as on a complex and fluctuating system of feudal relationships in which lesser nobles and others accepted the status of vassals in exchange for a degree of protection. Some of the rulers were more successful than others in imposing their will in their regions: one of the key factors in the eventual success of the Capetians in uniting the country under their rule was their ability to exercise control in their own demesne.

As a general rule, appointments to both bishoprics and abbeys reflected the balance of power in their particular area, and bishops and abbots almost always came from the ranks of noble families. Bishops were often elected by cathedral chapters, and abbots by monks.

At the end of the eleventh century, as a result of the reforms introduced by Pope Gregory VII, the Papacy came to have a greater say over Church appointments, which it exercised through papal legates. In France the Capetians had traditionally had the power to appoint about one-third of the bishops, but they were careful to avoid clashes with Rome on the issue. So there was nothing comparable to the confrontation that took place between Gregory and the German Emperor, Henry IV.

For their part, the monasteries had been an increasingly important part of the European scene since Carolingian times. Charlemagne had followed a deliberate policy of building up the monastic system, and this was continued by his successors.

So in the closing years of the tenth century, when the conditions of life began to improve after the period of chaos which followed the collapse of the Carolingian empire, monasteries came to play a larger and larger role. They were revived or newly founded by the great families of the day, and generously endowed by them, generally on the understanding that the families would retain control over them.

There were some exceptions. When William the Pious, Duke of Aquitaine, founded the Burgundian abbey of Cluny in 910 (see page 63), he specified that it should be independent of both secular and Church authorities, and subject only to the Pope. This was an important factor in the influence it acquired. Cluny came to head a sprawling empire of abbeys, priories and other such institutions across Europe, and its abbot was regularly an important counsellor of popes, emperors and kings.

The Cistercians, whose order was founded in 1098 by Benedictines who believed that Cluny had become too self-indulgent, were equally independent, and they too quickly spread all over western Europe. St Bernard of Clairvaux, the most prominent of the Cistercians, was a highly influential figure, both in Church affairs and on the wider international scene.

Capetian policy began to pay off during the reign of Louis VI (1108-37), and he was able to be more assertive beyond the royal demesne. Louis was indefatigable in travelling round his demesne to enforce his rights, and his success in doing this gave him the authority to intervene further afield. In 1122 he led an army to Auvergne to reinstate the bishop of Clermont, who had been expelled from his see, and in 1127 he led another to Bruges to avenge the murder of a count of Flanders.

He had his greatest triumph in 1124, when Henry V, the German Emperor, invaded France, and many of the most powerful French nobles answered Louis's call to rally at Rheims, either by sending military contingents or by coming themselves. Henry withdrew rather than face a battle, and Louis drew strength from this affirmation that he was recognized as overlord of the French nobles, and was more than just *primus inter pares*.

His chief minister was Suger, abbot of St-Denis on the outskirts of Paris, a hugely talented man whose abbey church, which he rebuilt in the 1130s and 1140s, was the first to introduce the new style that became known as Gothic. St-Denis had been the royal burial place since the days of the Franks, and Suger was a strong believer in the powers of a centralized monarchy. So he worked with Louis and later with Louis's son and successor, Louis VII, to expand royal influence throughout the regions of France.

One of their objectives was to present the Capetian kings as the successors of Charlemagne, and to play on a greater sense of French nationalism. This was reflected in the great epic, *The Song of Roland*, much of which was written at that time.

One particular move that Louis VI and Suger made was spectacularly unsuccessful, however. They arranged for the younger Louis to marry Eleanor of Aquitaine, daughter of the Duke of Aquitaine and heiress to a vast region of western France. But personal relations between Louis and Eleanor were bad from the beginning, and though the marriage survived Louis's accession to the throne in

1137, the couple was divorced in 1152 after Suger's death. Eleanor immediately married Henry Plantagenet, who was already Duke of Normandy and Count of Anjou, and transferred all her lands to him.

This meant that for most of the second half of the twelfth century the King of England was nominally the ruler, not just of Normandy, but of that vast expanse of France from Anjou to Auvergne, and from Poitou to Gascony. Le Mans, Tours, Poitiers, Clermont, Le Puy-en-Velay, Périgueux, Angoulême and Bordeaux were all subject to Plantagenet rule, and each of the four main pilgrim routes to Santiago de Compostela had stretches that passed through their territory.

But though Louis VII's demesne was dwarfed by the concentration of land in English hands, this situation did not last long. Louis and his successor, Philip II, known as Philippe Auguste, were able to capitalize on fears of Plantagenet power, and resentment of the foreign presence. They also took advantage of the fact that nobles and prelates from all over France were only too keen to submit differences to the royal courts, or to offer homage in exchange for royal protection. As a result, the royal demesne grew steadily.

The big advance came in 1204 when Philippe Auguste seized Normandy from King John of England, and went on to take over Maine, Brittany, Anjou, Touraine and Poitou. This gave the French king control of a huge part of what is now France. The process was taken further in the Albigensian War (1208-29), which effectively ended the autonomy of southern France. The result was that most of the French nobles came to acknowledge the pre-eminence of the Capetian king.

The monasteries

Monasteries were a major feature of life in the Middle Ages. The monks who lived in them had great economic, political and cultural influence in the wider world. The result was that many of the most magnificent Romanesque buildings – at Vézelay (see page 93), Conques (see page 174), Moissac (see page 262), St-Benoît-sur-Loire (see page 154) and in many other places – were originally built as abbey churches surrounded by a complex of monastic buildings.

This would have surprised the first Christian monks who created the idea of monastic life in the deserts of Egypt and the Near East, and who saw it as a way of withdrawing from the world in order to pursue a religious vocation. But it came about because of the turmoil in western Europe after the collapse of the western Roman Empire, and the significant role played in it by the Church.

The Church, and the monasteries in particular, provided one of the few

Abbey church of St-Michel-de-Cuxa, from the south (see page 338)

elements of stability and continuity in the breakdown of society which followed the invasion of the empire by Goths, Franks, Lombards, Burgundians and others. The Church, too, suffered from the invasions, since the various peoples involved, largely Germanic, were pagan, but its organization held, and one by one the invaders were converted, though not always initially to Catholicism.

Clovis, the leader of the Franks, was baptized a Catholic at Rheims in 496, and from then on there was a firm bond between the Church and the Franks. So when Charlemagne, also a Frank, was attempting in the late eighth and early ninth century to restore order and harmony in the sprawling Carolingian empire – and to re-establish the grandeur of ancient Rome – he gave the monasteries a central role, not merely in spreading uniform Christian beliefs, but in providing a material basis for economic, cultural and administrative revival.

This policy was applied both in the lands which had been part of the Roman Empire, where Christianity had long been established, and in the Germanic heartlands further east which were still largely pagan. It gave the monks a role that went well beyond their purely religious activities, and although they suffered again during the upheavals of the later barbarian raids in the ninth and early tenth centuries, which played their part in the collapse of the Carolingian empire, they maintained that role.

As the invasions came to an end, and the economy of western Europe picked up from the late tenth century on, monasteries were revived or founded in increasing numbers by the great potentates of the day, and generously endowed. Such people saw them partly as a means of ensuring the future well-being of their souls, and those of their families, and partly as a good investment for more practical reasons, since they often retained a degree of control over their activities, and their income. For their part, many of the monks and nuns themselves came from aristocratic or well-to-do families.

The result was that while the monks and nuns were poor individually, the main monastic communities in which they lived became rich and powerful landowners, playing an important part both in the economic development of the countryside and in wider issues – and possessing the means, as well as having the need, to put up large new buildings in the style of the day. Many of them were sufficiently knowledgeable in the ways of the world to make themselves felt in the politics of the time.

The monasteries also maintained their position as repositories of learning, copying books in their *scriptoria* and owning libraries that included not only the great works of the Christian Church, but many of the works of classical antiquity. Up until the Renaissance of the twelfth century, monks were generally the most learned people in western Europe.

But it was all a far cry from the deserts of Syria, Palestine and Egypt, where early Christians had begun to withdraw from the world in search of solitude and the spiritual life in the third century.

Two traditions had evolved in those early days, principally in Egypt: that of the solitary hermit, and that of the organized community of ascetics. The communal, or cenobitical, principle is said to have originated with Pachomius, a Coptic-speaking Egyptian, and it was this that was transmitted to western Europe in the fourth century, when monastic groups began to form.

There were a number of influential actors in this process. One was John Cassian, a Scythian monk who described the ideas of the desert communities in a widely-read work, *Conferences*, and who eventually settled near Marseille, where he established two communities, one for monks and the other for nuns, in the fifth century. Another was Honoratus, a Gaul, who founded a monastery on the Lérins islands off the coast of Provence at about the same time, which was active in setting up monastic communities throughout the region.

An earlier figure was St Hilary, or Hilaire, the much-travelled Bishop of Poitiers in the fourth century, who encouraged a community of ascetics in that city. St Hilary influenced St Martin, who settled initially in a hermitage at Ligugé, near

Poitiers, and went on to become Bishop of Tours and play an important part in the spread of the monastic movement.

The most influential figure in the history of western monasticism was, however, St Benedict, an Italian, whose Rule provided the basis on which monasteries across Europe were established and run. Firm facts about his life are elusive – though much was written about the miracles he was believed to have worked – but it seems that he was born in Nursia, the modern Norcia, in Umbria in the late fifth century and became a hermit, living in a cave near Subiaco, east of Rome.

There he attracted disciples, whom he organized into communal groups, before moving to Monte Cassino, a hilltop between Rome and Naples, where he established a fully-fledged monastery, and where he died in the middle of the sixth century. It was for Monte Cassino that he drew up his Rule. It laid down a comprehensive list of principles, such as who could be admitted to a monastery and on what terms, the pattern of daily life for monks and nuns, the overriding importance of humility and obedience, and the role of the abbot and the procedure for electing a new one.

One of the assumptions of the Rule was that monks, and sometimes even their abbot, were not ordained. This had been so from the beginning, since the first monks had not been part of the Church hierarchy, and it continued to be the case for centuries, so that even in the eleventh century not all Benedictine monks were ordained, although by then most of them were.

St Benedict's Rule was only one of several that were composed for monasteries at the time, and he seems to have drawn on at least one earlier one. But it was particularly coherent and comprehensive, and moderate in its demands on monks and nuns, setting out the austere ideals of the eastern ascetics in a typically Roman framework of written rules.

Monte Cassino was sacked by the Lombards in 577, not long after St Benedict's death, and lay in ruins for the next 140 years or so. But his name was widely known, and in about 672 a group of monks from the monastery of Fleury, on the Loire upstream from Orléans, pulled off a bold coup when they travelled to Monte Cassino, dug up the bones of St Benedict and his sister, St Scholastica, and took them back to Fleury, which they renamed St-Benoît-sur-Loire.

This gave St Benedict and his Rule a central place in the land of the Franks, and while he was promoting monastic life Charlemagne set out to make the Benedictine Rule the standard for all the abbeys in the Carolingian empire. He made some progress in this, but was not completely successful.

The process was taken further by his son, Louis the Pious, who ruled from 814 to 840 and, with the help of the second St Benedict, from Aniane in southern

Gaul, imposed the Rule on all monastic establishments in the empire north and west of the Alps. St Benedict of Aniane, a Goth whose original name was Witiza, believed in a rigorous interpretation of the Rule, and his ideas were embodied in a number of decrees issued in the ninth century by Louis from Aachen, the imperial capital.

The Carolingian empire collapsed, however, in the course of that century, and with it the general application of the Benedictine Rule as the monastic communities suffered in the chaos – and lay founders and abbots went their own ways. Monasteries were pillaged by the invaders, and monks often had to flee with their relics to what they hoped would be safer centres.

The monks of Noirmoutier, an island off the Atlantic coast, fled inland with the relics of St Philibert in 836, settled in five different places, and only found a permanent home in Tournus (see page 86), in Burgundy, in 875. Similarly in England the monks of Lindisfarne moved from place to place with the relics of St Cuthbert before settling in Durham in 995.

The most significant event of the period – though it would not have been appreciated at the time – was the foundation in 910 by William the Pious, Duke of Aquitaine, of the new monastery at Cluny (see page 61), also in Burgundy. Duke William appointed as the first abbot Berno, later St Berno, who was already the head of the small and remote abbey of Baume, in the Jura mountains, in which the Benedictine Rule was observed. As normal monastic life resumed, Cluny became not just the leading Benedictine community but one of the most important institutions of the Middle Ages.

From its early days the abbots and monks of Cluny were called in to advise on the re-establishment of the Benedictine Rule in other monasteries, including Fleury, and, as we have seen, over the years the abbey became the centre of a vast though loosely linked empire made up of some 1,450 monastic institutions, great and small, principally in France, Italy and Spain, but including Germany and even England. Some of these were priories directly subordinate to Cluny, and others, like Vézelay and Moissac, were largely independent abbeys; but they all observed similar Benedictine principles.

Part of Cluny's success was due to the fact that it was run by a number of outstanding abbots – in particular, St Odo (926-44), St Mayeul (965-94), St Odilo (994-1048) and St Hugh (1049-1109) – and part to the fact that at its foundation it had been given complete freedom to run its own affairs independently of both secular and Church authorities, and subject only to the Pope in distant Rome, as I have said. Its abbots became leading international statesmen, having close relations not just with successive popes but with emperors and kings.

Cluny was an active promoter of the pilgrimage to Santiago de Compostela. Several of its leading figures became popes themselves, including Urban II, who launched the First Crusade in 1095.

The great church at Cluny itself, the third to be built on the same site, was largely destroyed in the years after the French Revolution, but what is left gives an idea of the excellence both of its architecture and of the sculpture that was part of it. Funds for the church's construction, which began under St Hugh in the late eleventh century, came from a wide range of donors, including Henry I of England and Alfonso VI of León and Castile, the latter riding high after his capture of Toledo from the Moors in 1085.

Other Cluniac churches were built in varying styles, but the lovely basilica of Paray-le-Monial (see page 73), on the banks of the river Bourbince some miles west of Cluny, was built at about the same time as the main church, in similar style but on a smaller scale. St Hugh was also responsible for the exquisite little chapel at Berzé-la-Ville (see page 64), across the hills to the south-east of Cluny, with its frescoes in Byzantine style.

Further afield, the abbey of St-Pierre at Moissac, on the Tarn north of Toulouse, was an example of a monastery given new life after being taken into the Cluniac system by St Odilo. With its magnificently carved south porch and cloister, Moissac demonstrated the attention paid in the Cluniac system to putting up beautiful buildings and decorating them with paintings and sculpture, which were used to convey Christian teaching.

Cluniac monks also attached great importance to the liturgy, and the music that went with it, as I have mentioned. Much of their time was given to church services, and the stone vaulting of their churches was specially designed to produce a rhythmical echo for the distinctive Cluniac chant.

As time went by, such attitudes came to be regarded as self-indulgent, and the opulence of the Cluniac monasteries was criticized as a departure from the ascetic principles of monastic life, and specifically from a strict interpretation of the Benedictine Rule. Individuals and groups withdrew to remote spots where they were able to find seclusion and devote time to manual labour and private meditation. A number of influential movements were born which aimed to embody the spiritual experience of the desert in permanent form.

These included the Carthusians, and also the monastic community at Fontevrault, or Fontevraud (see page 147), on the Loire, whose abbey church eventually became the chosen burial place of the Plantagenet dynasty.

At the same time there was an increase in the number of canons regular, clerics who chose to live in a virtually monastic community, often attached to a collegiate church or cathedral, and who often followed the Rule of St Augustine, a modified version of principles enunciated by St Augustine of Hippo in the late fourth and early fifth century. The Premonstratensians, founded by St Norbert at Prémontré, near Laon, in the early twelfth century, were an example.

The most prominent of the critics of Cluny, and the most successful in numerical terms, were the Cistercians. They were founded in 1098 by a group of dissident monks, headed by Robert of Molesme, who were determined to revive an austere interpretation of the Benedictine Rule. They took their name from Cîteaux, an out of the way place south of Dijon where they set themselves up, and from which the 'White Monks' proceeded to expand rapidly.

Within half a century the Cistercians had more than 300 abbeys scattered across Europe, and they continued to grow after that. Like Cluny, they subscribed to the Benedictine Rule but they criticized the Cluniac monks for not observing the Rule strictly enough, and there was a high-level controversy between the two groups.

St Bernard, Abbot of Clairvaux, became the most prominent and most out-spoken of the Cistercians, and strongly worded public letters were exchanged between him and Peter the Venerable, Abbot of Cluny. St Bernard became an influential figure in the church politics of the twelfth century, attracting a wide range of adherents from all sectors of society through his calls for a more austere life than that led at the great Cluniac abbeys.

He made himself famous by his virulence, and in particular by his attacks on the beasts and monsters that were often a feature of the carved capitals in cloisters and elsewhere. 'What profit is there,' he wrote, 'in those ridiculous monsters of deformed comeliness and comely deformity? To what purpose are those unclean apes, those fierce lions, those monstrous centaurs, those half-men, those striped tigers, those fighting knights, those hunters winding their horns?'

The Cistercians led a simple life, most often in secluded areas, where they emphasized the value of manual labour and devoted less time than the Cluniac monks to elaborate liturgy. They were innovative not merely in religious matters but also in their architecture, because, after a short period when they were not interested in the style of their accommodation, they came to realize that they needed suitable buildings in which to conduct monastic life.

So a standard model was drawn up for the layout of their monasteries – although it had inevitably to be adapted in its details to local conditions.

As a result, the early Cistercian churches have noticeable similarities, including, very often, slightly pointed barrel vaulting over quite broad naves; and while they have none of the decoration of the Cluniac churches, they have an austere beauty of their own, with their well-balanced proportions. They were Romanesque, but

Romanesque with a difference. Their clear lines and absence of ornament for ornament's sake anticipated Gothic, which was, of course, already being developed in northern France at the time when they were being built.

It is also worth noting that in the twelfth century these churches would have seemed revolutionary in a way that is not immediately obvious today. This is because Romanesque churches tended to have colour everywhere in addition to, and often on top of, whatever sculpture they may have had. So the plain Cistercian style would have seemed all the more austere when contrasted with that.

One outstanding example of an early Cistercian church is Fontenay (see page 68), in Burgundy. There are others in Provence: Sénanque, Silvacane and Le Thoronet (see page 303). But there are Cistercian abbey churches, or their ruins, as far afield as Fountains Abbey and Rievaulx in England, Chiaravalle outside Milan, and Poblet, Santes Creus and Vallbona de les Monges in Catalonia; and they show how, from their simple beginnings, they became more elaborate over the years.

This was true of the Cistercian movement in general. In its heyday it had responded more vigorously than other monks to the religious fervour that had begun to be in evidence across Europe at the end of the eleventh century. But over the years it became successful and increasingly rich as a result of its huge endowments, and it too became a wealthy and influential landowner, similar in many ways to the much-criticized Cluny.

Pilgrimages

Travel in the Romanesque period, and for a long time afterwards, was extremely uncomfortable and often dangerous. Yet many thousands of pilgrims, rich and poor, used to set off every year for Santiago de Compostela, making the long journey from every corner of Europe and taking months to reach that distant city – and then more months to return home.

Those travelling from Britain or Ireland might do the greater part of the journey by sea. Ships sailed from the south coast of Cornwall, for instance, to Corunna on the Galician coast, from where it was only about fifty miles overland to Santiago. Other pilgrims sailed to Soulac, near Bordeaux, where they joined one of the main continental routes.

But the great majority travelled the whole way overland, and while a few – kings, aristocrats, church leaders – could afford to go on horseback, often with an accompanying escort, the rest went on foot.

They had to negotiate bad roads (even the old Roman ones had been neglected for centuries), thick forests, swamps, mountains and rivers without bridges. They might be attacked on the many desolate stretches by bandits or wolves. They could be fleeced or worse by toll-keepers, ferry-owners or innkeepers.

Understandably, they travelled as light as possible. The traditional pilgrim's equipment consisted of a broad-brimmed hat, a long cloak, a small pouch or scrip for some food and personal belongings, a gourd or something similar to carry water, sandals, and a long staff tipped by an iron ferrule to serve both as a walking stick and as a weapon in case of attack. It was only after they had reached Santiago that pilgrims were entitled to wear the cockle-shell which was the symbol of the pilgrimage.

Spring was the usual time they set off, as described by Chaucer in *The Canterbury Tales*, in the hope that there would be several months of reasonable weather. But there was no certainty of that, and the summer could be hot. One can easily imagine the exhilaration they must have felt when, after the hardships of days of walking, they arrived at a town, monastery or hospice.

The contrast between the rigours of the road and the magnificence of much of the architecture that they encountered must have been extreme. This was particularly true at a time when most people were illiterate and hardly ever saw images of any sort, so that the impact of the buildings, with their paintings and sculpture, must have been far greater than they would be today.

In such places they were able to take advantage of the benefits that, for many, made such a pilgrimage possible. There was a general requirement that pilgrims should be offered hospitality, and that applied particularly to monasteries and other religious institutions, which had hospices for them. But in spite of that the pilgrims had to pay for much of their board and lodging along the way. There were also, of course, the many temptations that might be met in a town.

The making of a pilgrimage had long been part of the Christian tradition (as it later became a tradition in Islam). Pilgrims used to travel to the Holy Land from the earliest days of Christianity, and there is a surviving account of a journey undertaken in the first half of the fourth century by an anonymous pilgrim from Bordeaux. So, as the conditions of life improved with the ending of the barbarian raids in the tenth century, and people became better off, the practice grew.

There were a number of reasons for making a pilgrimage, not least the desire to make a statement of Christian faith by undertaking a strenuous journey, or sometimes to carry out an act of penance. But the main, underlying one was the belief in the power of relics. People believed that if they travelled to venerate the relics of a saint, that saint would intercede in some way on their behalf, either in this life or the next – and sometimes with a miracle.

Pilgrimage church of Orcival: church and village in their wooded setting (see page 183)

Those who could travelled to the Holy Land or to Rome, where there were shrines containing the relics of St Peter and St Paul. But many more travelled to shrines that were nearer home, where they knew that the relics of other saints, often with local associations, were held. There were many of them across Europe.

This meant that it was important for a church, cathedral or monastery to have saintly relics, and as many as possible of them. The great church of St-Sernin in Toulouse (see page 274) did not only have the relics of St Saturninus, the martyred bishop of Toulouse to whom it was dedicated (Saturninus had become Sernin in the local dialect), but claimed to have relics of many other saints, including the two St Jameses, St Philip, St Bartholomew, St Simon, St Jude and St Barnabas, and even of St Peter and St Paul, these having been given to it by Pope Calixtus II.

It also meant that churches or monasteries that did not have relics had to set about acquiring some, not always by scrupulous means. In the seventh century, for instance, a group of monks from the abbey of Fleury on the Loire (see pages 30 and 154) travelled secretly to Monte Cassino and brought back the bones of St Benedict and St Scholastica, as I have said. Similarly in the ninth century a monk from Conques (see page 174), just south of the Massif Central, removed the relics of St Foy, a young girl martyred in the early fourth century, from her shrine in Agen.

There was often recrimination, and in the case of the relics of St Benedict it lasted for centuries. But both Fleury and Conques, whose magnificent church is dedicated to St Foy, flourished on the strength of the relics they had acquired.

The discovery of the bones of St James at what came to be known as Compostela was a landmark event in the Middle Ages. It took place in about 813, when, according to a later account, Theodomir, the bishop of Iria Flavia, a Roman foundation on the west coast of Galicia, and Pelagius, a local hermit, were led by a star to a field in which they found a tomb containing three sarcophagi.

The two men had no doubt that one of the sarcophagi contained the remains of St James, and it was not long before their discovery became known across Europe. Compostela was proclaimed an apostolic shrine, almost on a par with Rome.

The belief was that St James had been charged by Christ himself with converting the people of the Iberian peninsula, and that he had actually spent a brief if unsuccessful time in the peninsula before returning to Palestine. There he was condemned to death by Herod Agrippa I and beheaded in AD 42 or 44.

Two companions, St Athanasius and St Theodore, then put his remains into a boat, and they and the coffin were carried by wind, tide and divine guidance across the Mediterranean, through the straits of Gibraltar and north to the coast of Galicia, where they came ashore near the modern town of Padrón after a seven-day voyage. St Athanasius and St Theodore were eventually buried with St James, and their remains were in the other two sarcophagi found almost eight centuries later.

The name of Compostela is often said to be a corruption of *Campus stellae*, or 'field of the star', and to refer to the way in which the tomb had been found, though this is disputed. An alternative explanation is that it derives from a Latin word for a cemetery.

In any case, the discovery of the remains of St James was particularly significant because he was the only Apostle to be buried in western Europe outside Rome. Compostela quickly became a local pilgrimage centre, and soon a Benedictine monastery was established there. Within fifty years the festival of St James, on 25 July, was listed as far away as Metz in the cathedral's martyrology, and in due course the pilgrimage to Santiago de Compostela became one of the most important in the Christian world.

There was another, political, factor involved in the prominence achieved by Compostela. The discovery of the tomb of St James came almost exactly a century after the Arab-led forces, all of them Muslim, had invaded and occupied almost the whole of the Iberian peninsula; and Galicia was in the front line in the battle against them. Alfonso II, King of Asturias and Galicia at the time of the discovery of

St James's tomb, needed support from elsewhere in Europe, as did the rulers of the other tiny kingdoms in the north of Spain, and they encouraged the pilgrimage.

In 844, Alfonso's successor, Ramiro I, received support from St James himself when a knight in shining armour mounted on a charger and bearing a white standard with a red cross upon it appeared at the battle of Clavijo and helped him defeat the Moors. The knight was recognized as St James, and from that moment the Apostle was converted into 'Santiago Matamoros', the Slayer of Moors, and became the champion of the Christians in the centuries-long war against the infidel. He is seen in that martial role, cutting down the enemies of the Church, in sculptures in Santiago cathedral and elsewhere.

It was against this background of a holy war that the pilgrimage developed, with the encouragement of Cluny (see page 61) and other monasteries, which also supported the *reconquista*, or reconquest of the peninsula. In the early days, the pilgrims followed the coast road to Galicia after passing the Pyrenees because that was safer – and just how dangerous it could be was shown in 997, when al-Mansur, the Muslim commander, sacked Santiago de Compostela, destroying the cathedral and carrying off its bells to Córdoba (they were eventually recovered when the Christians recaptured Córdoba in 1236).

Later on, however, as the Moors were gradually driven south, the inland route that passed through Burgos and León became safe and was used more often. It was known as the *camino francés* because it was generally used by French pilgrims. Over the years roads were repaired or even re-directed in order to pass through particular towns, and bridges were built. Monasteries were founded along the route, and hospices and inns built to accommodate the pilgrims; and there were even new towns that sprang up, for which artisans of all sorts were needed.

By the twelfth century the four main pilgrim routes through France were well established (see page 7). Three of them merged just north of the Pyrenees, which they crossed by the Roncesvalles pass, and the fourth used the Somport pass further east. There was a final junction at Puente la Reina where the bridge, which still stands, was built on the orders of a Queen of Navarre in the eleventh century – though it is not known which. From there a single route crossed northern Spain to Santiago de Compostela.

Clearly not all pilgrims would have stuck to every yard of these main routes. There were also innumerable minor ones that often passed through lesser pilgrimage centres nearby. But each of the main routes had the advantage of beginning at a pilgrimage centre that was important in its own right, and that made it a suitable starting-point, particularly for foreigners who might already have travelled a long way. And they passed through other such centres on the way to Compostela.

The four routes were described in a remarkable document, *The Pilgrim's Guide to Santiago de Compostela*, written in Latin and thought to have been compiled in the 1130s. This early guidebook was one section of a collection of manuscripts known variously as the *Codex Calixtinus* and the *Book of St James*, all of them to do with the cult of St James. It gave practical information on some of the hazards pilgrims would meet, the nature of the regions through which they would travel, the people who inhabited them, and the important shrines en route. It included a detailed description of the cathedral in Santiago as it was at that time.

The *Guide* is an engagingly subjective work in which the principal author does not hesitate to be extremely critical, and even offensive, about some of the people who would be encountered. It is not necessary to believe every word he writes. At one point he appears to believe that Cornishmen have tails. But that gives it its appeal.

The author seems to have been French and is often said to have been Aimery Picaud, a priest from Parthenay in Poitou who is named twice in addenda to the *Guide*. This is not universally accepted, but it does appear certain that, whoever he was, he travelled along one of the main routes, the one that began at St-Denis, near

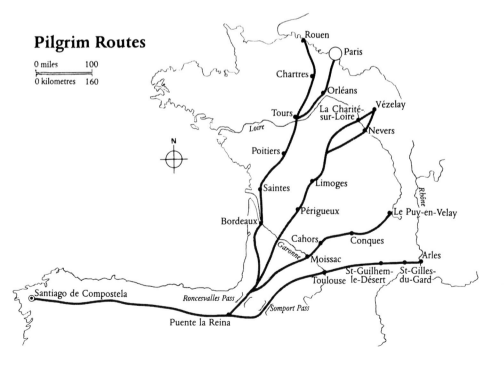

Pilgrim Routes

0 miles   100
0 kilometres 160

Paris, and that – given the time he took to cover the distances – he was on horse-back.

He gives full descriptions of the main shrines on the Paris route but omits several important shrines on the other routes. He seems to have relied on written sources for those routes, as he did for his sometimes lengthy biographies of saints.

There are some lively passages. On rivers, for instance. 'At a place called Lorca, in the eastern part, runs a river called the Salty Brook. Be careful not to let it touch your lips or allow your horse to drink there, for this river is deadly. On its bank, while we were going to Santiago, we met two men of Navarre sitting sharpening their knives. They are in the habit of skinning the mounts of pilgrims who drink that water and die.

'When questioned by us, these liars said that it was safe to drink. We therefore watered our horses, and immediately two of them died, which these people skinned on the spot.'

Ferries were another hazard. In Gascony: 'Many times, after receiving the money, the ferrymen take on such a throng of pilgrims that the boat tips over, and the pilgrims are killed in the water. Thereupon the ferrymen rejoice wickedly after seizing the spoils from the dead.'

The author describes the Navarrese and the Basques as being similar, and does not like either of them. The Navarrese, he writes, are 'a barbarous race unlike other races in customs and in character, full of malice, swarthy in colour, evil of face, depraved, perverse, perfidious, empty of faith and corrupt, libidinous, drunken …', and so on. He adds that they practise 'unchaste fornication with animals'.

Not everything is negative, however, and no praise is high enough for the people of Poitou, who are 'valiant heroes and fighting men, very experienced in war with bows, arrows and lances, daring in the front line of battle, very fast in running, elegant in their dress, distinguished of face, shrewd of speech, very generous with gifts, lavish in hospitality'. It is hardly surprising that the author is assumed to have been a Poitevin.

He writes interestingly about the various shrines, which he describes with due reverence, and is lyrical as he reaches the Roncesvalles pass, which he calls by another name, the Port de Cize: 'The ascent of it is eight miles, and the descent is similarly eight. For the height of the mountain is so great that it seems to reach the sky. To him who ascends it, it seems that he can touch the sky with his own hand. From its summit can be seen the Sea of Brittany and the Western Ocean, and also the territories of three regions – that is, Castile, Aragon and France.'

Modern pilgrims may well share this sense of exhilaration, even if they do not recognize other areas in his account.

Burgundy

Burgundy has some of the outstanding churches from the Romanesque period, including some of the earliest. The region was centrally placed, on roads running between the valleys of the Rhône and the Loire, and it also had links to Germany in the east. So it quickly adopted the First Romanesque style as it spread from Lombardy (see page 17), and churches survive that date back to the early eleventh century and even before that.

The lovely old abbey church of St-Philibert in Tournus has parts that were built in the late tenth century, and there are early Romanesque churches dotted around the rolling countryside, often dominating villages.

But there are also magnificent churches from the twelfth century, among them Autun cathedral and one of the most beautiful of all Romanesque creations, the basilica of Vézelay. Although the great abbey church at Cluny, Cluny III, was largely demolished in the aftermath of the French Revolution, the part that survives gives an idea of its past grandeur.

The Burgundians had been among the first to take the important step of building stone vaults over the naves of their churches. They had seen their churches go up in flames, whether as a result of a raid by Magyars – as at Tournus in 937 – or from other causes, and stone was safer than timber. It was also more pleasing to the eye and, because of the acoustic qualities of barrel vaulting, to the ear, too – this last being something that appealed to the music-loving monks of the abbey of Cluny.

Monasteries were in fact one of the most important features in the Burgundian scene. Cluny, which became such an influential institution across western Europe in the eleventh and early twelfth centuries, is in southern Burgundy, where it was founded in 910, as I have said. Its liking for pointed arches was shown not just in Cluny III but in Autun cathedral and the priory churches of Paray-le-Monial and La Charité-sur-Loire that were built under its influence.

Cîteaux, home to the Cistercian Order, is also in Burgundy. It was founded in 1098 and, with its austerer view of monastic life, it soon became a rival to Cluny.

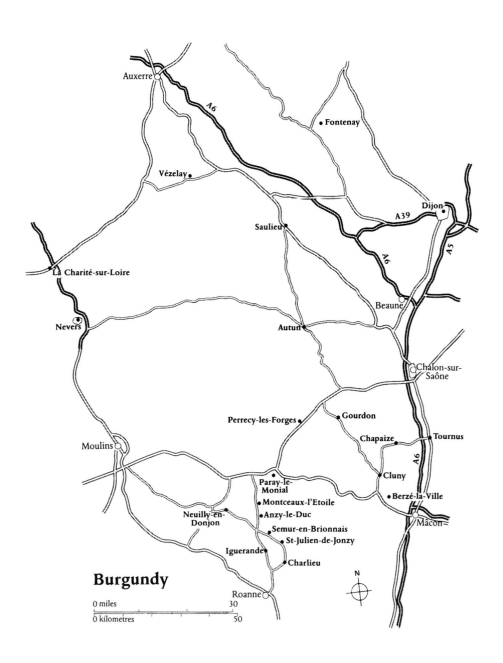

Auxerre

A6

• Fontenay

Vézelay•

Dijon
A39

Saulieu• A6 A5

La Charité-sur-Loire

Beaune

Nevers

Autun

Chalon-sur-
Saône

Perrecy-les-Forges• • Gourdon

Chapaize• Tournus

Moulins

A6

Cluny

Paray-le-
Monial

• Berzé-la-Ville

• Montceaux-l'Etoile

Neuilly-en-
Donjon •Anzy-le-Duc

Mâcon

•Semur-en-Brionnais

•St-Julien-de-Jonzy

Iguerande•

•Charlieu

Burgundy

N

0 miles   30

0 kilometres   50

Roanne

Little is left of the original monastery of Cîteaux, but the twelfth-century abbey of Fontenay in northern Burgundy is a splendid example of the bare beauty of the early Cistercian churches, with their minimal decoration. Like the Cluniacs, the Cistercians used pointed arches.

Interestingly, the church at Vézelay, though built at a time when its monks were briefly linked to Cluny, does not have the Cluniac arrangement of a pointed barrel vault. Instead, it has groin vaulting over its nave, an attractive but less stable system which is also found in two smaller Burgundian churches, Anzy-le-Duc and Gourdon.

Burgundy produced some of the most accomplished sculpture of the Romanesque period as well. If much of the sculpture of Cluny III has been lost, a few fine pieces survive, on display in the former granary; and the sculpture of Autun, Vézelay and the smaller priory church of Saulieu includes some of the masterpieces of Romanesque art, among them the great tympana of Autun and Vézelay and a large number of superb column capitals.

There is more exceptional sculpture to be found in small country churches, particularly in the Brionnais area in south-western Burgundy and some nearby villages. There, too, there are carved tympana – at Charlieu, St-Julien-de-Jonzy, Montceaux-l'Etoile and Neuilly-en-Donjon. At Perrecy-les-Forges the tympanum is the central feature of a narthex with carved capitals.

Anzy-le-Duc, Montceaux-l'Etoile and Neuilly-en-Donjon

The village of Anzy-le-Duc, in the Brionnais region in the south of Burgundy, has one of the most appealing churches in an area that is particularly rich in them. It has a beautiful Romanesque bell-tower, visible from miles away across the countryside, and its interior is a harmonious succession of round arches, decorated with some lively and imaginative capitals.

The honey-coloured stone in which the church is built adds to its charm. The same is true of a smaller church in a neighbouring village, Montceaux-l'Etoile. This was a parish church that came under the influence of the priory of Anzy-le-Duc in the Romanesque period, and it has an outstanding tympanum, depicting the Ascension, over its west door.

And yet another remarkable tympanum, of a later date, is to be seen a few miles away in Neuilly-en-Donjon, a village on the far side of the Loire valley. This is carved in the same honey-coloured stone and is a work of striking originality. It has the Adoration of the Magi as its main theme.

Priory church of Anzy-le-Duc, from the south

The priory at **Anzy-le-Duc** was founded in the late ninth century on land donated by Letbald, a local nobleman, and Altaric, his wife. Its first prior was Hugh of Poitiers, later St Hugh, a prominent monk who had been a member of the monastic community at St-Savin-sur-Gartempe (see page 241) and played an important role in the monastic reform movement, including the creation of the abbey of Cluny in 910 (see page 61). In later years, the priory was always linked to Cluny.

Hugh died at Anzy in about 930, and his tomb attracted so many pilgrims that a larger building was needed. The present church was largely erected in the course of the eleventh century, with some additions in the early twelfth century. The design is similar to that of the church that was built at the same time in Charlieu (see page 58), a few miles to the south, which it may have influenced. It retained the tenth-century crypt in which St Hugh was buried, that has recently been rediscovered under the eastern part of the church.

It has a simple and satisfying form, dominated on the outside by its bell-tower, which is built over the transept crossing. The tower is octagonal with three almost identical tiers, one above the other, of elaborate double arches, each topped by Lombard bands – the panels of tiny blind arches that often served to decorate early Romanesque churches (see page 18). It is a most attractive design, reminiscent of some Italian *campanili*.

The *chevet* is thought to have been the earliest section of the church, as so often, and to date back to the early eleventh century. It has a simple arrangement of chapels with round arches, built in parallel and all facing east.

Some of the best views of the church and its bell-tower are to be had from the courtyard on its south side, which is surrounded by the surviving buildings of the priory. The view along the line of trees leading to its west front is also impressive. The façade is largely plain but the bell-tower can be seen above it, and the central feature of the façade is the elaborate doorway that was added in the late eleventh or early twelfth century, perhaps in two phases.

The doorway is badly damaged. But the carving of Christ in Glory on the tympanum, with the mandorla in which he sits supported by two angels, still has power and poise; while below on the lintel is a lively scene from the Ascension, with the Virgin Mary and Twelve Apostles, each of them in a state of agitation, carved in low relief. In style, the work stands midway between the greater stiffness of the earlier, similar work in Charlieu and the greater fluency of the tympanum in Montceaux-l'Etoile.

The inner archivolt has carvings of the Elders of the Apocalyse, each carrying his viol and cup of perfume (see page 263). This has been even more badly damaged than the rest of the doorway, but several of the Elders can still be seen – and they are engaging figures, as they always are. Enough survives to show that this was an accomplished work that had perhaps been carried out by a sculptor from Cluny.

There were usually twenty-four Elders, and not all of them appear on the archivolt. A few were carved on the two capitals below it, and one of those in particular is well preserved. There are also attractive corbels under the lintel, each showing a man straining to hold up the stone above his head, in a decorative setting of formal plant designs, with an animal at one side.

Inside the church, the nave has a succession of round transverse arches that lead the eye to the apse and the semi-circle of arches below it. More round arches divide the nave from the side-aisles, and light comes in from small windows above them.

Anzy-le-Duc has groin vaulting over each of the bays of the nave, as well as in the side-aisles; and the church is thought to have provided a model for similar vaulting elsewhere, especially in the great basilica of Vézelay (see page 93) in northern Burgundy. The choir and the two arms of the transept, all built in an earlier phase, have round barrel vaulting.

Down below is the newly discovered crypt, also covered by groin vaulting, a dark and simple place.

The church's capitals are one of the glories of Anzy-le-Duc. They are placed all over the nave, transept and choir, some of them consisting of formal designs, some with human, animal and religious scenes, and they have a vigour which, as is common in Romanesque churches, makes them an integral part of the architecture.

As you walk down the nave, they stand out on the columns supporting the arches on each side, and also, less prominently, high up under the vault: Samson grappling a lion, a diabolical figure playing a flute for other people to dance to, St Michael attacking a snarling monster with sword and shield, an acrobat bent over backwards while two snakes begin to devour him.

Just before the transept, a capital shows the rivers of Paradise flowing out of upturned chalices, each of them held by a small seated human figure. Opposite is one that depicts two men grabbing one another by the beard in a fierce tussle, while on either side of them there is a large human face with a long tongue and beard, and behind them are two simian figures kissing each other. Elsewhere Daniel sits between two lions.

The oldest capitals are in the choir, which is thought to date from the first half of the eleventh century. They include plants, animals and birds, among them pairs of eagles and lions, and there are two that stand out, one on either side of the apse. On each of them a crouching man supports the weight of the stone above him with raised arms, while other men sit looking contemplative on either side, and monkeys look on from behind.

There is more lively carving in the corbels on the outside of the church where the sculptors have made the most of the small space available. And there is another carved doorway to be seen on the far side of the courtyard, on what used to be the south entrance to the priory. This is a late work, from the middle of the twelfth century, and is generally regarded as illustrating the decline of sculpture in the Brionnais towards the end of the Romanesque period.

It does, however, have a delicate presentation of the Adoration of the Magi, alongside the story of Adam, Eve and the serpent in the Garden of Eden; while the lintel has some horrifying scenes of Hell, including a huge coiled monster which is devouring sinners. A capital on one side shows a man being beheaded, and on the other a man being strung up by his hands and feet.

There is a happier theme in **Montceaux-l'Etoile**. There the church is smaller and simpler than Anzy-le-Duc's, and the inside is of limited interest. But it has a pretty bell-tower, and a view out over the valley of the Arconce. It is well worth going there merely to see the west doorway and its tympanum. This was carved a few years later than the one over the west doorway in Anzy-le-Duc, and is one of the best in the Brionnais.

Both the tympanum and the lintel are devoted to the Ascension, and they make one continuous scene that is carved from a single block and alive with movement. Christ stands in a mandorla holding a cross, and is clearly being borne upwards by the angels on either side. Down below, two central figures point upwards towards him and address the Apostles, who gesture excitedly and talk among themselves.

It is a lively scene, and there is more to be seen on the doorway. The two corbels both show diabolical figures. The left-hand one is particularly forceful, with an armed St Michael striking down a cringeing monster. The left-hand capital has another fighting figure, while the one opposite has a mysterious scene in which an angel

Montceaux-l'Etoile: capital on the west doorway showing St Michael battling a monster

addresses a small person, apparently a saint, while pointing to the ascending Christ.

The tympanum is also the outstanding feature of another small, quite simple country church at **Neuilly-en-Donjon**. It too is much later, from the end of the twelfth century, but it is in a different style and is a strange and inspiring work, with elongated figures, carefully poised.

The centre of the tympanum has the Adoration of the Magi, with a large star above their heads, and the Virgin Mary sitting on a high throne with the infant Jesus on her knee. The tall, stylized figures of the Magi seem almost to be in movement, and the first of them is especially elegant as he performs a half-bow and offers his gift to the young child. Four angels blow huge, curled horns, two on either side of the central scene.

Below are two large animals, a bull and a lion, both of them winged and carved with great verve. These beasts have been interpreted in different ways, sometimes as monsters representing the evil in the world, now overcome. But it would seem more probable that, as in so much Romanesque art, they represent two of the evangelists, St Luke and St Mark, and that the tall winged figure holding a book behind the Mary's throne is the third, St Matthew (see page 263).

Tympanum of Neuilly-en-Donjon: the Adoration of the Magi

The main difficulty about this interpretation is that the eagle, which represents the fourth evangelist, St John, is not shown, which would be quite unconventional. It has been suggested that the Magi are intended to take St John's place. This is not really satisfactory, and so the role of the two great beasts remains a mystery.

The tympanum is, nonetheless, the work of a very great sculptor, and it is complemented by the carvings below, on the lintel and the two capitals. The left-hand capital shows the sufferings of two sinners, one at the hands of a grinning devil, the other perhaps Simon Magus plunging to earth at the instigation of St Peter. The right-hand one, easier to interpret, shows Daniel in the lions' den.

Across the lintel are two endearingly naive scenes: first, Adam and Eve in the Garden of Eden and, beside them, a stylized meal which combines features of the supper at the house of Simon the Pharisee – since it shows Mary Magdalene weeping at the feet of Jesus – and of the Last Supper. It is a static scene that contrasts well with the fluid scene above, and the details are all worth studying: the crouching figure of Mary, the folds of the Apostles' clothes, and their different attitudes and expressions.

Autun

The most prominent feature of Autun cathedral, as you approach this old Roman city, is its tall spire, built in the fifteenth century. But most of the inside is Romanesque of the first half of the twelfth century, and it is one of the finest churches of that period, both for its internal architecture and for its sculpture.

The tympanum over the west door is an unforgettable example of Romanesque art, a treatment of the Last Judgment which combines strange, elongated figures with a vivid depiction of the horrors of Hell. Within, there is an exceptional series of column capitals, most of them thought to be by the same sculptor as carved the tympanum, including scenes from both the Old and the New Testament.

For once, we may even know the name of the sculptor since on the tympanum, under the feet of the central figure of Christ, is an inscription: 'Gislebertus hoc fecit' (Gislebertus made this). Nothing more is known of Gislebertus, but if he was the sculptor, he was very gifted.

Autun was originally built by the Romans in the first century on an almost empty site on the bank of the river Arroux, and called Augustodunum. It was among the most important cities in Roman Gaul, and continued to be important in medieval times. Today, the old part is attractive to walk around, with its narrow, winding streets, and there are still impressive remains of the city's Roman past: among them, two monumental gates and the ruins of the theatre.

Christianity is believed to have reached Autun in the late second century, and to have been introduced by St Symphorian, who was martyred there. But the real boost to its prestige as a religious centre came from the claim that the remains of Lazarus, the friend of Christ whom he brought back to life, had been brought to Autun in mysterious circumstances in the late tenth century.

Early in the twelfth century Etienne de Bâgé, Bishop of Autun, decided that a new church dedicated to St Lazarus was needed to provide a suitable setting for such unique relics, and to attract pilgrims, and it was largely built between 1120 and 1146, in the architectural style developed by the abbey of Cluny (see page 61), south-east of Autun. Since 1195 it has been the cathedral.

Most of the exterior is now Gothic, and even the two bell-towers of the west front, which are Romanesque in style, were built in the nineteenth century, with the towers of Paray-le-Monial (see page 73), fifty miles to the south, as a model. But when you climb the steps beneath them, you enter the open two-bay narthex, built towards the end of the twelfth century, and that is dominated by the magnificent Last Judgment, carved about 1135, over the doorway into the church.

In the centre is Christ, a serene figure with outstretched hands and flowing

Tympanum of Autun cathedral: weighing of souls in the Last Judgment

draperies, who is enthroned in a mandorla, itself supported by angels, with the symbols of the sun and moon above him. On his right are the Virgin Mary and, below her, the happy elect, including a group of Apostles who crane their heads towards him, and St Peter, who is helping a small, naked figure to enter the narrow arcade which leads to Paradise.

On Christ's left are two unidentified saints, or perhaps Old Testament prophets, and below them the scene, familiar in Romanesque art, which is the most vivid: the weighing of souls and the agonies of the damned. The weighing of souls is derived from an ancient Egyptian motif in which the souls of the dead were weighed in the presence of Osiris. In Autun, St Michael and a grimacing devil confront each other on either side of the scales, while other devils grab hold of those found wanting and thrust them down into a sort of funnel.

The tympanum is one of the most dramatic, and distinctive, of the period because of the elongated forms of the main figures and the attitudes they strike. Four angels blow huge trumpets from the outer rim, and there is more drama on the lintel. The blessed, including clearly identified pilgrims, are ushered forward by angels on the left, and the damned, among them a miser carrying his bag of money and a woman whose breasts are being gnawed by serpents, meet their fate on the right. A pair of huge hands is throttling one of the sinners.

The tympanum is in good condition chiefly because it was plastered over in the eighteenth century, and so survived the French Revolution, when many churches and abbeys were damaged. It was rediscovered in 1837 and restored, but the head of Christ, which had been removed by the plasterers because it protruded too much, was missing, and it was only found in 1948, when it was put back in place.

The two archivolts provide an intriguing frame. The inner one has formal flower and foliage designs, and the outer one a sequence of signs of the Zodiac and little scenes illustrating the work appropriate to each month. The *trumeau*, or central pier of the doorway, dates from the nineteenth century, but there are some appealing twelfth-century capitals on either side, including one in which St Jerome extracts a thorn from the paw of a huge but well-disposed lion.

Inside, the nave of the cathedral is a compelling sight, tall, narrow and well-lit, with high windows on either side and others in the aisles. It is much as it was built in the twelfth century, and like other churches influenced by Cluny has a high barrel vault supported by pointed transverse arches, with more pointed arches dividing the nave from the aisles and supporting the groin vaulting in the aisles.

The apse at the east end of the cathedral was mostly rebuilt in the Gothic period, but there are still two tiers of round Romanesque arches, enclosing windows, at the lower levels. There is no ambulatory, which was uncommon for the time.

Capital inside Autun cathedral: the Temptation of Christ

The pointed arches of the nave and aisles look ahead to Gothic. However, there is also a foretaste of the Renaissance, as at Cluny itself and at Paray-le-Monial, in the elegant arrangement of the nave elevations. The architect of Autun was clearly influenced by the decoration of the city's surviving Roman gates, and he makes full use of fluted pilasters, Roman style, to achieve such near-Renaissance effects.

Some of these pilasters decorate the main arches on either side of the nave, and some the smaller arcades of the triforium. Others run all the way up to the base of the vault, culminating in the clerestory, where there is a single round-topped window in each bay.

The architect is entirely Romanesque, on the other hand, in the masterly use he makes of the sculpture of the capitals. Like many other Romanesque churches, Autun has finely carved capitals in the nave, the transept and the choir, which provide focal points of interest while helping to articulate the structure. And they are of very high quality.

Most are thought to be by Gislebertus, or whoever carved the tympanum, and they range widely in subject-matter, including stories from the Old and New Testament, and also mythological creatures, morality themes and much else, all of them vigorously and graphically presented. There are said to be 101 capitals in all, of which 49 are historiated, and it is worth taking time to walk round and look at them one by one.

Scenes from the Old Testament include Noah's Ark perched on top of Mount Ararat, Abraham's sacrifice of Isaac and Samson pulling down the temple. From the New Testament are the Nativity, the Temptation of Christ, Christ's appearance to Mary Magdalene after his Resurrection, and the stoning of St Stephen.

Other subjects are the dramatic fall of Simon Magus, the apocryphal magician, a surprisingly sensual evocation of Lust, Music as represented by a man carrying a string of bells, and a cockfight.

A handful of outstanding capitals was taken down in the nineteenth century because they were damaged, and

Capital inside Autun cathedral: dwarf in battle with a monstrous bird

replaced by copies. But the originals are now on display in the chapterhouse, which can be reached from inside the cathedral, and they are a feast for the eye, all the more enjoyable because they can be seen from close to.

They include the Adoration of the Magi, the engaging Awakening of the Magi, in which the three Wise Men are asleep under a single blanket, wearing their crowns, and are about to be woken up by an angel, a touching version of the Flight into Egypt, and the horrific Hanging of Judas. The Autun chapterhouse is itself one of the high points of Romanesque sculpture.

There is more sculpture to be seen in the Musée Rolin, just by the cathedral, and that includes another masterpiece: the figure of Eve, which was originally on the lintel of the north doorway of the cathedral, dismantled in the eighteenth century, and which is also thought to be the work of Gislebertus. Eve is a suggestive, naked figure, lying full-length and reaching out to pick the apple from the tree, with the serpent just visible to one side.

In the same museum are statues from the tomb of St Lazarus, which once stood in the cathedral sanctuary and formed a focal point for pilgrims but, like the north doorway, was dismantled in the eighteenth century. They include the figures of Martha and Mary Magdalene, and are dated to the first half of the twelfth century.

La Charité-sur-Loire

La Charité-sur-Loire is a picturesque old town that is dominated by the remaining parts of its large and ornate priory church, which in the second half of the twelfth century was one of the biggest in France, second only to the abbey church at Cluny (see page 61). Several stretches of the town's medieval ramparts still survive, and so does the sixteenth-century stone bridge that crosses the main arm of the Loire to an island close to the far bank.

The church at La Charité was one of the main stops for pilgrims on the route from Vézelay, in Burgundy, to Santiago de Compostela (see page 39), and as they walked on towards Bourges they, like the modern visitor, would have been able to look back across the Loire to the attractive jumble of church towers, monastic buildings and other houses ranged on the slopes above the river.

Cluny had founded a priory at La Charité in 1059 on a site with a tradition of monastic activity, and it became known as one of Cluny's five 'eldest daughters', with about fifty daughter houses of its own across Europe, including several in England. The first Cluniac church was consecrated by Pope Pascal II in 1107, and dedicated to the Virgin Mary, and it was rebuilt in parts and extended through much of the first half of the twelfth century.

One of the church's western towers survives, with its tiers of blind arches and arched windows now topped by a later spire. So does the whole of its east end: the magnificent *chevet*, with its radiating chapels, the two arms of the transept, and the octagonal tower over the crossing. They are all elaborately decorated, and give a good idea of how the church as a whole would have been.

Today's nave is a rather pedestrian seventeenth-century reconstruction, put up more than a century after a disastrous fire in 1559, and it is only four bays long, compared with the ten bays of the twelfth-century church. But the space left by the six bays that have vanished is now a pretty, open square, with the surviving western tower in one corner and a few ranges of finely carved arches from the original building high up on the walls.

From it, one can walk round the outside of the southern arm of the transept for a closer view of the carvings on the transept, the choir and the crossing tower; and then come out onto an open space to the east of the church. This is now a happy hunting ground for archaeologists, who have discovered traces of an earlier church. From there the whole *chevet* can be seen. It is a grand sight, with the Gothic chapel that protrudes from the easternmost point of the ambulatory

Priory church of La Charité-sur-Loire, from the north-east

providing the only discordant note. The walk continues through the remains of the monastic buildings to the north of the church, and another pretty square below the western bell-tower.

At the foot of the tower is one of two surviving tympana from the twelfth-century west front of the church (the other is inside). The stonework is damaged in parts – and was recently home to three large and well-established birds' nests. But there are some delightful carvings: of Christ receiving the Virgin Mary into Heaven and, on the lintel below, the Annunciation, the Visitation, the Nativity and the announcement to the shepherds.

The scenes on the lintel are noticeably similar to a sequence on the *portail royal* (royal porch) of Chartres cathedral (see page 102), and there was presumably some link between the sculptors who worked on the two tympana, although there is disagreement on what it was, and who may have influenced whom.

There is also uncertainty over whether there was ever a second western tower, which would have balanced the one that survives and, together with it, created a grand west front for the church. The assumption is that a second tower was intended, and it may have been built and then destroyed in a fire in 1204. But there is no firm proof of that.

Perhaps the most notable feature of La Charité as a whole is the rich and detailed decoration of the church, both outside and in. Outside, most noticeably, there are ranges of blind arcading in which the polyfoil arches show the artistic influence of Islamic Spain, and there is a great variety of patterns on the square pilasters between the arches. Sculptures in relief of saints fill several of the niches on the outside of the choir and the crossing tower.

Most surprising, perhaps, is the almost baroque shape of the buttresses round the choir, which curve out, bow-shaped, over the roof of the ambulatory.

Inside the church, it is the powerful effect of the tall, pointed arches of the crossing and the choir, characteristic of later Cluniac architecture, that is immediately evident. The cupola over the crossing is supported on squinches, and the choir itself is both stylish and decorative, with a ring of columns supporting pointed arches, a blind arcade of polyfoil arches, and rounded windows above that. The transept dates from an earlier phase in the building of the church and has rounded arches at its lower level, as well as chapels with apses on the eastern side.

There are well-carved column capitals both in the choir and elsewhere in the church, many with formalized plant decoration, but also including lions, birds and monsters. There is a cycle of other imaginary beasts, with the Paschal Lamb at their centre, carved in relief round the wall of the choir.

The second tympanum from the west front is now in the wall of the south arm

La Charité-sur-Loire: the choir and apse

of the transept, where it was brought for protection in the nineteenth century, and it is another powerful work, full of movement. The principal scene is of the Transfiguration, with Christ at the centre in a mandorla, Moses and Elijah on either side, and three Apostles showing their astonishment. Below, on the lintel, are two more intimate scenes: of the Three Wise Men offering their gifts to the Virgin and Child, and of the Presentation in the Temple.

Charlieu and St-Julien-de-Jonzy

Very little is left of the eleventh-century priory church that once stood in Charlieu, an evocative old town just south of the borders of Burgundy. But the narthex which was added to the west end of the church in the twelfth century still stands, and it has three remarkable doorways which, in their different ways, show the skills of the Romanesque sculptors in and around Burgundy's Brionnais region.

The two most striking doorways are, unusually, on the north façade of the narthex, and though they are much damaged, demonstrate the 'baroque' exuberance of the Brionnais sculptors of the second quarter of the twelfth century. They have very lavish decoration, exquisitely carved, over much of their surfaces, and

Tympanum of Charlieu priory church: Christ in Majesty

there is a Christ in Majesty on the tympanum of the larger doorway whose complex design and flowing lines give it a strong sense of movement and drama.

The contrast with the third doorway, which is inside the narthex and also has a Christ in Majesty on its tympanum, could hardly be greater. This one is part of the original west front of the eleventh-century church, and dates from the second half of that century. It has almost no decoration on the flanking columns and the archivolts apart from some simple carved capitals, and the figures on the tympanum and the lintel, while they have a quiet power of their own, are largely static.

Taken together, the three doorways show the progression that took place in barely half a century. The theme of Christ in Majesty, often linked with that of the Ascension, was a recurring one, and after the first version in Charlieu it was taken up by sculptors in Anzy-le-Duc and Montceaux-l'Etoile (see page 43), who treated it with increasing freedom. The larger of the two northern doorways at Charlieu represents the culmination of the school before it went into decline.

The same is true of a tympanum in St-Julien-de-Jonzy, a village a few miles north of Charlieu, which is in the same style as the two doorways, and the church is worth visiting in order to see it.

Charlieu is on the river Sornin, and was long a crossroads for traffic between the Saône and the Loire, with a history going back to prehistoric times. It was settled in the Roman period. It acquired its present name in the late ninth century, when monks fleeing from the Viking raids up the Loire established an abbey there, and called it 'carus locus' (lovely place), which became Charlieu.

The abbey was linked to the Burgundian abbey of Cluny (see page 61) about 930-40, and in due course downgraded to a priory. But it flourished under the new dispensation, and a new church similar in style to that of Anzy-le-Duc was consecrated in 1094.

Only the westernmost bay of that church survives, the rest of it having been demolished after the French Revolution. There is now just an open space under which the foundations of the body of the church and those of its predecessors on the site have been excavated – flanked by an imposing defensive tower of the late twelfth century and a complex of buildings, of various dates, which survive from the priory.

The single bay has some entertaining capitals, including an acrobat so contorted that his head appears through his legs, and the scene of a fight between a man on horseback and a centaur. But the most interesting part is the eleventh-century western doorway. This shows Christ sitting in a mandorla, which is supported by two standing angels, while down below, on the lintel, are the Twelve Apostles, each sitting in a small niche.

Tympanum of St-Julien-de-Jonzy: Christ in Majesty

The two twelfth-century doorways on the north façade of the narthex stand side by side, and are a tour de force. The sculptors of the larger one showed great inventiveness in devising a range of patterns that cover the upright columns on either side of the door itself, as well as the archivolts above it. And there are not only patterns but floral designs, harpies, angels and the figure of a nearly naked woman being devoured by a snake and a crab, who represents lust and its punishment.

The figure of Christ in Majesty on the tympanum is surrounded not just by two angels who support the mandorla in which he sits but by the creatures that symbolize the four evangelists – the lion of St Mark, the bull of St Luke, the eagle of St John and the winged man of St Matthew (see page 263). The lintel has the Virgin Mary in the centre, with an angel on either side, and flanked by the Twelve Apostles, while at the top of the main arch is the Lamb of God.

Below, at each end of the main arch, is the delicate, flowing figure of an angel playing a stringed instrument; and at either end of the lintel a capital showing one of the benefactors of the priory, each carrying a tiny building in his hands.

The smaller doorway is less dramatic but carved with the same verve – though it too is badly damaged. On the tympanum is the Marriage at Cana, with Christ and the other guests seated at a slightly curved table, and below on the lintel the scene of an Old Testament sacrifice, where animals are being led to the altar. Above them on the main arch are the six participants in the Transfiguration, all vigorously carved, but all unfortunately disfigured in the nineteenth century – from left to right, St James, St John, Christ himself, Moses, Elijah and St Peter.

The church in **St-Julien-de-Jonzy** is not far away, and it has a spectacular setting on a hilltop looking out over the surrounding countryside as well as a pretty bell-tower. Much of the church has been rebuilt but the tower, which once covered the transept crossing, dates from the first half of the twelfth century, and so does the beautifully carved doorway below it.

The style of the doorway with its poised figures and intricately carved capitals is so close to that of the two northern doorways in Charlieu that it appears to have been carved by the same team. It has even been suggested, without any firm proof, that it may originally have been intended for Charlieu.

In the tympanum, as so often in the Brionnais, is Christ in Majesty, sitting in a mandorla which is supported by two angels with flowing robes. On the lintel is the Last Supper, with Christ and the Apostles sitting at a long table, and every fold of the table-cloth carefully outlined. At one side Christ washes the feet of St Peter. At the other, some of the Apostles follow his example.

Cluny and Berzé-la-Ville

The Benedictine abbey of Cluny, in southern Burgundy, was the most influential monastic institution in Europe in the eleventh and early twelfth centuries, as we have seen. At its peak it had some 1,450 abbeys, priories and other religious communities associated with it, spread across western Europe, and in Cluny itself it had a church whose dimensions and style matched its spiritual and political importance.

Cluny III, the Romanesque church which was the third and last to be built on the site by its monks, most of it between 1088 and 1130, was for centuries the largest in the Christian world – until St Peter's in Rome was rebuilt in the sixteenth century. When it was finally completed in about 1230, it was more than 600ft long, its vault was almost 100ft high, and its many towers, built over its two transepts and its west front, made it a breathtaking sight from miles away.

Today, very little is left of this huge church since the greater part of it was pulled down in the aftermath of the French Revolution. But the south arm of the main transept still stands, together with the two towers built over it, and that gives at least an idea of the scale of the church and of its elegant style, both inside and out.

Abbey church of Cluny: south arm of the main transept, the only surviving part

A few other pieces survive, not least the capitals which used to decorate the choir, and which are now on display in the abbey's former granary. And there is another outstanding survival from the great days of Cluny: the tiny chapel at Berzé-la-Ville, out in the country a few miles away, which has some of the most compelling and beautiful frescoes of the Romanesque period.

It should be added that Cluny itself is another atmospheric little town which originally grew up alongside the abbey, and has an array of old houses, some of them dating back to Romanesque times. The main gateway into the abbey, which was built in about 1100 and is reminiscent of a Roman triumphal arch, with two round arches, each flanked by columns, remains standing.

Cluny was founded in 910 by William the Pious, Duke of Aquitaine, on land which he owned and which he handed over to the abbey – he was also, among other things, Count of Mâcon. He stipulated that it should observe the Rule of St Benedict, drawn up in the sixth century, and that it should be subject only to the Pope, with the freedom to run its own affairs without interference from either civil or church authorities, as I have mentioned.

The building of Cluny III was set in motion by one of the greatest of its abbots, Hugh of Semur, later St Hugh, who held the office from 1049 to 1109. The church had a nave with two side-aisles on each side, two transepts, and a sizeable *chevet*, with an ambulatory and five radiating chapels. In a second stage a five-bay narthex was added at its western end, and two sturdy towers were built to frame the entrance.

Today, much of this is marked out on the ground, and it is possible to visualize the size of the church. But the dominant feature is the surviving arm of the main transept, with its tall and beautiful bell-tower, known as the Holy Water Bell-Tower (*clocher de l'eau bénite*), which rises from the truncated transept, flanked by the smaller Clock Tower.

The Holy Water Bell-Tower is octagonal, with two tiers of skilfully carved arches below its conical spire. It was originally balanced by a similar tower on the north arm of the transept; and in between them was an even larger, square tower built over the crossing. There was also a smaller tower over the crossing of the smaller transept, which was to the east of the main one. So the view of the *chevet* from the east was a complex and magnificent one.

The inside of the transept is now just a shell, and its rough floor and bare walls show the battering it has undergone over the years. However, with its high vault, it has not lost the soaring quality that the whole church must have had, and it still has the pleasing arrangement of arches, windows and carved capitals high up on its three walls. Like churches elsewhere built under the influence of Cluny, it has a slightly pointed barrel vault on either side of the cupola that supports the bell-tower, while it seems to foreshadow the Renaissance with its round arches, columns and fluted pilasters.

Most of the other surviving buildings at Cluny were built or rebuilt in later centuries, including the abbots' lodgings, the cloister, and a long, east-facing façade that dates from the eighteenth century. It is a harmonious ensemble, which includes a park, and in many places is still surrounded by the old abbey walls, together with towers of various shapes.

The former granary is a handsome Gothic building on two levels built in the thirteenth century. The upper floor, with its intricate timber vaulting, is now used to display the capitals from the Romanesque church's choir, and they show the talents of the sculptors at Cluny's disposal. There are two with biblical scenes on them, Adam and Eve in the Garden of Eden and Abraham's Sacrifice of Isaac, while the other eight have a range of subjects, mostly allegorical, on each of their four sides. They include some exquisitely carved human figures, set in the frame of a mandorla and surrounded by foliage.

There has been much debate about the dating of the capitals – about whether they are late eleventh or early twelfth-century – and about the identity of some of the figures. But the figures on one capital clearly represent the four winds, and those on another four virtues – love, faith, hope and justice. Another of the capitals has the four rivers of Paradise, which gush out over naked young men, with fruit trees standing between them.

Two capitals have musicians of various sorts on each of their four sides, and they are especially engaging. They are thought to represent the eight modes of plainsong, something that was much cherished at Cluny. Together with the other capitals from the choir, they are another of the high points of Romanesque sculpture in Burgundy.

The frescoes in **Berzé-la-Ville** are a further high point of the period. This simple but shapely little Romanesque chapel, which stands on a spur of rock in the countryside south of Cluny, surrounded by farmland and farm buildings, has paintings in its apse which are anything but rustic. They show the influence of both Byzantine and Ottonian art, and were clearly the work of one or more of the leading artists of the day.

They make an immediate impression when you walk into the chapel. The whole apse is filled with paintings in a rich mix of colours, and in its centre, dominating the chapel, is the figure of Christ in Majesty seated in a mandorla which seems to stand out from the hollow of the apse. He looks out fixedly at the world with an expression that is both stern and gentle, while on either side of him stands a group

of Apostles, each of whom leans attent-
ively forward towards the figure of
Christ.

Down below are formal portraits of
six female saints, each in an angle between the arches, and at the bottom
head-and-shoulders portraits of several
early Christian martyrs. But the most
arresting are two complete paintings,
each depicting a martyrdom, which are
in the blind arches on either side of the
windows. On one side is the imprison-
ment and beheading of St Blasius, a
fourth-century Anatolian bishop, on
the other the roasting on a grill of
St Vincent, a third-century Spanish
deacon.

The chapel is known as the Monks' *Chapel of Berzé-la-Ville, near Cluny*
Chapel, and had a special relationship
with Cluny in medieval times. It stands on land that was acquired by the abbey in
1093 when Hugh of Semur was abbot; and the priory that he built there is said to
have been a refuge for him towards the end of his life, away from the bustle of the
abbey.

The frescoes in the chapel do not date from Hugh's lifetime, it seems, but were
painted soon after his death in 1109, probably in the following fifteen years or so.
They too show the quality of the artists employed by Cluny at the height of its
power, and give an indication of how the abbey church itself would have been
decorated in the twelfth century. The painter or painters could have seen Byzantine
work in Italy, perhaps in Ravenna or in the monastery of Monte Cassino, south of
Rome, while the Ottonian influence must have come from the German Empire,
with which Cluny had close links.

The power of the frescoes comes partly from the warmth of the colours – blue
for much of the background and a range of reds, ochres, browns and greens –
and also from their composition and draughtsmanship. The figures have a formal,
hieratic quality that is typical of Byzantine art, but there is also an expressiveness
in their faces and gestures. This is true of the two groups of Apostles, and also of
four other figures just below the mandorla: on one side two deacons, on the other
two bishops.

The two scenes of martyrdom are moving and powerful. In the one devoted to St Blasius a widow is shown visiting the saint in prison in the upper part of the painting. She is offering him the head and legs of her pig to eat because, many years before, he had helped her by rescuing the pig, then only a piglet, from a wolf. Then at a lower level St Blasius is shown being beheaded.

The painting of the martyrdom of St Vincent has another, different effect. The saint is at the bottom, lying naked on the grill, while the fire blazes underneath and the two executioners prod him with long metal-tipped staves. The Roman procurator, Dacianus, sits at one side, a huge figure balancing a sceptre on his knee. The executioners' staves and Dacianus's sceptre are almost parallel, and they form diagonal lines that cross the painting from top to bottom.

Little is known about the later history of the chapel, but the frescoes disappeared from sight and were only rediscovered by the local priest in 1887, covered with plaster. This had probably preserved the freshness of the colours.

The plaster was removed and they were eventually restored, but not until a British archaeologist, Joan Evans, later Dame Joan Evans, had bought the chapel herself to prevent it from being sold and dismantled, and made a gift of it to the Académie de Mâcon.

Dijon: St-Bénigne

Only the crypt survives of one of the most original buildings of early eleventh-century Burgundy – the three-tier rotunda at the east end of the former abbey church of St-Bénigne in Dijon, now the cathedral. Today St-Bénigne is largely Gothic, but steps at the side lead down to the eastern end of the crypt, which is Romanesque, and at its centre is an open circular space with a forest of columns arranged in three concentric rings.

These columns are the lowest of the three levels of the rotunda, which was built in the first years of the eleventh century in imitation of the Holy Sepulchre church in Jerusalem, also circular. Now, the crypt is windowless and dark, but it is possible to imagine the grandeur the whole rotunda must once have possessed, when the two upper levels were still in place, each of them with more rings of columns, and when light came in from above.

The crypt held the relics of St Bénigne, a shadowy figure who is believed to have brought Christianity to the Dijon region in the second century, and to have been martyred there. So the rotunda became the focal point of the abbey church, and it was preserved when the rest of the upper church was rebuilt in the Gothic period. The two higher levels were only demolished in 1792, after the French Revolution.

In the process the lowest level of the rotunda was filled in, and it was not rediscovered until some fifty years later when a new sacristy was being built. The whole of the eastern end of the crypt has been cleared and restored, including several chapels and a small sunken area between the two arms of the transept which has the lower part of an ancient sarcophagus, thought to be that of St Bénigne.

West of that – excavations have shown – are the remains of the crypt's Romanesque nave, which stretches under the nave of the upper church. But it was filled in long ago, and has not been dug out.

The site is an ancient one that dates back to Roman times. As so often, the cult of St Bénigne grew up in the cemetery which was on the edge of the Roman town, and in which Bénigne was presumably buried. In due course a monastic community was formed, and in 989 William of Volpiano, one of the great reforming abbots of the period, arrived in Dijon at the instigation of Cluny (see page 61), the abbey in southern Burgundy, to run the affairs of St-Bénigne.

William was there for forty years, and the rotunda was conceived as the masterpiece of his architectural work. It was a complex building but, compared to later Romanesque churches, its decoration is quite simple since most of the columns have plain capitals.

Two of the capitals, however, have a naive but haunting design which is considered to be contemporary with the building. It shows the head and arms of a bearded man with staring eyes who appears to be praying. The design is repeated with variations on each of the faces of one capital. The other has some simpler, almost abstract versions of the same design, which could have been early sketches for it.

There are other capitals elsewhere in the crypt which are well worth noticing, although they are probably not contemporary with the rotunda. Some of them, which are largely abstract, perhaps date from the earlier, Carolingian period. Others, which have

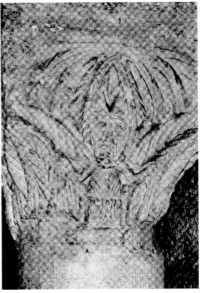

Dijon cathedral: capital in crypt

fairly complex and sophisticated designs, including monsters, demons and animal masks, are almost certainly later.

Fontenay

The former abbey of Fontenay in northern Burgundy stands out in a number of ways: for the beauty of its site, for its austere but harmonious architecture, and for the fact that it is the best surviving example of an early Cistercian foundation.

The abbey church was built between 1139 and 1147 in the plain, unadorned style favoured by St Bernard of Clairvaux – well-proportioned but with very little decoration; and it has a large and handsome cloister that was built at the same time and is only a little more decorative, on its south side. Several of the other monastic buildings also date back to the twelfth century, and they have the same elegant simplicity.

As elsewhere in Burgundy, the Fontenay builders used the pointed barrel vault and pointed arches in the nave of the church, and so to a certain extent fore-shadowed the later Gothic style. But the style of the church is Romanesque, of the distinctive kind that was introduced by the first Cistercians, and particularly by St Bernard.

Cistercian abbey of Fontenay: the cloister

The Cistercian order had had its beginnings in 1098 when Robert of Molesme and his fellow monks established themselves at Cîteaux, south of Dijon, to follow their own rigorous interpretation of the Rule of St Benedict, as we have seen. They were joined in 1112 by Bernard of Fontaine, the future St Bernard, and in due course he became the most prominent member of the order.

Bernard became the founding Abbot of Clairvaux, a daughter-house of Cîteaux, in 1115, and in 1118 or 1119 he sent out monks to found Fontenay as a daughter-house of Clairvaux. Following Cistercian practice, they looked for a site that was remote but had a ready supply of water, and though the first place they found was not satisfactory, by 1130 they were established in the present site, where they channeled the stream that flowed through it.

Fontenay is still off the beaten track, in a wooded valley with its stream, and it consists of a complex of buildings of different periods set in a small park. It mainly owes its survival to the fact that after being sold off in the years after the French Revolution it was used as a paper-mill, and so not demolished. It has been owned by different branches of the same family since 1820, and during the twentieth century they set about extensive restoration of the abbey buildings.

The policy of the Cistercians was to avoid anything that was ostentatious or superfluous, and it is noticeable that the church is hardly taller or more prominent than the other monastic buildings. It has, for instance, no bell-tower. It is a long rectangular building with a nave and two side-aisles, and a flat *chevet*, or east end, rather than the more elaborate apse or apses often found in Romanesque churches.

In spite of its simplicity, however, it is far from dull, partly because of the balance between its various features. The sloping tiled roofs of the nave and aisles end in decorative cornices on either side of the church, with windows below, and at both the east and west ends of the church there is a typically Cistercian arrangement of tall round-topped windows.

The west front is largely plain apart from these windows but it has a characteristic design. Two solid buttresses mark the division between the nave and the aisles, and the windows are placed between them, beneath the gable. Down below is the central doorway, which is also round-topped and relatively unadorned. There is just one decorative touch: slim columns with formal capitals that flank the doorway and the largest of the windows, in the centre at the top.

The inside of the church goes beyond simplicity and achieves an austere grandeur which, again, is distinctively Cistercian. The long barrel vault, supported by the pointed transverse arches, stretches the length of the nave as far as the transept, with a line of pointed arches on either side. A flying screen, with five windows in it, makes the transition to the choir, which has a lower vault, also pointed, and the flat wall beyond the sanctuary has six windows, arranged in two rows of three.

Decoration is minimal, as I have said. Engaged columns are set into the pillars of the nave, forming clusters around them, and their capitals provide focal points as in other Romanesque churches. But there is only the barest of formal carving on the capitals, and there is no triforium or clerestory. The powerful effect of the nave is created by the simple lines of the structure, culminating in the characteristic form of the vault.

The nave itself has no windows, but it is well lit by the windows at each end, east and west, and also by the windows in the aisles. These have transverse barrel vaulting in each bay, with pointed arches between the bays, an arrangement similar to that in the nave of the church of St-Philibert in Tournus (see page 86).

The cloister, by way of contrast, has round arches on all four sides, and is a large open space with views not just of the church and other buildings but of the wooded hillside beyond. There are wider openings in the centre of each side, but the arches are mainly in pairs, resting on small, rather squat columns, with a wider relieving arch above each pair. Here again the proportions are well judged, making it a beautiful and imposing place.

As in the church, the carving of the capitals is of the simplest, following the belief of St Bernard that the monks should not be distracted from their prayers by 'ridiculous monsters' and the like (see page 33). But the columns on the north side, below the church, and in particular the buttresses between each pair of arches, are more intricately carved than the others, some of them with fluting.

Other abbey buildings can be entered from the cloister. One shapely doorway, which has been given four archivolts, leads into the chapterhouse, and that is connected with the *scriptorium*, where the monks copied manuscripts. Both rooms are of approximately the same date as the church, and it is interesting that they have rib vaulting.

Above them, on the upper floor, is the monks' dormitory, which stretches the whole length of the building, and is now covered by a wooden ceiling of the sixteenth century.

Not the least interesting of the abbey buildings is the forge, another long and well-proportioned building which dates from the late twelfth or early thirteenth century, and has a fast-moving stream running along its far side. This too has rib vaulting in its various rooms. The monks used the water from the stream to work the iron deposits found locally.

An inscription records that this was the first metallurgical factory in Europe, and the place where the hydraulic hammer was invented.

Nevers: St-Etienne

Clustered on a hill overlooking the Loire, at a key crossing point over the river, Nevers has been a city of some importance since Roman times. During the Romanesque period the counts of Nevers made it their business to extend their power over the surrounding region, the Nivernais, and the city itself was the seat of a bishop, with a cathedral as well as a number of other churches and abbeys.

It was also a stopping-point on one of the lesser pilgrim routes to Santiago de Compostela, which branched off the main route that began in Vézelay (see page 39), in Burgundy, and linked up with it again after crossing the river Creuse north of Limoges.

The elegant priory church of St-Etienne, in the old part of Nevers, is a survivor from those days, and its interior is one of the best preserved and most satisfying of the eleventh century. With its tall, barrel-vaulted nave and the intricate arrangement of its choir and transept, it is a fine example of a Romanesque church of its date, when the style had reached maturity.

Priory church of Nevers: the 'chevet'

St-Etienne has unfortunately lost its two western towers and the tall octagonal tower over the crossing, which were pulled down during the French Revolution. That has robbed the exterior of much of its impact. The west front is now almost entirely bare, having also lost its porch and the sculptured tympanum inside it; and the short crossing tower is much less inspiring than it must once have been.

But the *chevet* is a masterly example of its kind, with a high apse surrounded by the ambulatory and chapels. So are the two tall arms of the transept, each ending in a decorative façade. And the main body of the church is essentially as it was when it was consecrated in 1097 by Yves, Bishop of Chartres, by which date it is thought to have been more or less complete.

Today, it contrasts with Nevers cathedral, which is in another part of the old city, a large church that still has Romanesque parts but much that is Gothic, or even later, in style. An interesting feature is that it has two apses, one at the east end and one at the west – an arrangement much commoner in Germany than France – and the western one is Romanesque like the crypt underneath it and much of the transept.

The Benedictine priory of St-Etienne was one of many established by Cluny (see page 61) after the site had been presented to it by William I, Count of Nevers, in 1068. Its church was, therefore, built primarily for the use of the monks rather than as a shrine for pilgrims, but with its ambulatory and radiating chapels it has much in common with the pilgrimage churches of the period.

The first impression is one of darkness, as in many Romanesque churches, and of an array of lofty, rounded arches leading from the nave to the semi-circle of the apse and chancel. But as in many such churches, the light is subtly contrived, and St-Etienne has a feature that is uncommon for a barrel-vaulted church. It has a clerestory high up on either side of the nave, above the galleries, and that provides a direct source of light for the nave, in addition to the light filtered in through the main arches and the galleries above them.

There is more light in the transept, each arm of which has windows on all three of its sides, and a flying screen consisting of five small arches borne by a wide arch, an architectural device that also serves to let in light. It is a stylish arrangement, similar to that in several of the Auvergne churches (see page 162).

St-Etienne has little in the way of surface decoration – only a handful of column capitals with formalized plant designs, beautifully carved, most of them in the ambulatory. The rest of the capitals are plain. The builders chose to concentrate on line, proportions and the play of light.

Paray-le-Monial

The basilica of Paray-le-Monial in southern Burgundy, once part of a priory linked to the abbey of Cluny (see page 61), is a particularly graceful church, and a good example of Cluny's style of Romanesque architecture in the twelfth century. If there has been some restoration on the outside, it has been sensitively done, and the inside remains as impressive as it must always have been – with a tall nave and transept and the subtle use of light and decorated stonework.

Work on the church began early in the twelfth century, on the instructions of Hugh of Semur, the influential abbot of Cluny from 1049 to 1109, later St Hugh. It continued for several decades, and was more or less contemporary with the building of the great church at Cluny itself – Cluny III – which was also set in motion by Hugh. As a result, Paray-le-Monial was in many ways a smaller version of that church.

It is interesting for the way that, like other Cluniac churches, it looks ahead to the Gothic style with its pointed arches and its sense of upward movement. But at the same time, many of its features, not least the very handsome arrangement of tall columns in the sanctuary, which are linked by round arches and have a semi-circle of round-headed windows above them, seem to anticipate the Renaissance.

The church has a picturesque setting on the banks of the river Bourbince, and on a calm day its three towers are reflected in the slow-moving water: the two square towers of the west front and the larger octagonal bell-tower over the transept crossing, all topped by the conical spires of the Romanesque period. There are gardens in front of the church and, to one side, the eighteenth-century priory building, the last to be put up by the Cluniac monks before the dissolution of their order.

The church also has a magnificent *chevet*, best seen from the north-east. As in other Romanesque churches, the various parts – the radiating chapels, the ambulatory, the apse, the choir and the transept – build up, level upon level, to the climax of the bell-tower over the transept crossing, and Paray-le-Monial is one of the most splendid examples of the style.

The only slight reservation must be over the bell-tower itself, because this is a nineteenth-century structure that was built to replace a bulb-shaped tower which had itself replaced the original tower, destroyed in a fire in the fourteenth century. But it was closely modelled on the surviving bell-tower at Cluny, and is presumably similar to the original.

The two western towers and the narthex beneath them are older than the rest of the church, dating from the eleventh century. This is because the origins of the

Priory church of Paray-le-Monial, from the north-west

priory go back to the late tenth century, when the land on which it stands was offered to Cluny, and the twelfth-century church was the third to be built there by the monks. The narthex and the two towers were the western end of an earlier church that had been erected on the same site, and rather than pull them down, the monks kept them as part of the new one – even though it had a slightly different orientation.

Like the main bell-tower, the two towers had their spires remade in the nineteenth century. But this too was sensitively done, and the west front of Paray-le-Monial is both distinctive and appealing. The southern tower is simple and well proportioned, with pairs of small arched windows, the northern one more elaborate and particularly handsome, with larger, more ornate arches, flanked by columns and capitals.

The narthex itself was thoroughly remodelled in the nineteenth century, after centuries of being walled off, and so was the chapel dedicated to St Michael on the floor above it. Both have the pure lines of the Romanesque style, with round arches. The vaulting of the narthex is supported by two clusters of columns, each with capitals based on Romanesque originals.

The nave itself is relatively short, only three bays long, but its height is all the more striking for that. Pointed transverse arches support a barrel vault, and there is a harmonious view along the length of the church, to the tall semi-circle of columns and arches behind the sanctuary.

High, pointed arches divide the nave from the side-aisles, which are groin-vaulted and also have pointed arches between the bays, and there is a triforium of blind arches above them. Small, round-headed windows fill the clerestory that runs above that. This arrangement continues in the choir and in the two arms of the transept, which have the same height as the nave.

The semi-circle of columns in the sanctuary is one of the most beautiful parts of the church. Beyond it is the ambulatory, with three chapels radiating off it, and this creates a complex arrangement of round arches that contrasts with the pointed arches elsewhere.

The nave and the transept are quite dark since the only direct light for them comes from the windows of the clerestory, high up on the side walls. But this appears to have been deliberate, and is part of the appeal of Paray-le-Monial. As so frequently in Romanesque churches, the light is carefully controlled, and the relative darkness of the nave and the transept creates an element of drama, conducive to devotion, before the transition to the brightness of the sanctuary.

One of the notable features of the church is the extent to which the stonework is decorated. This is not so much a matter of the capitals, because although there are many of them in Paray-le-Monial, they chiefly consist of formal plant designs, together with a few animals and birds, and a handful of human figures.

It is rather the patterning that is found on the arches all over the church, most often with a succession of tiny egg shapes, and the fluting on the many engaged pilasters, which are common in churches influenced by Cluny. Together with the articulation of the engaged columns and pilasters that run up the sides of the nave, transepts and choir, they show the sophistication of the builders from Cluny.

Some of the church's most lavish decoration is on the outside, on the doorways at either end of the transept. The north doorway is the more remarkable, and the more accessible, but each of them is covered with intricate carving, with a variety of designs on the door frame, on the columns on either side, on the archivolt and the lintel. There is little doubt that, like other Romanesque work, they were influenced by the artistry of Muslim Spain.

Perrecy-les-Forges and Gourdon

Perrecy-les-Forges and Gourdon are two of the many villages dotted across Burgundy's rolling countryside which still have churches from the eleventh and twelfth centuries. They are only a few miles apart, in southern Burgundy, and while their churches are different from each other, they both have features that make them stand out.

Perrecy has a narthex at its western end with some particularly appealing carving, on the doorway and on the capitals of the columns, as well as a tall and shapely bell-tower above. Gourdon is a church of great charm which is one of the few to have preserved some Romanesque frescoes, with their characteristic style and colours, and also has some naive but engaging capitals.

Both churches are of monastic origin. **Perrecy**'s history goes back to Carolingian times, and the eighth-century struggle against the Arab invasion, because it was part of a domain that was given by Charles Martel, who had defeated the Arabs near Poitiers in 732, to Childebrand, his brother, in recognition of a victory Childebrand had won four years later. Eccard, Childebrand's son, founded a priory there, which he left in his will to the important abbey of St-Benoît-sur-Loire (see page 154), and the present church was built under that abbey's auspices.

It makes a stirring sight when seen across the open fields to the west, a large sprawling church built in a mixture of styles. The *chevet* is Gothic, but the transept, crossing tower, nave and narthex are all Romanesque, and of different periods.

Narthex of Perrecy-les-Forges: capital with elephants

The nave, the south side-aisle and the transept crossing are the earliest surviving parts, built in about 1020-30, and they are in a simple early Romanesque style. A timber ceiling covers the nave, which has two rows of plain round arches along its south side, one above the other, and windows at the upper level on both sides. (There was once a north aisle, but it was later pulled down.)

The most interesting and telling feature is the four flying screens, consisting of small arches, all originally open, that are built into the stonework over each of the big arches that support the crossing tower.

It is the narthex, however, built a century later, that sets Perrecy apart. Its soaring bell-tower, decorated near the top with two tiers of round arches, three to a side and all with carved detail, towers over the church; and the sculpture in its porch is some of the best.

At the centre of the porch, on the tympanum over the door into the church, is a serene Christ in Majesty, sitting in a mandorla supported by two seraphim, that is, angels with six wings each. The subject and the style are similar to those in several churches in the Brionnais region, further to the south, but the use of seraphim rather than angels with two wings is unusual.

Below on the lintel, badly mutilated but still recognizable in most places, are scenes from the Passion of Christ. They include Jesus and the Apostles in the garden of Gethsemane, the kiss of Judas, the arrest of Jesus, and his appearances before the high priest and Pilate. They are carved with movement and vigour.

There are also carvings elsewhere, on the corbels supporting the lintel and on the capitals. One corbel has St Michael carrying a large spear as he calmly tramples on the dragon he has defeated – and apparently points the way into the church. The opposite one also has an angel, but he is fighting fiercely, wielding his sword and at the same time protecting a small human who is cowering behind his shield.

There is a similar contrast, and the same vitality, on the capitals on either side. Alongside St Michael is one depicting a peaceful scene: the meeting between two hermits, St Antony and St Paul. Opposite is a dramatic event that no one so far has satisfactorily explained. A warrior is preparing to attack a monstrous, three-headed bird. The warrior has goat-like legs, and a snake is apparently gnawing his belly. Behind the bird a woman is standing with her head in her hands.

There are more flights of fancy and moral lessons elsewhere in the porch. On one capital two elephants confront each other. They were clearly an unknown animal in twelfth-century Burgundy, since they have the hooves of cattle, the tusks of boars, tiny ears and long tails. But they are still recognizable and engaging beasts, surrounded by luscious foliage.

Other capitals have subjects that are more often treated in Romanesque sculpture: a siren with her legs wide apart, representing temptation; and a woman with her breasts being devoured by snakes, representing lust and its punishment. They, like the elephants, are surrounded by fine foliage, and are impeccably carved.

The foliage is in fact one of the most appealing features of the Perrecy porch. Not all the capitals have a story to tell, and there are several which consist solely of formal plant designs.

Gourdon, too, has a long history, since the village stands on the site of an ancient Gallic hill fortress, and it is known that there was a monastery there as early as the sixth century. The present church dates from the late eleventh and early twelfth centuries and, although it has lost the top of its bell-tower, it is still a satisfying building of that period, with a fine position high up on the edge of the village.

It has style and charm inside, with round transverse arches over the nave, pointed arches in the crossing and choir, and the round form of the apse at the eastern end. With their honey-coloured stone, the nave, choir and apse make an immediate impression when you enter the church through the west door.

The nave has a feature that is rare for Burgundy because, like Vézelay (see page 93) and Anzy-le-Duc (see page 43), it has groin vaulting; but unlike them, it has three levels on either side: round arches at ground level, pairs of blind arches above them and, at the top, small round-headed windows. To support all this, pillars run up either side of the nave, together with engaged columns, and the transverse arches rest on them.

It is a successful arrangement, which provides some direct light to the nave, at least at the top, and as is usual in Romanesque churches, the carved capitals provide focal points. They are simple but vivid, with carvings of birds, animals and humans, as well as foliage. There are pairs of lions and eagles head to head, human heads, grotesque masks, and a few capitals that point a moral: the common theme of a lustful woman being devoured by snakes, for instance.

The main focus, of course, is the apse at the east end of the church and the sanctuary below it, and this is where Gourdon is special because at least some of its twelfth-century frescoes can still be seen. They were only rediscovered in 1940, and they were not fully restored until the 1970s and 1980s. But though they are incomplete, they give an idea of how the church and others of its period would have looked when their walls were painted, as they always were.

In the apse, and dominating the sanctuary, is a stern Christ in Majesty, seated in a mandorla and surrounded by the figures symbolizing the four evangelists – the lion of St Mark, the bull of St Luke, the eagle of St John and the winged man of

Mural painting in Gourdon: the Nativity

St Matthew (see page 263) – as well as two angels. At a lower level, between the
windows, are formal portraits of unnamed abbots.

Some of the best paintings are on the north wall of the choir: the Annunciation
and the Nativity, each within an arch; and above them, a group of Apostles heading towards the figure of Christ. Opposite, on the south wall, is the scene of Christ
seated between the two pilgrims of Emmaus, and above it, another group of
Apostles, also heading towards Christ.

The frescoes have a soft range of colours, mainly reds and ochres, and they convey a sense of devotion and drama, with the figures formally but not stiffly drawn.
There would once have been more. Here and there there are other scraps of fresco
which have survived and give an idea of what has been lost: the head of a whale,
a man reaping his field, and another elephant with hooves and a tiny trunk, not
unlike the one in Perrecy.

Saulieu

The collegiate church of St-Andoche in Saulieu, some forty-five miles west of
Dijon, has a very individual collection of Romanesque column capitals of the first

Capital in collegiate church of Saulieu: the Flight into Egypt

half of the twelfth century, some with biblical subjects and others with animals, birds or exquisitely carved plant designs. Several of them are similar in subject-matter to those of nearby Autun (see page 49), but they are noticeably different in style, and they have an immediacy and decorative quality that put them in a class of their own.

The church itself is undistinguished on the outside. On the inside, its nave and two side-aisles are tall and stylish, in a manner clearly influenced by the abbey of Cluny (see page 61). The nave has barrel vaulting supported by pointed transverse arches, and there are more pointed arches along its sides, with an arcade of smaller round arches in the triforium and a single round-topped window in each bay of the clerestory. The aisles have groin vaulting, also with pointed arches between the bays. The apse is a later reconstruction.

Although there are similarities, however, to Autun and to what is left of Cluny itself, Saulieu's nave has little surface decoration on the stonework – no fluted pilasters, for instance – and so the capitals stand out strongly against a relatively austere setting. They are also set relatively low, and that means that they are easy to see.

St Andoche is believed to have been a Greek who brought Christianity to Saulieu, or Sedelocum, in Roman times and was martyred there. An abbey was established later on the site of his tomb, but in the ninth century it was put under the authority of the Bishop of Autun; and in about 1139 the monks were replaced by a college of canons.

It is thought that Etienne de Bâgé, who became Bishop of Autun in 1112, and began the building of Autun cathedral, was responsible for the building of Saulieu, too, though the dates are uncertain.

One point of dispute is whether the capitals at Saulieu were carved before or after those at Autun. Art historians have argued both cases. Recent thinking is that the Saulieu capitals were later, and they certainly have an ornate quality which is almost baroque, with much use of decorative foliage. Many of them are also carved in greater depth, with the figures standing right out from the rest of the capitals.

One of the most engaging is of Balaam, the Old Testament figure whose ass saw an angel with a sword blocking the way ahead and refused to go any further. It actually spoke to Balaam to complain. Both Balaam and the ass are sympathetic-ally portrayed, and seem entranced by the sight of the angel brandishing a sword.

The Flight into Egypt also has great charm, with Mary and the baby Jesus wide-eyed as Joseph leads the donkey on which they are riding – though the scene lacks the pathos of the similar one in Autun.

The other biblical compositions are also treated dramatically. One capital shows

Christ's appearance to Mary Magdalene after his Resurrection, and he has a haunting, supernatural appearance as he looks down on an astounded Mary, his hands raised in the air. Another, which shows the Temptation of Christ, has a particularly evil-looking devil offering a serene Christ a stone – and a curvaceous tree in the background which seems to evoke the tree of the Garden of Eden.

As at Autun, a grim note is introduced by the capital showing Judas's suicide: a snarling devil pulls on the rope with which Judas has hanged himself – and to which his bag of money is attached.

Foliage appears on many of the capitals in Saulieu, whether or not they

Capital in Saulieu: the suicide of Judas

are historiated. On one capital an owl is perched on the acanthus, and on another an original effect is obtained by having human and animal masks emerging from the tips of the leaves.

Animals, birds and monsters also feature. One capital has two large animals confronting each other, variously interpreted as boars or as bears whose fart is said to announce the arrival of spring. Another has a cockfight, and a third a pair of eagles. Yet another has a confrontation between two winged monsters.

A common feature of all the Saulieu capitals is the vigour of the carving, which is combined at times with typically Romanesque fantasy and humour.

Semur-en-Brionnais and Iguerande

Semur-en-Brionnais is a hilltop village which was once the capital of the Brionnais region in the south of Burgundy, and it still has the remains of the castle in which the ruling family lived. It also has a majestic Romanesque church, built in the middle and later twelfth century – a time when the Romanesque style in Burgundy was entering its final phase but had not yet lost its vigour.

The view of the *chevet*, seen across the open space between the castle and the

Semur-en-Brionnais: lintel over the west door showing triumph of St Hilary

church, is one to cherish. A stocky but well-formed octagonal bell-tower rises over the transept crossing, with the tiled roofs of three small apses below it, and the three-dimensional effect is enhanced by tall triangular gables which stand at the end of the choir and each arm of the transept.

The church also has a richly decorated west doorway which is similar to the larger doorway on the north side of the narthex in Charlieu (see page 58), not far away. The decoration is a good example of the later, more lavish Romanesque style but the tympanum at its centre lacks the fluency and sense of design of the one in Charlieu, and appears to mark the setting in of decline.

The Brionnais is remarkable for its concentration of Romanesque churches, most of them well preserved, and they can be found in villages across the region. Just below Semur, and visible from it, is St-Martin-la-Vallée, a handsome country church which sadly needs restoration inside. A few miles away, on a hill above the Loire, is the village of Iguerande, whose church has been well restored in recent years, and is another good example of country Romanesque.

Semur-en-Brionnais is best known for having been the birthplace of Hugh of Semur, later St Hugh, who was a member of its ruling family and, as abbot of Cluny (see page 61) from 1049 to 1109, was one of the most influential men of his time, as we have seen. The church in Semur was not built until after his death, however. Work on it began in about 1130 and was set in motion by a nephew or great-nephew, and continued with interruptions well into the second half of the century.

The *chevet* came first, including the lower and less ornate level of the bell-tower, to be followed by the nave, which is higher, and by the upper level of the tower, with its pointed arches. Altogether three of the church's doorways have some form of decoration, but the western one has the most detail and, unlike the others, has a pointed arch.

Like the doorway in Charlieu, it has the Lamb of God at the top, and also like Charlieu, it has a Christ in Majesty in the tympanum, with Christ surrounded not just by two angels who support the mandorla in which he is sitting but by the figures that represent the four evangelists – the lion for St Mark, the bull for St Luke, the eagle for St John, and the winged man for St Matthew (see page 263). The design is cramped, however, and lacks the movement and drama of Charlieu.

The lintel underneath presents not a biblical event but the story of St Hilary, or Hilaire, the fourth-century Bishop of Poitiers. Hilary was exiled to Asia Minor for his opposition to the Arian heresy but succeeded in triumphing over his opponents at the Council of Seleucia in 359. According to legend, the anti-Pope Leo, who had been elected by those opponents, then withdrew and, suffering from intestinal trouble, died 'shamefully' in the latrines.

This story is told with gusto on the lintel, concluding with a scene which shows Leo dying. He is seated, presumably on a latrine, and his soul, conventionally represented by a small, naked body, is leaving his mouth, to be seized by gleeful devils. The lintel has been criticized for being tasteless, and the case is made stronger by the fact that to its right is a capital with an obscenely naked man on it, representing licentiousness. All the same, it tells a lively tale with graphic vigour.

Inside the church, the nave is tall and like the outside it makes a statement of its own. It has a triforium made up of rows of small arches resting on columns with carved capitals, and these continue round the west end of the nave. There they lead to a most original tribune, shaped like an inverted beehive, which juts out over the nave.

The church shows the influence of Cluny in the fluted pilasters that run up the sides of the nave, and the pointed arches that line it on either side. The barrel vault, too, was originally supported by pointed arches. It collapsed in a fire in the sixteenth century; and when it was eventually remade in the nineteenth century a round vault was installed.

Most of the sculpture in the church has formal floral designs but there are two carvings at the entrance to the choir, each of a devil supporting the weight of a pillar on his shoulders, which are very different. One has an insinuating sneer, and they are almost modern in the direct, suggestive way in which they look out at the twenty-first-century visitor.

If **Iguerande** is not far from Semur-en-Brionnais by road, its church is a long way from it in style. It was built around 1100, and is a sturdy building in an exposed position which had to be buttressed to prevent it from subsiding. Even so, it has the proportion and balance that are characteristic of Romanesque, with a simple bell-tower, and it has a remarkable collection of corbels around its two apses: animals, birds and humans in a variety of postures.

Inside, it has round arches throughout, both in its nave and in the two side-aisles, and there is a harmonious view up the length of the church.

Perhaps the most distinctive features of Iguerande, however, are its capitals and, unusually, the carvings at the foot of some of the columns. Many of the capitals are more or less conventional – eagles, pairs of lions, and some pretty foliage patterns. But there are strange and fascinating capitals on the north side of the nave which show the head of a monster playing a tiny harp, another one-eyed creature playing Pan pipes, and small human figures playing horns.

The carvings at the foot of the columns are more obviously rustic. One has the head of a calf and, beside it, the head of a devil. Another shows the head of a calf which, for a reason known only to the sculptor, is lying upside down.

Tournus and Chapaize

The abbey church of St-Philibert in Tournus, in southern Burgundy, has an architectural style and a special charm that make it stand out among the many achievements of the Romanesque period. It is one of the earliest Romanesque churches, with parts that may date back to the late tenth century, and it has a serenity and a power that immediately affect the visitor.

A few miles away, in the village of Chapaize, is another early church, which dates back to the first half of the eleventh century and has its own appeal, and it is worth visiting at the same time. Like Tournus, it demonstrates the flowering of early Romanesque architecture in Burgundy.

Tournus itself is a delightful old town on the banks of the river Saône, and today the church's two tall bell-towers, added in the twelfth century, are a landmark for miles around. The town dates back to Roman times, and it still has several of the abbey buildings, including defensive towers that formed part of the walls which once surrounded the abbey.

Abbey church of Tournus: the west front

It is the inside of the church, however, which makes Tournus different. The entrance is itself unlike that of most churches since you walk through a dark and atmospheric narthex whose low vaults are supported by massive round pillars, made up of roughly cut stone. From there you emerge into the nave, which is soaring and spacious, and above all bathed in light. More massive round pillars, also made of rough stone, line the nave, but they are tall, and tinged with the pink of the local stone, and they support a succession of high, transverse arches which lead to the apse at the east end.

The arch-stones are also carved from the pink stone, but several of the arches have alternating stones of a deep red, and they add an extra touch of colour.

The luminosity of the nave is due to the system of vaulting, which appears to have been invented in Tournus. In each of the bays there is a barrel vault that runs across the line of the nave, from north to south, and rests on the transverse arches on either side.

In this way the weight of the barrel vaults is borne by the arches and the pillars of the nave which support them. So it was possible to insert windows high up in each bay of the nave, above the line of the side-aisles. The aisles are also tall, and are lit by more windows, but have more conventional groin vaulting.

Much is mysterious about Tournus, and in particular the dating of the various parts of the church. It is known that it is a very old religious centre. St Valerian is said to have brought Christianity to it towards the end of the second century, and after being beheaded to have been buried on the site of the existing crypt. His tomb attracted pilgrims, and a monastery was founded there, probably in the sixth century.

In 875 the existing monks were joined by another monastic community, which had had to flee from the island of Noirmoutier, off the Atlantic coast, to escape from the Viking raids. Their monastery had been founded by St Philibert, and they travelled from place to place for almost forty years, carrying his relics with them, before being granted the abbey and town of Tournus by Charles the Bald.

Not surprisingly, relations between the two communities seem to have been difficult at times. And monastic life was disrupted by a series of disasters: a Magyar raid in 937, in which the abbey was sacked; a fire in 1006 which destroyed much of the church that existed at the time; and a devastating famine in Burgundy in 1030-3. But the abbey survived, the church was built, and Tournus continued to be an important pilgrimage centre. Significantly, it remained independent of two younger and better-known abbeys, Cluny and Cîteaux, both of them also in Burgundy.

The oldest part of the church is the crypt, which may well have been built

Tournus: the nave

before the end of the tenth century, though there is no definite proof of that. It is certainly early work, however, and it is a dark and evocative place, with an ambulatory, three rectangular chapels that radiate outwards from it, and a central area with two rows of columns, all topped by some beautifully carved capitals.

Just what happened next, and when, is disputed. What is certain is that the western and eastern ends of the church are built in different styles. The narthex and the nave are in an earlier style, and so must at least have been begun in the opening years of the eleventh century, while the choir, the ambulatory and the transept are largely in the style of the late eleventh or early twelfth century.

What is not certain is whether one part was built after the other. So it is possible that work on the two parts was carried out independently, perhaps even simultaneously, and the church as a whole only completed in 1120, when it was re-consecrated by Pope Calixtus II, a Burgundian.

In any case, the two parts combine well together. The bare grandeur of the nave leads to the more ornate choir and apse, which are built in white stone and have an arrangement of round arches, supported by columns and pilasters. More arches and columns are ranged high up under the cupola built over the transept crossing, and there are some capitals with human and animal designs on the sturdy pillars that support the cupola.

The ambulatory is particularly appealing. It has curved barrel vaulting, supported by round transverse arches, and is separated from the choir by a semi-circle of columns, each topped by a carved capital. From it, there are views of the stonework of the choir, and of the whole length of the nave.

The ambulatory and its rectangular chapels were built on the foundations of the crypt, and have the same dimensions. The assumption, therefore, is that they were originally built soon after the crypt, but that they, and the eastern end of the church as a whole, were radically rebuilt later.

The narthex is one of the outstanding features of the church, and that is only partly because of the very moving character of the three bays of its ground floor – where there are still a few traces of medieval painting, including a twelfth-century Christ in Majesty flanked by two angels in the vaulting over the central doorway into the church proper.

Just as impressive is the tall and spacious upper level, which is dedicated, as such high places often were, as a chapel of St Michael, the archangel. Today it is bare, and it too has the roughly cut wall-surface of early Romanesque, and solid round columns. But its high barrel vault, supported by transverse arches, gives it a lightness that the ground floor does not have, and the whole area is lit by rows of round-topped windows.

From this upper level you can look out over the nave and its stately line of columns. The central opening is now blocked by the organ, but the columns on either side of it have some extraordinary early capitals. Most of the carvings are of plant designs. However, on one side there is a human face, and on the other a bearded man holding a sort of hammer in one hand and blessing with the other. The second of these may be an abbot called Gerlannus, since an inscription on the arch names him, but that is not certain.

Just when the narthex was built is not known. It was early, and work on its ground floor may even have begun before the end of the tenth century. There was an interval before the upper level was built but that too dates from the early eleventh century.

Work on the nave must also have begun early in the eleventh century. When it was completed is not known. There is an attractive Romanesque statue in one of the chapels off the southern side-aisle – a twelfth-century Virgin and Child known as Notre-Dame-la-Brune, carved in wood in the style of Auvergne.

The outside of the church reflects the various periods of building. The two bell-towers, for instance, a large one over the transept crossing and a slightly smaller one on the north end of the west front, were the last of the Romanesque additions to the church, and may date from the second half of the twelfth century. Both are good examples of Burgundian late Romanesque, with two tiers of round arches complete with capitals high up under a pyramid-shaped spire, and they contrast with the greater simplicity of earlier periods.

The contrast is particularly noticeable on the west front. The greater part of this is in the relatively plain style of early Romanesque, with Lombard bands, the rows of tiny blind arches set in panels (see page 18), providing the main decoration. The portal and the crenellated walkway between the two towers are unfortunate nineteenth-century restorations. The south end of the façade is still topped by the simple turret, decorated with Lombard bands and arched windows, that was built in the eleventh century.

The north end, on the other hand, now has the twelfth-century bell-tower, which was built over a similar eleventh-century turret that still survives in part. This tower breaks the symmetry of the west front but it does not spoil the archaic appeal of the west front as a whole; and it is possible to envisage the severe but stylish façade that the church once presented.

The bell-tower is, besides, a very handsome structure, which is also built in pink stone, and stands out against a blue sky. It has some elongated human figures – now replaced by copies – in the place of columns.

The best place to see the larger bell-tower is from what is left of the cloister.

Only one side of this remains, running along the side of the church, but it is a tranquil place which now looks out over a little garden and some of the remaining abbey buildings. It has round arches, together with groin vaulting and some early capitals, and dates back to the first half of the eleventh century.

Up above is the south side of the church, stretching from the west front to the transept, and although it is relatively plain, the stylistic differences are clearly visible. The large bell-tower over the crossing, on the other hand, has stone of different colours in its upper tier and and some carved capitals – which are hard to see from the ground.

The *chevet* also shows evidence of the origins of this ancient church. It is made up of the central apse, the ambulatory and radiating chapels; but since the chapels were built on the foundations of the crypt, they are rectangular, without the smaller apses which were usual in later churches, and they are built in roughly cut stone. The stone of the main apse, which was built later, is smooth.

There are thick woods between Tournus and **Chapaize**. Chapaize stands in an extensive clearing, with stone houses and a cluster of trees, and as you approach there is a magnificent view across the fields of the church's tall bell-tower, which stands out above the village. The tower has two tiers of round arches high up

Priory church of Chapaize, from the south

under a pyramid-shaped top, and, as you come closer, you can see the decoration, so typical of early Romanesque, which lightens the effect of this substantial structure – pairs of twin arches on each face and, below them, Lombard bands.

Like Tournus, Chapaize has a history that goes back to Roman times since it stood near the junction of two Roman roads and was known as Capasia. In the Romanesque period there was a priory belonging to the abbey of St-Pierre in Chalon-sur-Saône in the village, and the church was part of that. Building began in about 1030, with the bell-tower dated to the 1050s, and the church must have been completed soon afterwards. Alterations were made in the twelfth century, but they did not alter the basic character of this handsome eleventh-century church.

The west front is largely plain, apart from a panel of Lombard bands, and the whole church is solidly constructed and well proportioned, with the classic Romanesque design of a tall nave, two side-aisles and a *chevet* with three round apses. The *chevet* was rebuilt late in the twelfth century or perhaps in the early thirteenth century, and is majestic. The apses and the gable of the choir form a three-dimensional complex at the foot of the bell-tower, which soars above them.

The inside of the church also has a massive quality and an appearance of rustic simplicity that give it atmosphere and charm. On either side of the nave are squat and powerful pillars built of roughly cut stone, which are topped by simple triangular shapes instead of capitals. They support the walls, which are also of roughly cut stone and have round arches between them.

The rustic impression is enhanced by the fact that some of the nave columns lean outwards, particularly on the north side. And there is more rusticity in the side-aisles, which each have a succession of round transverse arches, with groin vaulting between them, since some of the arches are noticeably depressed.

The nave originally had a round barrel vault but it collapsed in the mid-twelfth century and was replaced by the present vault. It is slightly pointed, and higher than the original one, but it does not detract from the appeal of this early Romanesque church.

Vézelay

The abbey church of Vézelay, which towers over the small Burgundian hill-town, and is visible for miles around, is one of the most moving in the Romanesque world. At the peak of its fame in the twelfth and thirteenth centuries, Vézelay was a very important pilgrimage centre, as well as acting as a starting

Tympanum in narthex of Vézelay: Christ's Mission to the Apostles

point for a principal pilgrim route to Santiago de Compostela (see page 39). To enter the church today is to enter a world where religious devotion was combined with one of the great architectural achievements of the time.

Like some other Burgundian churches, Vézelay has a three-bay narthex at its western end, and this is dominated by a twelfth-century tympanum, showing Christ's Mission to the Apostles, over the central doorway into the church itself, and two smaller tympana, one on either side. Beyond them, through the central doorway, can be seen the great nave, ten bays long, whose vault is supported by a procession of round transverse arches made of stone of alternating colours, white and reddish brown.

At the far end, the choir and the apse are early Gothic, and were built in the late twelfth and early thirteenth century. But they complement the grandeur of the Romanesque nave, and together they are an unforgettable sight.

Romanesque churches can sometimes be dark, but Vézelay's nave is bathed in the light that comes from the windows high up in the clerestory on either side. This shows up the many different shades of the stone, and the textures, and the alternating colours of the arch-stones give a touch of exoticism, with echoes of the architecture of Muslim Spain (see page 11).

The capitals of the nave are another of the glories of Vézelay. They cover a wide range of subjects, including events from the Old and New Testament, the lives of saints, allegorical scenes, strange beasts and, not least, some ferocious devils, all of them carved with graphic vigour.

Vézelay is a peaceful place, but over the centuries it has gone through turbulent times. It is said to have taken its name from a certain Vercellus, a landowner of the fourth or fifth century, in the closing years of the Roman Empire. In the ninth century it became a religious centre when Girard de Roussillon, a heroic figure whose exploits in battle against the Saracens in Provence became legendary, founded a convent at the foot of the hill where the village of St-Père is now.

Dates are uncertain. Within a few years the nuns had been replaced by monks, and when the monastery was sacked by the Vikings, they took refuge on the hilltop where the church and town of Vézelay stand. A new monastery was established there towards the end of the ninth century, and the monks never returned to St-Père.

Vézelay's rise to fame began in the early eleventh century, when the monks let it be known that they had the body of Mary Magdalene, brought to them from St-Maximin in Provence, where she was believed to have died. This claim was upheld by a papal bull of 1058, and although it was fiercely contested by the monks of St-Maximin, it was supported by a further bull in 1103.

From then on Vézelay attracted pilgrims in their thousands, drawn both by the relics of Mary Magdalene and by the town's role as a meeting point before they set off on the long journey to Santiago de Compostela. In 1146 St Bernard of Clairvaux launched the Second Crusade with a speech at Vézelay, and in 1190 two of the leaders of the Third Crusade, King Philippe-Auguste of France and King Richard Lionheart of England, met there before setting off.

Not everything went smoothly for the abbey. There were constant struggles with the bishops of Autun whom the monks were determined to prevent from intervening in their affairs. There were conflicts between the monks and the townspeople, who objected to the taxes imposed on them – and in 1106 murdered the abbot, a certain Artaud. And there were fires, including a particularly disastrous one in 1120 which devastated the abbey and was later said to have killed more than a thousand worshippers.

Finally in 1279 the monks of St-Maximin had their revenge. They announced that they had rediscovered the bones of Mary Magdalene, which had been hidden long before, and this time they were backed by Pope Boniface VIII, allegedly to do a favour to Charles II of Anjou, the then ruler of Provence. This was a stunning blow to Vézelay's position as a pilgrimage centre, and it never fully recovered. By the end of the eighteenth century the abbey and its church were in a sorry state.

The church was restored in the nineteenth century, however – by Viollet-le-Duc, the much-criticized architect – and the greater part of it has survived from Vézelay's days of glory. This includes the nave, which was perhaps begun before the fire of 1120 and in any case was largely completed by 1132; the narthex, which was begun soon after that and perhaps completed about 1150; and the Gothic choir and apse, which were built between 1185 and 1215, replacing the Romanesque structures that had been there before.

One interesting feature of Vézelay is the way that the juxtaposition of Romanesque and Gothic illustrates some of the differences between the two styles. The Romanesque nave is supremely elegant, but it has, in contrast to the choir, a certain sturdiness. It has an upward movement, but also a three-dimensional quality, with some strong horizontal lines. Above all, it is fully decorated, with the alternating stones in the vault and the carving of the capitals, and its lighting is soft and diffused.

The choir and apse, on the other hand, have the lightness and upward movement of Gothic, and the strong lighting that comes from the windows. But they have almost no carved decoration, apart from some rudimentary capitals, and no stained glass in the windows. So their appeal comes from the clean upward lines and the skilful use of space.

Today, it is best to approach the church on foot. It is a joy to walk up through the streets of the town, past old fortifications and buildings of different centuries, to the open space at the top where the church stands, and the sweeping views out over the surrounding countryside from the gardens at the eastern end.

The outside of the church is disappointing since it too is in a mixture of styles, and was much damaged over the centuries before being extensively reshaped by Viollet-le-Duc. The west front is imposing, with its single tower and its large central gable, but it shows signs of having been rebuilt, and perhaps the best view is of the Gothic *chevet* from the gardens.

While the west front was originally Romanesque, built about 1150, the central gable, including a five-light window and statues, was added in the thirteenth century, and is in an ornate Gothic; and there is a Gothic bell-tower of approximately the same date at the south end of the façade. Much of it was remade by Viollet-le-Duc, including the windows of the central gable and the bell-tower, and he had an uninspiring tympanum, representing the Last Judgment, carved in neo-Romanesque style for the central doorway.

He also remade the other bell-tower, dating from the early thirteenth century, which stands on the south side of the church, in the angle between the nave and the transept, and he rebuilt the eastern gallery of the cloister just below it.

On entering the narthex, however, you are in the world of the twelfth century, and much closer to what the pilgrims of the time would have seen. The narthex is a fully decorated space with a nave and two side-aisles at ground level, and an upper level containing a chapel dedicated to St Michael. It is interesting that, unlike the nave of the church itself, the narthex has pointed arches, and even a rib vault over the tribune that covers the easternmost bay – although the arch leading to the central doorway is round. These are pointers to its slightly later date.

But what catch the eye are the three doorways into the church itself, each of them an exquisite work of art with a carved tympanum in the middle. The central tympanum, in particular, is a powerful work which represents one of the peaks of Romanesque sculpture, but the two smaller ones both have a vigour and an appeal of their own.

The central scene is generally described as showing Christ's Mission to the Apostles, given when he spoke to them in person after his Resurrection. It is also said to represent the events of Pentecost, which took place after his Ascension. In a sense it can be seen as a conflation of the two events, since Christ is shown as inspiring the Apostles by flashes of light, rather as happened at Pentecost, even though he was not then physically present.

In any case, it is a dramatic scene, full of movement. Christ sits in a mandorla, dressed in a robe that swirls around him, and lightning-like flashes radiate from his outstretched arms, directed at the heads of each of the Apostles. There are six of them on either side, each in a different position as they are caught up in the excitement of the event, and each with an elaborately carved robe.

The Apostles' mission, of course, was to go out and spread the Christian message, and in compartments around the edge of the tympanum are small groups of people, many of them with exotic features, who are usually interpreted as representing the various peoples of the world that the Apostles were to evangelize.

Beyond them is a ring of tiny round medallions, each enclosing either a sign of the Zodiac or the labour of one of the months of the year, while below on the lintel are two processions, one of participants in a pagan sacrifice, the other of representatives of more exotic races, among them pygmies and the so-called Panotii, a people with huge ears.

It is interesting that two figures, St Peter and St Paul, are shown descending from the tympanum to the lintel – from the world of the Apostles to that of the pagans who are to be converted. More Apostles are shown on the capitals on either side of the door, including another meeting between St Peter and St Paul, and John the Baptist is given a prominent place on the *trumeau*, or central pier. The work is badly damaged but he can be seen to be holding the Lamb of God.

All three tympana are surrounded by formal decoration, largely floral. The right-hand one focuses on the events surrounding the birth of Christ, from the Annunciation to the Nativity itself, the arrival of the shepherds and the Adoration of the Magi. The left-hand one illustrates Christ's appearances after his Resurrection: his encounter with the two pilgrims walking to Emmaus on the lower level, and his meeting with the Apostles – or possibly the Ascension – on the upper.

If the capitals in the narthex are a little later in date than those in the nave, they have a similar range of subjects and, like them, show the vigour and charm of Burgundian Romanesque sculpture. They include the stories of Joseph and Potiphar's wife, of Cain, John the Baptist, St Benedict and many others.

The view from the narthex of the nave of Vézelay is one of the great experiences offered by the architecture of that period. This is partly because of the dramatic effect of the arches which span the nave, with the reddish-brown archstones alternating with the white ones, and partly because of the rare overall design, which is not found elsewhere in a church of this size and makes it exceptionally wide.

When they set out to build a large new abbey church in the early twelfth century, the architects deliberately chose not to use the design identified with the abbey of Cluny (see page 61) and other monastic institutions linked to it: a barrel vault with pointed transverse arches, and a three-part elevation on each side of the nave, made up of a tall arcade, a triforium and a clerestory. This is surprising, since at the time Vézelay was itself briefly linked to Cluny; but it illustrates the determination of its monks to be independent.

Instead, they employed a design used a few years earlier in the smaller church of Anzy-le-Duc, in southern Burgundy (see page 43). This had groin vaulting over each of the bays of the nave, with round transverse arches between the bays, and a side elevation of only two parts – an arcade and, above it, a clerestory. It was adopted at Vézelay, and it left space for the quite large windows in the spaces between the transverse arches supporting the vault.

In the long run, the structure did not prove stable, and the vault had to be supported later by flying buttresses. But the nave has survived in all its grandeur, with the light still coming in through the windows; and the two side-aisles, which also have round transverse arches and groin vaulting in each bay, have a harmony of their own, especially when seen through the two smaller doorways from the narthex.

The decorative features of the nave include bands of formal patterns that are set into the stone of the various arches, both in the vault and in the side elevations, and above all the many capitals. Those at Vézelay are outstanding, and it is worth

Capital in Vézelay: the Mystic Mill

taking the time to study them in all their elaborate detail. There are said to be about a hundred in the nave alone.

Many take their subjects from the Old Testament: Adam and Eve in the Garden of Eden, Noah building his ark, David killing Goliath, Moses and the golden calf (which has a savage-looking devil emerging from its mouth), Cain and Abel. There are fewer from the New Testament – St Peter being freed from prison is one – but this is made up for by the lives of saints. St Martin is shown ordering the cutting down of a tree worshipped by pagans, St Hubert receiving his revelation while out hunting, St Eugenia baring her breasts to prove that she was not a man when accused of rape.

Interestingly, there are even a few capitals with stories from classical literature: the rape of Ganymede, for instance, and the education of Achilles.

Less surprising are the capitals which point a moral. One tells the story of Dives and Lazarus, and elsewhere there are figures representing lust and despair, perfidy and avarice. Devils and monsters are prominent and suitably gruesome, and on some capitals they have the scene to themselves as they fight each other.

Some capitals have proved difficult to interpret in modern times. One particularly fascinating one shows various figures crouched over bellows-like objects, and it has often been interpreted as representing the winds. But there is an alternative explanation: that it depicts the country craft of bee-keeping

One of the most vivid, and uncontroversial, capitals is generally described as the Mystic Mill. In it one man pours grain into a small mill and another collects the flour that comes out of it in a sack. The first man is believed to be Moses, and the grain the law of the Old Testament. The mill is Christ, who transforms the grain, and the flour represents his teaching. The second man, who collects the flour, is St Paul.

The scene is simply and feelingly presented, with the two men intent on their task and a few large leaf clusters in the background. It shows the mastery achieved by the sculptors of Vézelay, and their talent for conveying a story and a message in visual form.

Paris Region

The Paris region, and the Ile de France in particular, is best known as the birth-place of the Gothic style, which eventually replaced Romanesque. But there were Romanesque churches here before the advent of Gothic, and some churches which today are predominantly Gothic still have parts that date from the Romanesque period.

Chartres cathedral, for instance, still has its Romanesque crypt; and the *portail royal* (royal porch) and the lancet windows on its magnificent west front can be classified as either late Romanesque or early Gothic. In Rheims, in addition to the cathedral, there is the monumental basilica of St-Remi, dedicated to the saint who

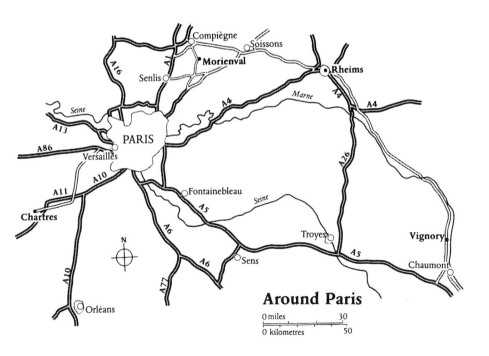

Around Paris

was its Bishop in the late fifth and early sixth century, and parts of that are Roman-esque, including the nave.

There are also a few churches that are almost pure Romanesque. One of the best is in the village of Morienval, north-east of Paris. It is an inspiring sight from the outside, with its three bell-towers, and inside it has the characteristic style and the intimate feel of a Romanesque church, together with some capitals of great originality.

Further afield, in the village of Vignory in the upper valley of the Marne, there is another Romanesque church that is well worth visiting. It dates from the eleventh century, and has an unusual arrangement in which the nave has no bays but is divided from the two side-aisles by a continuous wall pierced by three tiers of arches. The apse, with its semi-circle of alternating columns and pillars, is framed by a 'triumphal arch'.

Chartres

Chartres is one of the supreme Gothic cathedrals, famous for its stained-glass windows, and for the two very different spires that are visible for miles around across the flat farming countryside. The low hill on which it stands appears to have been a religious centre since pagan times, and the Gothic cathedral, which was mainly built after a disastrous fire in 1194, was only the last of several buildings on the site.

Not everything was destroyed in the fire, however, and the Romanesque parts are survivals from the earlier church. Apart from a few later modifications, the crypt remains essentially as it was when it was built in the early eleventh century as the lowest level of a Romanesque cathedral – and incorporated parts of an even earlier ninth-century church.

It is an atmospheric place, redolent of its long past, and is interesting as having one of the earliest examples of an ambulatory with chapels radiating off it. This was the arrangement specially designed for pilgrims coming to venerate saintly relics.

The ambulatory circles round the east end of the ninth-century church, and en-closes an ancient well into which, according to tradition, early Christian martyrs were thrown; and there are still two long vaulted corridors which run from it under the aisles of the existing cathedral. There are three chapels that radiate off the ambulatory, all of them survivals from the Romanesque period, and one has a row of paintings of saints from the twelfth century.

The most striking survivals at Chartres, however, are the *portail royal* and the three lancet windows in the centre of the west front. The *portail* is a triple door-way which is dated 1145-55 and which has art historians divided on how to classify it. Some describe it as late Romanesque, others as early Gothic, and others again as standing somewhere between the two.

It is in any case a beautiful and powerful work, which clearly draws on the achievements of Romanesque sculptors in Burgundy, Aquitaine and Languedoc, while providing a model for later Gothic artists. It illustrates the transition from Romanesque to Gothic that was taking place in and around Paris, and in northern France generally, in the middle years of the twelfth century.

Up above are the three windows, and glass which also dates from the middle of the twelfth century. It was possibly put in just after the *portail royal*, and is the most complete set of stained glass to have survived from that period. It too is re-garded by some art historians as being Romanesque in spirit, and it is in any case a wonderful display of glass-making that shows how early the famous blue colour of the windows of Chartres was created.

So the greater part of the west front is the product of a mid-twelfth-century building programme which followed an earlier fire, in 1134. The programme in-cluded the two towers – apart from the spire of the northern one, which dates from the sixteenth century.

Because of this much later spire, the northern tower has come to be known as the 'new bell-tower'. But it is in reality the older of the two towers, as is clear from the relatively plain decoration at its lower levels. The southern tower was built a little later, and is more elaborate. With its well-judged proportions and its tall spire, it shows the prowess of twelfth-century builders in northern France, and is still classified by some writers as Romanesque.

The most remarkable feature of the *portail royal* is the sequence of tall, elongated figures, impassive but far from lifeless, and decked out in formal, flowing draperies, which flank the three doorways. These stately figures represent the ancestors of Christ, several of them kings and queens, which is why the *portail royal* has its name, and they have both a religious and an architectural function.

In the religious scheme they provide the Old Testament foundation for the Gospel story, which is illustrated in the three tympana above; while visually, with their severe lines, they serve as supporting columns for the whole complex design.

Such elongated statues had been carved before, for the abbey church of St-Denis outside Paris, and for Notre-Dame-du-Fort in Etampes, and were an inno-vation that went beyond the traditional Romanesque style. Those at Chartres are singularly beautiful, and the doorway as a whole shows how artists in northern

Chartres cathedral: ancestors of Christ on 'portail royal'

France were making their own synthesis of regional Romanesque styles as they moved towards Gothic.

They took the carved tympanum and lintel from Burgundy and Languedoc, and the decoration of the archivolts with converging human figures that frame the central scene from Poitou and the Saintonge, in western France. With the addition of the statue-columns, and a frieze that runs across the capitals above them, they created a rich combination, drawn together in a single design.

It is thought that there was one master craftsman in overall charge, and that he was responsible for the whole central doorway, and for the statue-columns on both sides of the heavy pillars that flank it. Other craftsmen carved the statue-columns on the outer pillars, and the tympana and archivolts of the two side doorways.

It is noticeable that the Nativity scene, for instance, on the lintel above the right-hand doorway is very similar to one at the Romanesque priory church at La Charité-sur-Loire (see page 54), on the edge of Burgundy; and there are other similarities to earlier Romanesque works.

The design of the *portail royal* is thought to have been carefully planned in co-operation with the city's theologians and, since the cathedral was dedicated to the Virgin Mary, gave prominence to her. The tympana represent three essential phases of the Gospel story, and Mary is the dominant figure, holding the child on her lap, in the right-hand one, which depicts the Incarnation. The Ascension is on the left, and in the centre a climactic scene in which Christ, seated in a mandorla with the four beasts of the Apocalypse around him (see page 263), announces his Second Coming and the end of the world.

These scenes are powerfully carved – though they have been damaged over the centuries – and are surrounded by a wealth of detail, including not just human figures, but formal plant designs and patterns, and all of it absorbing:

  in the central doorway, angels and the Twenty-four Elders of the Apocalypse (see page 263) are on the archivolts, and Apostles on the lintel;

  in the right-hand doorway, teachers and thinkers representing the liberal arts (in itself an innovation) are on the archivolts, and the Nativity and the Presentation at the Temple on the lintels;

  in the left-hand doorway, the seasons and the signs of the Zodiac are on the archivolts, and jubilant angels telling the Apostles the good news on the lintels.

Down below, on the frieze that runs across the capitals, there are tiny biblical scenes, vividly presented: the Massacre of the Innocents, the Flight into Egypt, the Entry into Jerusalem, and many others.

Altogether there are a huge number of carved figures, large and small. A farmer reaps his corn. Cancer, the crab, puts in a daunting appearance. Pythagoras crouches over his writing frame. And in the outermost archivolt of the central tympanum, in a typically Romanesque touch, tiny human faces peer in through the foliage.

The *portail royal* is one of the most inspired works of the period, whether or not it can be strictly classed as Romanesque.

The three windows above it are also compelling. They have sequences of small biblical scenes, vigorously depicted, and their themes are similar to those of the *portail royal*, although the arrangement is different. All show the moving simplicity characteristic of the period, and throughout there is the range of clear colours – yellows, greens, reds and purples as well as the brilliant blue that is the hallmark of Chartres.

In the central window the theme is the Incarnation, and here again the Virgin Mary is the main figure, sitting at the top in a mandorla, with the infant Christ on her knees. The story runs from the Annunciation and the Nativity to Christ's Entry into Jerusalem, and is told in twenty-four diminutive narrative scenes, set in alternating round and square frames, and each surrounded by decorative features.

The window on the right has the Tree of Jesse as its theme, and once again represents the ancestors of Christ, while giving prominence to Mary. Jesse reclines at the bottom with a stem rising from his groin, while up above in the branches are, one after another, four kings flanked by Old Testament prophets, Mary, and at the top, the seated Christ.

The theme of the left-hand window is the Passion and Resurrection. It begins with the Transfiguration and ends with Christ's meeting with his two disciples at Emmaus.

There is one other window that survives from the twelfth-century cathedral and was inserted in a window in the south ambulatory when the Gothic cathedral was being built. Once again, it has the Virgin Mary crowned and seated, with the infant Christ on her lap, and is one more indication of the importance that Mary has long had at Chartres, not least in Romanesque times.

Morienval

The church at Morienval is near Crépy-en-Valois, some forty-five miles north-east of Paris, and is one of the few survivals of the Romanesque period in the Ile de

France. The village is in a rural setting just south of the Forest of Compiègne, and the church, though much restored over the years, has retained many of its original Romanesque features from the eleventh and twelfth centuries.

The most immediately noticeable of them are the three tall bell-towers, one standing at the west end and the other two at the east, on either side of the choir. All three towers have pairs of rounded arches rising in tiers one above the other, with some simple decoration, and the overall effect, especially from the park that lies below the church to the east, is majestic.

There is a good view from there of the two eastern towers, each relatively slender and topped with a stone pyramid, which flank the apse, and of the more massive western one behind them. The eastern towers date entirely from the eleventh century, as do the lower levels of the western one, while the more ornate upper level of the western tower is from the early twelfth century. The steeply sloping roof on the top of the western tower is much later.

The apse has a semi-circle of small round-topped windows, also simply decorated, and is ringed by what appears from outside to be an ambulatory, making a characteristically Romanesque *chevet* – though the apse roof too is later, and higher than it would have been in Romanesque times.

Little is known about the early history of Morienval, except that a Benedictine abbey was founded there in the ninth century, and that the present church was largely built in the middle of the eleventh century – while changes and additions continued to be made until the late nineteenth century.

Today, the main approach to the church is from the west, and it is also a rewarding one, leading down through the village and across an open square lined with trees. In front is the great west tower, which originally stood more or less on its own at the western end of the nave, but is now flanked on both sides by seventeenth-century buildings, including a grandiose doorway to the north.

Inside, the church has recently been cleaned, and retains the charm and the intimate feel of a Romanesque church – even though the rib vaulting over the nave dates from the seventeenth century. The sides of the nave, with rounded arches supported on engaged columns, are from the original eleventh-century church, and so are the carved capitals which are one of the glories of Morienval.

These capitals have designs which combine spiral patterns, formalized plants, human masks, mythical beasts and birds, and much else. They are complex and sophisticated, and there is speculation that the motifs derive from ancient folk traditions in the region, perhaps Celtic or Merovingian.

The transept crossing still rests on three plain, round arches from the eleventh century, together with a later pointed one, and there is a simple flying screen of

Abbey church of Morienval, from the west

five small arches above the main nave arch. Beyond are the choir and the altar area, which are the focal point of the church, and make an attractive climax.

The choir has an early rib vault built in the first part of the twelfth century, and the apse itself dates from the late nineteenth century. But the ring of four broad arches below the apse is a strong and typically Romanesque feature, if with a difference. The arches are not symmetrical – only one is rounded, and the others are pointed – and they are given a sense of depth by the arrangement of the vaulting behind them.

This is where some art historians have seen an ambulatory – perhaps built for the worship of the relics of St Annobert, which were brought to Morienval by monks from Normandy in the twelfth century – and they have even identified an early Gothic feature in the rather primitive rib vaulting over the narrow passageway running round the altar.

Other writers have countered that the passageway is not a true ambulatory since it does not communicate with the body of the church, which it would have to do if pilgrims were to use it, and that it is in any case exceptionally narrow. They also reject the Gothic claim. The most likely explanation, they suggest, is that the east end of the eleventh-century church was in danger of collapse early in the following century because of the steep slope immediately below it, and that the 'pseudo-ambulatory' was simply built as a neat way of preventing the threatened collapse.

Certainly the east end of the church is one of the most alluring parts of the church, with its arrays of engaged columns and, above them, more carved capitals, which are similar in style to those in the nave, though later in date.

Rheims: St-Remi

The city of Rheims has its Gothic cathedral, mainly a creation of the thirteenth century, but the basilica of St-Remi, which was originally built in the first half of the eleventh century, is another large and magnificent church. And the Romanesque parts, which survived later rebuilding – and devastation during the First World War – are still very much in evidence.

The nave, for instance, is extraordinarily impressive. It is long and wide, and apart from the two westernmost bays it is predominantly Romanesque, with a three-tier elevation, dating back to the eleventh century, on either side. There are eleven bays from that period, with broad round arches at ground level, a triforium above that consisting of pairs of smaller arches which open onto a gallery, and at the top a clerestory of small, round-topped windows.

Abbey church of St-Remi in Rheims: the nave

The nave was given a Gothic rib vault, to replace the original timber ceiling, in the second half of the twelfth century, and the two Gothic bays at the western end took the place of a Romanesque porch which had stood there. The whole eastern end of the church was also rebuilt in early Gothic style, with a choir, ambulatory and radiating chapels, and the tomb of St Remi behind the altar.

But the round Romanesque arches still march along either side of the nave for the greater part of its length, and the two styles combine well. The nave is quite dark since the clerestory windows are small, but all the more satisfying for that. And the two arms of the transept have also retained their three-tier Romanesque elevation, similar to that of the nave.

The church was badly damaged during the fighting in 1918, and it was not until 1958, forty years later, that the restoration was completed – including the rebuilding of the rib vault and of much of the south side of the nave. But the work was carefully done, and St-Remi stands as a powerful record of Rheims's history.

St Remi was Bishop of Rheims in the late fifth and early sixth century, and is known for having baptized Clovis, the Frankish king who eventually conquered most of Roman Gaul. The baptism took place in 496 according to tradition, but may have been a year or two later. It was an important historical event, and after

Remi's death in 533 pilgrims flocked to his tomb near the site of the present church. In the eighth century a Benedictine monastery was established there.

It was the monks who began the building of the present church in 1007, and they completed it in 1049, when it was consecrated by Pope Leo IX. It was an imposing place, and the nave retains the grandeur of that time. The main arches rest on clusters of engaged columns, which have simple but appealing capitals carved with floral, animal and bird designs. In the triforium, the pairs of arches are divided by a slender column, with a relieving arch above.

Much of St-Remi is now Gothic as a result of the features added in the second half of the twelfth century. The side-aisles, for instance, were given rib vaulting, and so were the galleries above them. A small round window, or oculus, was opened above each of the clerestory windows in the nave when the rib vaulting was built over the nave, and a blind pointed arch was built into the wall above the triforium. But Romanesque style survives both in the nave and in the transept.

It can also be seen on the church's elaborate, and largely Gothic, west front. The central part of this façade, with its array of windows, replaced the Romanesque porch in the twelfth century, but the Romanesque bell-towers on either side were left in place. The tall and handsome tower at the south end, with its tiers of small round arches, has survived from the eleventh century – although its spire is later – and the north tower, while it is a nineteenth-century reconstruction, is also in the Romanesque style.

Vignory

The village of Vignory, which stands on a wooded hillside above the upper valley of the Marne in north-eastern France, has a church which even in the first half of the eleventh century was rather old-fashioned in parts. But it is no less inviting for that. It has a tall and handsome bell-tower, visible from miles away, and its interior has its own distinctive appeal, with a strong and imposing nave that leads to a more delicate, and slightly later, sanctuary.

The view from the western entrance of the church is unconventional for the period. As in many early churches, the nave has a plain timber ceiling, and below it along either side is a solid, continuous wall, with no marking out of bays. But each wall is pierced with round arches at three levels – single, relatively low ones at ground level, pairs of smaller and more ornate ones divided by columns with capitals above that, and small windows up at the top – and they give it an articulation reminiscent of a Roman aqueduct.

Priory church of Vignory: the nave

Marking the end of the nave is the broad 'triumphal arch', and that serves as a visual frame for the round apse beyond, and the ring of alternating columns and pillars which stands below it, beyond the sanctuary. The nave is lit by its own windows, but a stronger light bathes the ring of columns and pillars so that the eastern end of the church stands out dramatically.

One of the notable features of this arrangement is the importance it gives to the two side-aisles. Like the nave, each of them has a timber ceiling, high up above the second range of arches in the wall which divides the nave from the aisle. This means that they are both tall and interesting spaces in their own right, with views through the arches to the nave, and round arches at their eastern end.

The church in Vignory seems to have had a monastic function from its beginnings since its history goes back to 1032, when a college of canons was established there and building started. Only a few years later, by 1049, the canons were replaced by Benedictine monks, and Vignory became a priory subordinate to the important abbey of St-Bénigne in Dijon (see page 66).

The church was completed in 1057, and the change from canons to monks may explain the differences of style. Not everyone agrees, but it appears that the nave, which is closer to the earlier Carolingian style of eastern and northern France, is the oldest part, and was the work of the canons. The choir and east end, on the other hand, are influenced by the Romanesque style as it was evolving at the time in, for instance, Normandy and the Loire valley, and were built by the monks.

The church was thoroughly restored in the nineteenth century, and a number of its features were altered, or even added, in order to make it more uniformly Romanesque. The present west front, for instance, was built then to replace a Gothic façade, and the two rows of small round arches were pierced in the wall above the great arch at the east end of the nave. There were also a great number of less obvious alterations.

But the additions and modifications do not jar, and the styles of the two eleventh-century building periods combine together well.

It is even possible to see how one evolved into the other in the nave. For the greater part of its length the arches on either side are supported on solid pillars, but at the eastern end round columns take their place. There is also a change in the columns and capitals, which are chunky and quite crude, with abstract patterns, for most of the nave, but become more stylish towards the east.

This prepares the way for the eastern end of the church, which is generally in a lighter, less monumental style. The round apse over the sanctuary, the ambulatory that surrounds it, and the radiating chapels were features of Romanesque style as it evolved in France. In Vignory, as elsewhere, they make a most pleasing ensemble, with barrel vaulting in the ambulatory and little columns flanking the windows and the doorways into the chapels.

The semi-circle which encloses the sanctuary has an uncommon form because of the alternation of columns and pillars, with tiny round arches between them. But the arrangement is most effective. It is noticeable that there are carvings on the capitals of the two principal columns, which are still naive, but more sophisticated than those in the nave. One has pairs of lions against a formalized tree, showing Persian influence, the other just single lions with an inscription: 'Leo'.

Normandy

Normandy has a wealth of beautiful Romanesque churches, but it is different in a number of ways from the other regions where the style flourished. It is, of course, further north than most of them, but more important is the fact that during the Romanesque period the duchy of Normandy was a distinct entity, particularly well run and powerful – as was shown by the conquest of England in 1066.

So Normandy has some large churches which are notable for their scale, the quality of their stonework and their well-judged proportions but are unlike those elsewhere in having little sculptural decoration. The influence of Ottonian Germany can sometimes be seen, in the towering 'westwork' at Jumièges, for instance, and there are obvious similarities in style to the churches and cathedrals built by the Normans in England.

The abbey church of Jumièges, in the Seine valley downstream from Rouen, is mostly a ruin but none the less awe-inspiring for that. It was virtually complete by 1066, the year of the Battle of Hastings, and was consecrated in the presence of William the Conqueror the following year.

In Caen the presence of William is even more obvious. Two large and ambitious abbey churches, St-Etienne and La Trinité, were built there by him and his wife, Matilda of Flanders, respectively. There is also another, smaller church in a similar style, St-Nicolas, not far from St-Etienne.

The characteristic feature of the large Norman churches is their consistent use of three levels on either side of the nave – the main row of arches between the nave and the side-aisles, the triforium above that, and the clerestory with windows at the top. The detail is not always the same: St-Etienne, for instance, has a gallery at triforium level, whereas in La Trinité there is simply a row of blind arches. There are many successful variations on the three-level arrangement.

Another Norman feature was the use of a 'hollow wall', by which a walkway was built into the thickness of the nave or transept wall.

Norman churches were originally covered by a timber ceiling but both St-Etienne and La Trinité were given sophisticated sexpartite stone vaulting, which

Normandy

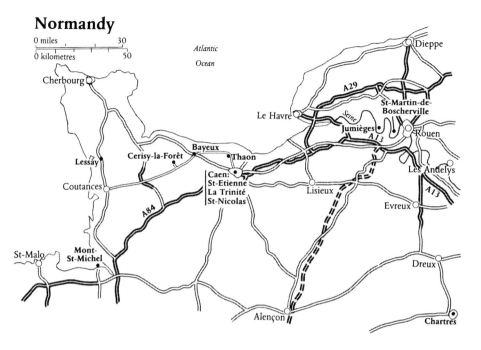

was a step towards Gothic. And Lessay, a lovely abbey church on Normandy's west coast, was one of the first Romanesque churches to be given rib vaulting over the nave – the technique which in due course became one of the basic features of Gothic.

One of the most appealing Romanesque churches in Normandy is the abbey church at St-Martin-de-Boscherville, which is also in the Seine valley downstream from Rouen, and also stands in a park. Another is Cerisy-la-Forêt, which is surrounded by fields west of Caen. And there are a number of smaller churches, including an enchanting one that stands by a stream near the village of Thaon, north-west of Caen.

Bayeux was important in Romanesque times, and it is full of character today. Its tapestry, which shows the events leading up to William the Conqueror's victory at Hastings, is on display there, and its cathedral, though now largely Gothic, still has parts that are Romanesque.

Certainly the most spectacularly placed of them all, however, is the church at Mont-St-Michel, built in the eleventh century and still largely Romanesque, which stands among the Gothic buildings of a later period, on the summit of the rock.

Bayeux and Thaon

Bayeux is the home of the famous tapestry, as I have said, which is one of the masterpieces of the Romanesque period. It is also a delightful old town which has the river Aure running through its centre, with old mills along its banks, and its centre is dominated by the cathedral.

The cathedral is now largely Gothic, but it has Romanesque decoration in the nave and, down below, a crypt that dates from an earlier church, built in the eleventh century.

Outside Bayeux, in the area to the east between it and Caen, there are several villages with Romanesque churches, and the one just outside Thaon is one of these. It is well worth seeing for its picturesque setting and for the carving along the outside of the south wall of the nave.

Bayeux's first Romanesque cathedral was built in the days of Odo, the turbulent half-brother of William the Conqueror who was Bishop of Bayeux and may well have commissioned the tapestry. The new church was consecrated in 1077 in the presence of William and his wife, Matilda, but was largely destroyed soon afterwards, in 1105, by the army of Henry I. Rebuilding stretched from the mid-twelfth to the early thirteenth century, so that it had both Romanesque and Gothic features.

The crypt and the bases of the two western towers survive from Odo's cathedral. The decoration of the stonework in the nave, covering the lower levels of both sides, dates from the early years of the rebuilding process, in the twelfth century, when the style was still Romanesque.

The crypt is simply decorated. It has two lines of short columns supporting the groin vaulting, and each column is topped with a carved capital of stylized foliage and, sometimes, human masks.

Two of the most interesting features are a pair of larger capitals from the eleventh-century church which were discovered under the central tower during reconstruction work in the nineteenth century and are displayed in the crypt. One represents the story of Doubting Thomas, with Christ in the centre, St Thomas reaching out to touch him on one side, and St Peter holding some enormous keys on the other. The other capital shows the salvation of a soul, with Christ holding a small, naked human figure on his knee and an angel on either side.

In the upper church, the decoration of the nave makes an immediate impression. The arches on either side have a range of patterns, including zigzags and fretwork, and the wall-space between them is also patterned, like a carpet. What particularly catch the eye are the little carved reliefs, including human figures and

Bayeux cathedral: carving in nave of a bishop pronouncing a blessing

Country church of Thaon, from the south-west

more or less fantastic beasts, which have been inserted in the angles between the arches.

Many explanations have been offered for these scenes but none of them has been wholly convincing. What is certain is that they include two bishops, each pronouncing a blessing, a man with a monkey on a chain, a bearded man standing on an animal head, and beasts in various picturesque contortions that are almost oriental in style – and are wholly fascinating.

A few miles away, the little church of **Thaon** stands in an isolated spot at the end of an overgrown lane, and brings you up short when you suddenly come upon it, surrounded by trees, with the stream in the foreground – a surprisingly ornate church in a remote country setting.

Its main feature is its pretty central tower, built in the eleventh century, but the effect is enhanced by the proportions of the church, and by the decoration that runs all round it. There are several tiers of arches, carefully arranged in the best Norman style, on its flat east end, and the design is continued, with variations, along the outside of the choir.

Particular care was given to the outside of the nave. Patterning fills the spaces in and between a row of largely blind arches running along the south side, and there is an array of splendidly grotesque faces under the cornice. The west façade has another elegant design, with an arch carved with geometrical patterns over the doorway, and more tiers of smaller arches above.

Thaon has suffered over the centuries. Its two side-aisles were removed in the eighteenth century, leaving the arches to the nave to be simply filled in, and the church is now in bad need of restoration. It is normally closed to visitors, but for those who succeed in entering, the interior is well proportioned, and has some simple carved capitals.

Thaon is worth visiting, however, if only for the views of the outside. The tower, which is the oldest part of the church, has two levels of arches and, above them, a pyramid-shaped top. The east end and the north side of the choir were built next, in the twelfth century, followed by the south side of the choir, the nave and the west front. It is noticeable that, as so often, the south side of the church has more decoration than the north.

Caen: St-Etienne, La Trinité and St-Nicolas

Caen was in many ways the creation of William the Conqueror, who treated it as the second capital of Normandy, after Rouen, and was buried there after his death

Abbey church of St-Etienne, Caen: the nave

in 1087. It is not surprising that there are three large churches there which date from the more than fifty years (1035-87) when he was Duke of Normandy, all of them chiefly or partly Romanesque.

The two principal ones are St-Etienne and La Trinité, both of them originally monastic churches that were built for the Abbaye aux Hommes and the Abbaye aux Dames respectively. St-Etienne was built over a period of years, and was much rebuilt in Gothic style in subsequent centuries. But the later builders were careful to respect the original design, and it still has its Romanesque west front and nave. In spite of the mixture of styles it is a compelling church.

La Trinité was not conceived on such a grand scale, and its nave, for instance, is markedly less tall. It is a beautiful church, however, with more decoration than most of those built in Normandy at that time. It too took some years to build, during the late eleventh and early twelfth centuries, and it has been much restored. But it is still largely Romanesque.

The third of the trio is St-Nicolas, which is not far from St-Etienne and was built as a parish church for that part of Caen – in a similar style but on a smaller scale. It is now deconsecrated, and normally closed to visitors, but it has a well-proportioned triple arch at the base of its west front, and there are good views to be had of its *chevet* from the cemetery that lies to the east of the church.

The two abbeys were founded by William the Conqueror and his wife, Matilda of Flanders, as a way of settling a dispute with the Church over their marriage, which had taken place in 1051 or 1052. They were distant cousins, and the Pope took the view that that pro-hibited them from marrying. They were excommunicated in 1053.

St-Nicolas, Caen: the 'chevet'

But in 1059, as a result of the negotiations conducted on their behalf by Lanfranc of Pavia, an influential figure in Norman affairs who was then abbot of Le Bec-Hellouin and later became Archbishop of Canterbury, Pope Nicholas II agreed to lift the excommunication – on condition that William and Matilda each founded an abbey. So William founded the Abbaye aux Hommes, and Matilda the Abbaye aux Dames. William was eventually buried in St-Etienne, and Matilda in La Trinité, and the sites of their tombs are still marked.

The building of St-Etienne began in about 1068, and the church had an initial dedication in 1077. It is an unforgettable sight when you see it across the gardens which lie to the south-west, with its array of towers and turrets and its Gothic *chevet*. But the eleventh-century church was more austere, and that is shown by its powerful but plain west front, which soars out of a smaller square on the far side.

This façade shows the Norman taste for proportion and precision rather than surface decoration. The lower part is no more than a balanced composition of thick buttresses and two tiers of plain, round-headed windows, ranged above three small, simple doorways (the carving on the central tympanum is modern). It is only in the two towers that the stonework becomes more detailed, with three tiers of quite richly carved arches on each.

The two Gothic turrets on the tops of the towers, which alter the proportions of the façade, were added in the thirteenth century. The lantern-tower over the transept crossing behind them is also not original, but a seventeenth-century reconstruction on a smaller scale of the eleventh-century tower, which collapsed in 1566.

Inside, St-Etienne has one of the most inspiring of the naves built in Normandy in the Romanesque period. As elsewhere there are three levels, but the arches of the triforium are, unusually, as tall and as wide as those at ground level, and open on to a wide gallery. Up above them is a decorated clerestory with a characteristic walkway running along it.

The arrangement of the engaged columns, which are placed around the main pillars and run up the side of the nave, is well judged. The capitals on top of the columns are carved, but with mainly formal designs, as was the Norman practice. Visually they serve as focal points when you look along the length of the nave.

St-Etienne originally had a timber ceiling. But this was replaced early in the twelfth century by the sexpartite rib vault, in a style that was transitional towards Gothic. The vault has a beauty of its own, however, and although alterations had to be made to the clerestory to accommodate it, it does not conflict with the style of the nave.

The same is true of the east end of the church, beyond the transept, which was completely rebuilt in Gothic style in the thirteenth century. The three levels of Gothic arches correspond to the arrangement and dimensions of the Romanesque ones, so that in spite of the difference in styles, there is a harmonious view, and a compelling one, the length of the church.

Abbey church of La Trinité, Caen: the nave

The building of La Trinité began earlier, in about 1060, and there was an initial consecration in 1066, just before the Normans set sail for England. It is a less spectacular building, particularly when seen from the outside. The west front, for instance, suffers from the incongruous balustrade placed on top of each of the two towers in the early eighteenth century, at the time of Louis XIV; and only the lowest part of the crossing tower retains the round arches of the Romanesque period. The carving on the central tympanum of the west front is also modern, as at St-Etienne.

The Romanesque design still covers most of the west front, however, and it is a handsome one, with a well-balanced arrangement of round arches on different levels, and in particular a cluster of tall, narrow arches on each of the towers. There is also a decorative line of round-headed windows, each flanked by two smaller blind arches, along the outside of the nave on the south side.

Inside the church there is, here as well, a fine view the length of the nave. As at St-Etienne, the original timber ceiling was replaced by a more complex stone vault early in the twelfth century, and this one is a 'pseudo'-sexpartite vault since it has a vertical diaphragm across the middle of the double bay rather than a transverse rib. But it too combines well with the original design.

The sides of the nave of La Trinité are especially ornate. There is a fretwork pattern over the main arches, a row of tiny blind arches in the triforium above them, and a clerestory with tall windows and a walkway that runs behind clusters of small columns. Unlike other, taller churches, it has essentially only two levels, the main arcade and the clerestory, but the row of tiny arches enables it to conform to the usual Norman style of three levels.

At the far end of the church, the choir still has its original groin vaulting, and it is quite dark, with expanses of plain wall on either side. But it provides the setting for a stylish arrangement of the apse. This has two semi-circular rings of arches, one above the other, and on both levels the columns supporting the arches are set a short way in from the outer wall and the windows, which creates a three-dimensional effect.

The two arms of the transept also have a special charm because of their decoration. They more or less repeat the design of the sides of the nave, but the row of tiny blind arches at the triforium level has more detailed work, with engaged columns topped by capitals instead of the plain arches of the nave. The view of each arm of the transept, seen through the arches of the crossing, is complex and rewarding.

The northern arm remains entirely Romanesque, while a Gothic chapterhouse was added to the southern arm in the thirteenth century.

This part of the church has some well-carved capitals, some on the pillars supporting the crossing, some on the columns of the apse. There are formal designs, but also some human figures, and rams with splendidly curled horns. One capital, in the apse, has a carving of an elephant in which, instead of a trunk, the animal has a short nose with a ring in it, to which a rope is attached so that it can be led like a bull.

Down below the east end of La Trinité there is a crypt, which is not common in Normandy. It is not normally open to visitors, but it is one of the oldest parts of the church, with sixteen columns ranged closely together, each with a simple and archaic carved capital.

Cerisy-la-Forêt

The abbey church of Cerisy-la-Forêt, which stands in open country south-west of Bayeux, not far from the forest of the same name, has suffered a great deal over the centuries – from the demolition of a large part of its nave and from unsympathetic rebuilding elsewhere. But it has retained much of the style of Norman Romanesque architecture of the late eleventh and early twelfth century, and it is still a grand sight across the surrounding fields.

Abbey church of Cerisy-la-Forêt, from the south-west

Inside the church, the nave, transept and choir are excellent examples of the Norman style of that period, with rows of arches ranged one above the other; and there is reconstructed timber roofing over much of the church, similar to what it would have had when it was first built.

The choir and the apse are particularly successful. There is Gothic vaulting over the apse, as there is over the transept crossing, but the overall effect is predominantly Romanesque and wholly memorable.

The history of Cerisy is thought to go back to the sixth century when St Vigor, later Bishop of Bayeux, is said to have founded a religious establishment there. What is certain is that in 1032 Robert the Magnificent, Duke of Normandy and father of William the Conqueror, founded a Benedictine abbey on the site, and that with ducal patronage it became influential in the monastic world of the time.

The present church was mostly built towards the end of the eleventh century, and originally had a nave of eight bays, compared with the three that survive today. In the thirteenth century it was given a Gothic west front. But the five westernmost bays and the west front were demolished in 1811, in the aftermath of the French Revolution, when the local parishioners, who had by then taken over the whole church from the monks, decided that they could not afford to maintain them.

The missing parts are marked out on the ground today, and that gives an idea of the scale of the original building. But the plain wall which forms the western end of the surviving church, first built in 1747, when the church was divided into two parts, is not a pretty sight.

There have been other changes, too. Only the two lower levels of the tower over the crossing date from the Romanesque period, the upper level and the spire having been added in the eighteenth century. Also, several of the windows of the *chevet* have been altered to make them conform with Gothic style, and buttresses have had to be added to the outside of the apse.

It is a tribute to the quality of the Romanesque design, with its arrangement of the various masses which make up the church, and its well-balanced proportions, that its main lines still stand out so strongly. The *chevet*, in spite of the changes, still has the charm of Romanesque style.

Inside, the three remaining bays of the nave are also as they were, and the effect is masterly. They have broad arches at the first level, pairs of narrower arches within a blind relieving arch in the triforium above that, and a clerestory with triple arches, a walkway and windows at the top. The side-aisles have groin vaulting.

The arrangement is characteristic of Norman style. No light comes in at the second level, but in Cerisy, as at St-Etienne in Caen (see page 119), the arches open onto a gallery that runs the length of the nave and continues beyond the transept, on either side of the choir. It is the windows in the clerestory that light the nave, while the walkway creates a three-dimensional effect within the thickness of the wall.

There is also another typically Norman feature in the transept: a raised gallery running across the end of each arm. The gallery at the end of the southern arm is especially attractive, with a row of small blind arches running across the top of the two main arches.

The choir and the apse were built later than the nave, in about 1100, and are even more striking. The choir has two bays of tall arches, which rest on a stretch of plain wall and open onto the gallery, and there is a continuation of the nave clerestory above them. The apse is Norman Romanesque design at its best, with three semi-circular ranges of arches, one above the other, and five round-headed windows in each.

The ribbed and segmented vault over the apse, added in the fourteenth century, is of course incongruous, and so is the pointed Gothic arch which precedes it. But the three ranges of Romanesque arches are largely intact. The windows are all set deep into the wall, with walkways at the second and third levels, and this achieves the three-dimensional effect found often in Normandy, as it does in the clerestory of the nave.

Cerisy has carved decoration over some of the arches of the nave, as well as in the south arm of the transept. However, as is usual in Norman churches, it is the overall design and the immaculate stonework which produce the main effect.

There are also carved capitals in various parts of the church, and a few of them, mainly at the eastern end of the church, have simple figures on them – some human and some animal, set against a background of plant patterns. But most of the capitals have formal designs, and they serve as focal points in the overall design, with its arrangement of arches, columns and engaged columns.

Jumièges

The ruined abbey church of Jumièges now stands in a park, and is another evocative sight which is evidence of the great ambitions and achievements of the dukes of Normandy in the eleventh century. It was originally a large Romanesque church, dedicated to Notre-Dame, but the eastern end was later rebuilt in Gothic style.

Much of the church was demolished in the early nineteenth century, after the French Revolution. But enough remains to give an idea of the scale and style of the Romanesque church, and of several other abbey buildings. These included a second church, dedicated to St Peter, part of which dates back to the tenth century and is therefore pre-Romanesque.

Today, the two western towers and what is left of the crossing tower, all part of the eleventh-century church of Notre-Dame, dominate the village of Jumièges, and are visible for miles around, rising out of wooded country in a loop of the Seine. Most of the Romanesque nave survives too, even though it is open to the sky, and its arrangement of arches and windows shows again the elegance achieved by the Norman builders of the period – both in Normandy and in England.

Ruins often have a special charm, and that is certainly true of Jumièges, which stands in an idyllic site, with the park surrounding it. The two western towers are striking, and so is the nave, which now has sunlight pouring in through the arches on its southern side, and a huge open arch, topped by two tiers of windows, under the crossing.

Abbey church of Jumièges: the west front

Jumièges's history reflects the upheavals that affected the Seine valley in the time of the Vikings, or Normans as they came to be known, and its subsequent recovery. An abbey had been founded there in the middle of the seventh century by St Philibert, a Frankish aristocrat, and it became a large and influential institution. But in the ninth century the prosperity of the Seine valley made it a target for the Vikings, and they set fire to the abbey more than once as they swept up the river to Rouen and Paris. The monks eventually abandoned the site, taking their relics and manuscripts with them, and settled near Cambrai.

In 911, however, Charles the Simple, the King of France, made a first grant of land to Rollo, a Viking chief, in what became Normandy, and after that conditions in the shattered region gradually improved. The Viking leaders not only converted to Christianity, but as dukes of Normandy began to encourage and finance the creation of monastic communities. So the monks returned to the ruins of Jumièges, and began the long task of rebuilding.

The reconstruction of Notre-Dame began in or about 1040, five years after William 'the Bastard', later William the Conqueror, became Duke of Normandy. It appears that the builders based their plans on the earlier church on the same site, because the design of Notre-Dame, with its two western towers and a third tower over the crossing, was a common one in the Carolingian period.

Also Carolingian, but less frequently found, is the high and relatively plain block of stonework which stands out from the centre of the western façade, and has a tribune on the upper floor behind it that looks out over the nave. This west-work was already archaic in France in the eleventh century and is not often found there, though there are examples in Germany.

Since the lower parts of the two towers are also mainly plain, the overall impression is austere, and massively monumental. But the effect is lightened by the fine quality of the decoration of the four upper levels of the towers. The two lower levels are square, the two upper ones octagonal, and each has a tier of small round arches, all different – some blind, some with windows inside them. The conical peaks that both towers once had have gone, but they are still impressive.

The nave is one of the most appealing parts of Jumièges, although sadly it is not possible to walk into it these days – for fear, it seems, of a collapse of part of the masonry. But it can be seen from outside, from the east and from the south, and it is possible to make out the characteristic three levels on either side: the broad arches at ground level, the sets of smaller triple arches above that, and at the top a row of windows.

One interesting feature of the nave is the alternation of simple columns and more robust pillars, with engaged columns on each face, at ground level on either side. This pattern is found elsewhere in Norman architecture – in Durham cathedral, for example.

Of the two side-aisles, only the northern one survives. It has groin vaulting in each of its bays, divided by transverse arches, and the southern aisle once had the same. The northern arm of the transept is also the better preserved of the two, and its western wall shows an early example of that other typical Norman feature – the walkway constructed high up in the thickness of the wall. There is a row of plain arches that open onto the transept and, behind them, the walkway.

It is noticeable that Notre-Dame, like many other Norman Romanesque churches, has an almost complete lack of sculptural decoration, in contrast to Romanesque churches in other parts of France. One or two simply sculptured capitals have been found – there is a delightful carving, for instance, of a bird surrounded by tendrils

at the north-west corner of the crossing
– but the majority are plain.

It is true, of course, that Notre-
Dame, like other Romanesque churches,
would have been extensively painted,
so that it would have had some decoration. But the Normans attached the
greatest importance to the pure lines of
their churches, and the quality of the
stonework, rather than to sculptural
decoration.

Jumièges: carving near the transept crossing

There is one example of decorative
carving to be seen on the western wall
of the cellar, the building to the south
of the church's western façade. The face
of a bearded man looks out quizzically
from a carved arch, and above him is a
row of tiny faces, with a range of expressions. It shows a lightness of touch
that contrasts with the monumentality of the church.

One of the best views of Notre-Dame is from the south, across what used to be
the cloister, although nothing of that remains. Since the southern side-aisle is in
ruins one can see into the nave, through the arches at ground level and the smaller
triple arches, each set inside a broader relieving arch, that are above them. High
above are the two western towers and, to the east, the surviving wall of the crossing tower, which also has arches set into it.

One of the buildings off the cloister site is the former chapterhouse, which was
built later than the church, in about 1100. It is now roofless, but still has a round
arch with carved capitals set into its wall.

Another, which is one of the most interesting of the abbey's surviving buildings,
is the church of St-Pierre. It too is now a ruin, and mainly Gothic, but the lower
part of its western front, and the first two bays of the north wall, are a rare surviving example of the architecture of the tenth century, when Normandy was still
recovering from the devastation of the Vikings.

It is simple work, but a small double arch set in a rectangular frame has been discovered in the west front, and there are traces of a relatively complex design inside
the church in the north-western corner. Two arches which once divided the nave
from the side-aisles can still be seen at ground level in the north wall, though they

Jumièges: remains of transept and crossing tower

are now blocked up, and above them are two double arches similar to the one in the west front.

Between the two are circles that are set into the stonework. Their purpose is unknown, but they are thought to have been decorative, with paintings or frescoes inside them.

Lessay

The beautiful abbey church of Lessay, a few miles inland from the western coast of Normandy, has the pure lines and balanced proportions of Norman Romanesque – and it also has one of the most remarkable survival stories.

It was severely damaged in 1944, when mines laid in the church by the retreating German army were detonated by Allied shells, but after a long debate about what to do it was lovingly rebuilt between 1945 and 1957 so as to come as close as possible to the crippled original building.

It was a huge job, as can be seen from photographs taken at the time. Almost all the vaulting had collapsed, as had the lantern tower over the crossing and much of the apse, choir and transept. So had most of the west front and the north side-aisle. But the architects and builders sifted through the rubble, retrieving as much of the original masonry as they could, and used similar building materials to replace what was missing.

Today the church is a serene and imposing building which is almost entirely Romanesque in style. Like other Norman churches of the period, it has a minimum of sculptural decoration, but, once more, makes its effect through the ordered elegance of its various parts – the apse, choir, transept and nave. Two ranges of round-headed windows march below cornices the length of the outside of the church, while a stocky and relatively ornate crossing tower, with sets of four arches, each with columns and capitals, provides a focal point.

One of Lessay's most interesting features is the rib vaulting over the nave, transept and choir. There are differences of opinion over the dating of this, but it was certainly one of the earliest uses of this technique, which subsequently became a key element in Gothic architecture. It could even, if the eleventh-century date is accepted, have been earlier than that in Durham cathedral, which is often seen as the first example of rib vaulting. But that is not certain.

Unlike Durham, which has slightly pointed transverse arches between the bays of rib vaulting, Lessay has round arches throughout the church. There is a superb view from the western end, along the length of the nave, the transept and the

Abbey church of Lessay, from the south

choir and culminating in the two ranges of round-topped windows set into the apse.

Lessay abbey was originally founded in about 1056 by Turstin Haldup, a Norman noble of Viking origin whose family was related to that of the dukes of Normandy, including William the Conqueror. His wife, Emma, and his son, Eudes au Capel – also known as Odo – were also associated with the foundation, which was formally confirmed in 1080 by William the Conqueror himself, and Eudes was buried in the church after his death in 1098.

It is thought that the eastern end of the church, including the apse, the choir, the transept, and the two eastern bays of the nave, had been completed by the time of Eudes's death, and that the five western bays of the nave were built later in a second phase, in the twelfth century. Certainly there are differences between the five western bays and the two eastern ones, even if they are not great enough to break the visual continuity.

The whole nave has the three levels which are found in almost all Norman churches of that time – broad arches at the first level, a row of smaller arches in the triforium, which has no windows, and a clerestory at the top with windows and a walkway in the thickness of the wall. The side-aisles have groin vaulting. But the two eastern bays, presumably built earlier, have three arches in the triforium, while the other five have only two.

More significantly, the eastern bays have only a single engaged column running up the side of the nave to support the transverse arch, and the cross arches of the rib vaulting fit rather awkwardly into the wall above the column capital. In the five western bays, on the other hand, there is a more solid pillar with an engaged column on either side, and so there is a wider capital which provides a base for the arches of the vault.

Neither of the two arms of the transept has the gallery which was often built there in Norman churches, although excavations carried out while the church was being rebuilt have shown that such galleries were originally intended. Both transepts are stylish structures, however, which continue the three levels of the nave, except with smaller arches in the triforium.

The choir, too, continues the three levels, and it leads to a fine apse which is also characteristic of Norman style. Unlike Cerisy-la-Forêt (see page 125), where the apse has three semi-circular rings of windows, Lessay has only two. But the five windows at each level are set deep into the apse wall to create the three-dimensional effect that we have seen the Norman architects aimed for. The lower level has arches with clusters of columns between them, the upper level the distinctive walkway.

There, as elsewhere in the church, the column capitals are carved, mainly with quite simple designs. Most of them have formal patterns, but there are a few human masks.

Mont-St-Michel

Mont-St-Michel, the high rock that rises majestically from the sea in the middle of a wide bay, its peak crowned by a church and other monastic buildings, is one of the most spectacular sites to be seen anywhere. Many of the buildings are in Gothic style, including the eastern end of the church, and the spire dates only from the nineteenth century. Enough is left of the Romanesque church, however, built between 1023 and 1085, to show that it was one of the great achievements of eleventh-century Normandy.

There were modifications in the twelfth century and later but the nave, the side-aisles and the two arms of the transept are all in the elegant style of Norman Romanesque; and there is nothing discordant when the style changes east of the transept to the soaring and exquisite Gothic of the chancel. This was constructed

Mont-St-Michel: Romanesque abbey church on the summit

in the fifteenth and sixteenth centuries after the Romanesque east end had collapsed in 1421.

Down below the church, and built onto the rock, are a pre-Romanesque church, probably dating from about 900, and two Romanesque crypts, one under each arm of the transept. There are also two vaulted rooms at the north-west corner of the church, one immediately above the other, that were built in Romanesque style for the use of the monks.

One of the most fascinating aspects of Mont-St-Michel is the way in which large and complex structures were put up on the small space available at the summit of the rock. The rock is thought to have been a holy one since prehistoric times, and to have attracted Christian hermits from the sixth century. There has been a continuous process of building and rebuilding on it ever since.

Like other high places, the rock came to be linked to St Michael, the archangel. A small church dedicated to him was first erected there by St Aubert, Bishop of Avranches, at the beginning of the eighth century, modelled on the shrine on Monte Gargano, in southern Italy, where St Michael was said to have appeared at the end of the fifth century. The Norman Mont-St-Michel soon became one of the main pilgrimage centres in Europe, as it continues to be.

A monastic community installed itself on the site, and by the eleventh century it was in the hands of Benedictine monks, with links to the great abbey of Cluny in Burgundy (see page 61). They decided to build a large new church, comparable to others elsewhere in Normandy. There was, however, a fundamental problem: how to construct a large church on such a small space.

The solution that was found was ingenious. Three crypts were built onto the bare rock around the summit, to the east, north and south, and at the same time the tiny church of Notre-Dame-sous-Terre, which already existed just below the summit to the west, was extended. Taken together, these new structures provided a big enough platform for the new abbey church, with the transept crossing and the bell-tower placed directly over the summit of the rock.

Two of the Romanesque crypts still survive – those under the two arms of the transept, dedicated to Our Lady of the Thirty Candles and to St Martin respectively – and so does the little church of Notre-Dame-sous-Terre, with its twin naves and its Romanesque extension. They are all simple, softly lit places. The eastern crypt is also still there but is different since it was remodelled in Gothic style when the choir was rebuilt in the fifteenth and sixteenth centuries, and is now known as the Crypt of the Big Pillars.

The Romanesque nave originally had seven bays instead of the four which survive, and the church must have been an impressive sight, from both outside and inside. The four surviving bays on the south side show how it looked inside. It had three tiers of round arches on each side, made of a dark granite with a reddish tinge. There were wide arches at floor level, a gallery with pairs of double arches above that, and large round-topped windows under blind relieving arches at the top.

Like other Norman churches of the time, Mont-St-Michel had a timber ceiling, as it still has, which meant that there was less pressure on the walls and greater scope for windows, both in the nave itself and in the side-aisles. There was little sculptural decoration, but the church had a certain number of carved column capitals, with largely formal designs.

The north side of the nave collapsed in 1103, not long after it had been built, and was rebuilt in a style which was close to that of the original structure but designed to be more robust. So there are differences in the dimensions of the various arches, and it is noticeable that the northern side-aisle has pointed transverse arches dividing the groin vaults in each bay whereas the southern aisle has round ones – with a pronounced sag.

It is also the southern arm of the transept which better shows its original design since the northern arm has been remodelled. It has a round barrel vault, a small apsidal chapel set in a broader relieving arch on its eastern side, and some fine windows in its south wall, framed in a sequence of archivolts, with tall outer arches rising from the floor. The transept has some of the most carefully worked capitals in the church, with plant designs.

The transept crossing has tall and well-proportioned round arches, which provide a frame for the transition to the Gothic chancel. They and the bell-tower above were remodelled in the nineteenth century.

Unlike many other former abbeys, Mont-St-Michel still has many of its monastic buildings, and they are a powerful presence, towering over the small village at their foot. The most spectacular are those of the Gothic period, which are understandably known as 'La Merveille', and include a pretty cloister with views far out to sea.

But the two Romanesque rooms that were built onto the rock to the north-east of the church, one above the other, are both worth visiting. The lower, known as the Hall of the *Aquilon*, or north wind, was the almonry of the abbey. It has pointed arches that rest on solid columns and support a series of groin vaults, and was probably remodelled in the early twelfth century.

Above it is another, slightly longer room known as the *Promenoir*, or covered walkway, which has an early example of rib vaulting, also probably dating from the early twelfth century. There is some uncertainty about the use to which this room was put, but it may have served as both refectory and chapterhouse for the monks.

One thing is sure. The monks had superb views out over the bay, with its tides and shifting sands, and the same is true for visitors today.

St-Martin-de-Boscherville

St-Martin-de-Boscherville, a village in one of the wooded loops of the Seine downstream from Rouen, has one of the outstanding churches of early twelfth-century Normandy. A former abbey church dedicated to St George, it stands on a gently sloping hillside above the river and, although it has some later additions, is a near-complete example of its kind, showing the sense of style and the craftsmanship of the Norman builders of that time.

Some of the best views of it can be had by walking up through the field at the back of the church or from the park in which it stands. These reveal a large and well-proportioned Romanesque church with apse, transept, nave and, dominating the scene, a powerful and decorative bell-tower, complete with spire, which rises from the transept crossing.

Abbey church of St-Martin-de-Boscherville, from the east

There is a seventeenth-century addition, built over the twelfth-century chapter-house, at the north end of the transept, but it does not obtrude. The only incongruous element is the pair of thin Gothic turrets, added in the thirteenth century, which spring out of the west façade.

There is the same harmonious quality inside the church. The nave, which originally had a timber ceiling, was given a Gothic ribbed vault, also in the thirteenth century, and so were the transept and the crossing. But the transverse arches are only slightly pointed and, with the three levels of rounded arches on each side of the nave, characteristic of Norman style, the eye is led easily to the transept and, beyond it, to a beautiful arrangement of the east end.

One of the most interesting facts about Boscherville is that it is a very old religious site, with a history that goes back more than 2,000 years to pagan times. Excavations have uncovered the foundations of a Gallo-Roman temple that was first built in wood towards the end of the first century BC, and later rebuilt in stone late in the first century AD. Sadly, there is no indication of the deity or deities to whom it was dedicated, though a number of votive offerings have been found.

The temple subsequently fell into ruin, but in the seventh century, during the time of the Merovingian rulers of Gaul, a Christian chapel was erected on the site, as often happened, and a large number of tombs, complete with sarcophagi and grave goods, have been discovered there, both inside the chapel and around it. The chapel and its cemetery continued to be used in the Carolingian period which followed.

In the eleventh century the site became the private property of a powerful Norman family which later took the name of Tancarville, several of whose members held the title of Chamberlain of Normandy. One of the most prominent members of the family was Raoul, who acted as tutor to William 'the Bastard', the young Duke of Normandy who later became William the Conqueror.

In about 1050 Raoul decided to install a college of canons, complete with a large new church and the necessary institutional buildings, in Boscherville, and he endowed it with property in different parts of Normandy. Early in the following century his son and successor, William, went one better. In 1113 he removed the canons, who had become discredited, and established a fully-fledged Benedictine abbey with monks, an even larger church and new monastic buildings.

It is thought that he undertook this costly operation because like William the Conqueror, he had run into criticism from the Church of his marriage – to Mathilde d'Arques, an heiress who had previously been married to one of his relations. So just as William the Conqueror agreed to finance the Abbaye aux Hommes and the church of St-Etienne in Caen because of criticism of *his* marriage (see page 121), William de Tancarville agreed to found a Benedictine abbey in Boscherville.

It is the twelfth-century church which he built then that very largely survives today. It towers over the village of Boscherville, and the park in which it stands provides a splendid setting.

Like most Norman Romanesque churches, Boscherville does not have the fine carving that is found in churches of the period further south. There were some sophisticated carvings in the cloister and the chapterhouse, which were later than the church, but the church itself has relatively few carved capitals.

On the outside, there are some historiated capitals on either side of the west doorway, and others on the ring of blind arches that runs round the base of the central apse at the east end. These include an original one that shows a man striking coins.

The appeal of Boscherville, like that of other Norman Romanesque churches, lies in its monumental quality, its balanced proportions and its immaculate stone-work – most distinctively, in the regular lines of round arches ranged one above the other, both inside the church and on the outside.

Inside, there is a magnificent view along the length of the church from the west door. The main arches on either side rest on a complex of engaged columns, set into substantial pillars. Above them is a triforium with a set of four tiny arches in each bay, and above that a clerestory with windows and a characteristic Norman walkway. Many of the capitals are simply carved, some with formal designs, some historiated, and they have the effect of articulating the wall surfaces.

As so often, the east end of the church is more elaborate. Many of the arches in the transept and under the crossing are decorated, mainly with zigzag patterns. There is also another characteristically Norman feature in each arm of the transept: a raised gallery supported by two arches. The central column of each gallery has a large capital, simply carved, and each has a tiny carved scene above that, in the angle between the arches: on one side, a bishop or abbot giving a blessing, on the other, two knights in combat.

The apse over and behind the sanctuary is one of the loveliest parts of the church. It has two semi-circular ranges of windows, one above the other, each window framed in round arches, and above them a ribbed vault. The upper range has a space between the inner columns and the outer wall which, as in the nave, leaves room for a walkway and creates a three-dimensional effect.

The outside of the church is just as inspiring. It is hard to assess the original effect of the west front because the central gable was made higher and more pointed in the Gothic period, and the two turrets were added. But it was well

St-Martin-de-Boscherville: the nave

proportioned, and more ornate than in earlier Norman churches. The doorway has no tympanum but it has receding archivolts, each decorated with geometrical patterns, and there are two rows of round arches above it, each enclosing three windows.

The outside walls of the nave were left relatively plain. But there is an austere beauty about these regular lines of round arches, and in the *chevet* they become more ornate.

The central apse, for instance, is a meticulous composition, with a balance between the three rings of arches, and it is flanked on either side by the arms of the transept, the smaller apses that emerge from the transept, and the side-aisles, all of which have decorative windows. They create a three-dimensional effect which one can admire from several angles as one walks round the *chevet*.

Up above, and providing a climax, is the great crossing tower with its two rows of arches, topped by the octagonal spire.

Almost nothing is left of the cloister, which was built in the later twelfth century on the north side of the church over the nave of Raoul's eleventh-century collegiate church. But a pair of capitals that were found on the site and are now in the Musée des Antiquités de la Seine-Maritime in Rouen show that it had some finely carved scenes, both biblical and secular, including musicians and dancers.

The chapterhouse, on the other hand, does survive. It was built in about 1170 over the choir of the collegiate church, and stands on the east side of where the cloister once was. Its upper floors were added on in the seventeenth century. It still has its formal entrance, made up of three decorated arches, and a late Romanesque interior, with a complex system of vaulting.

The arches had some lively carving, including biblical scenes on the capitals and some full-length figures similar to those on the *portail royal* at Chartres (see page 102), which may have influenced it. These figures, and the column capitals, have been completely remade in recent years, and although they are not original, give an indication of the style that the monastic buildings once had.

Loire Valley

The Loire valley has long been one of the main thoroughfares of France, and in the Romanesque period it was dotted with churches, many of them belonging to monasteries and convents. The church of St-Martin in Tours was an important pilgrimage centre in its own right, as well as a stopping-point on one of the routes to Santiago de Compostela.

Today only a few of them survive, and St-Martin is not one of them. But they include a graceful creation of the Romanesque period, the abbey church of St-Benoît-sur-Loire, and a number of small churches with some of the most vivid and moving wall-paintings, many of them only rediscovered in the twentieth century.

The most notable of these paintings are in the church at Tavant, a village on the

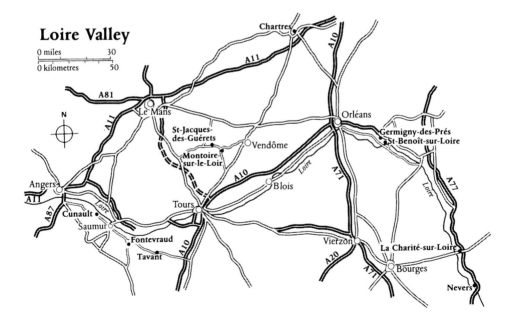

Vienne a few miles upstream from its junction with the Loire. There are others in the valley of the Loir, a tributary of the Loire, at Montoire-sur-le-Loir and St-Jacques-des-Guérets. They are all worth a visit because they are rare examples of the talent of the Romanesque painters.

St-Benoît-sur-Loire, upstream from Orléans, became famous because its monks succeeded in getting hold of the bones of St Benedict (see page 30), and they built a majestic church, complete with an elegant tower at the western end. But there were also other monastic institutions beside the long, broad river, and two of the most interesting are on either side of Saumur – Fontevraud to the south-east and Cunault to the north-west.

Fontevraud was an influential convent that was patronized by royalty and the nobility, and it is still an arresting place because not only the church but many of the other buildings still survive – not least the kitchens.

Cunault is an imposing hall church, like the churches of Poitou to the south, and it has a rare collection of more than 200 carved capitals, ranging from biblical scenes and floral designs to grimacing monsters.

Cunault

The church at Cunault, one of the charming villages on the south bank of the Loire, a few miles downstream from Saumur, is among the most impressive in the region. Formerly an abbey church, it has a tall nave and side-aisles which are well proportioned – and are especially striking when you look along the length of the nave from the west door. And its capitals are exceptional.

Some of them are in the naive and engaging style of the eleventh century, but most of them are the more sophisticated work of the twelfth. There is a wide range of subject-matter, including some purely decorative patterns, and they are all carved with considerable verve.

On the outside, Cunault towers over its surroundings, but it gives a disjointed impression since it lacks the harmony between its various parts that was character-istic of most Romanesque churches. This is mainly because of the sloping roofs that were clumsily built onto the church when it was being restored, possibly during extensive work in the nineteenth century. The roofs were laid across the various parts of the church – nave, aisles, chapels – without being related to dif-ferences in height and in form, as was usual in Romanesque style.

But the church still has a most attractive bell-tower, which dates from the second half of the eleventh century and is one of the oldest parts of the building.

It also has a fine twelfth-century chapel which extends from the north side of the *chevet* and, though truncated by the line of the roof, is still stylishly composed, with round forms in its windows and in the arcade of tiny blind arches above them.

The steeple of the bell-tower and the tiny turrets which surround it were added in the fifteenth century, but the rest of the tower, with its three tiers of rounded arches, many of them decorated with carving, is a fine example of the Romanesque architecture of eleventh-century Anjou. The doorway at its foot has two engaging capitals from that period, one showing temptation in the form of a mermaid holding out a fish to a fisherman, who reaches

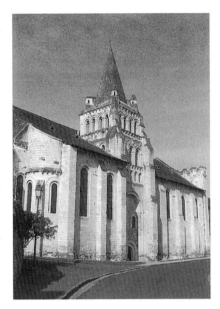

Abbey church of Cunault, from the north-east

out to grasp it, the other redemption through the Annunciation. In the latter, the Virgin Mary is sitting in a chair with a large sun behind her while the Archangel Gabriel touches her ear.

The history of the church goes back to the disturbed days of the ninth century when monks from the island of Noirmoutier, off the Atlantic coast, who were in flight from Viking raids, were given land in Cunault by the Abbot of St-Martin in Tours. They founded an abbey there but were still not safe, even in Cunault, and they moved on a few years later, taking with them the relics of two saints: St Philibert, who had founded the monastery on Noirmoutier, and St Maxenceul, who had brought Christianity to the Cunault region in the fourth century.

The monks eventually settled in the abbey of Tournus (see page 86), in Burgundy, but the link with Cunault was not broken, and its abbey continued to be a dependency of Tournus. With the advent of calmer times in the tenth century, some monks returned from Tournus, bringing with them the relics of St Maxenceul. The Cunault abbey was patronized by the powerful counts of Anjou, and it became rich and powerful, owning land on both banks of the Loire.

It also became a pilgrimage centre. The abbey church was dedicated to the Virgin Mary, and pilgrims came from far afield to venerate her.

A new church was built in the eleventh century, and the bell-tower survives from that. However, by the early twelfth century a larger building was needed, and that was when work began on the present church. The builders started with the *chevet*, as was usual, and worked westwards, and the church was only finished in the early thirteenth century, so that the vaulting of the three western bays of the nave shows the arrival of Gothic.

The western façade was last and is largely plain, but it has a rounded doorway with five archivolts, all undecorated; and in the tympanum is a carving of the Virgin and Child attended by two angels which, though a thirteenth-century work, is still partly Romanesque in style.

The greater part of the nave is Romanesque, with high, slightly pointed barrel vaulting supported by transverse arches, and it leads the eye easily to the sanctuary at the east end of the church, where there is a ring of tall, round arches, resting on multiple columns, each of which has beautifully carved capitals.

Cunault is built in the style of Poitou and, like many of the churches in that region, is a hall church – that is, the side-aisles are almost the same height as the nave. This means that the nave is not lit directly, but receives its light from the windows in the aisles. So the lighting of the nave is deliberately subdued, while the sanctuary, which receives direct light, stands out all the more prominently.

There are capitals throughout the church, in the nave and the aisles as well as the ambulatory, and they are one of the main glories of Cunault. Those from the eleventh century are in the oldest part of the church, under the bell-tower, and are simple carvings of plants, animals and monsters. Those from the twelfth century are in other parts of the church, and add a lively, decorative element to the overall design, although they are sometimes hard to see because they are very high up.

There are only a handful of biblical themes, but they include another Annunci-ation and two crude but powerful scenes which show the Flagellation and Christ weighed down as he carries the Cross. Elsewhere, Samson is shown fighting the lion and, later, lying on his back with his head on Delilah's knees while a Philistine prepares to put out his eyes.

There are also numerous action scenes. An armoured knight fights barbarians, another tackles a dragon, or a horseman charges towards the ramparts of a city. On one capital two warriors brandish swords, and are apparently about to attack each other. On another two naked men, each mounted on a winged monster, also seem to be challenging each other.

Monsters and animals are of course to be seen throughout the church, sur-rounded by carved patterns, and while they were undoubtedly intended to convey a moral message, they are decorative in their own right. On one capital animals are playing various musical instruments, and appear to represent the various vices.

On numerous others fantastic beasts with wings and twisted tails, or sometimes just grimacing heads, smile or snarl at the passers-by below.

The Cunault capitals are not unique in their range of story-telling and fantasy – nor in the many decorative motifs which surround them. But they are a vivid collection, and they are a distinctive feature of a beautiful church.

Fontevraud

The abbey of Fontevraud (also spelt Fontevrault) in the Loire valley was a rich and powerful institution in the twelfth century, patronized by aristocratic families and, not least, by the Plantagenet kings of England. It continued to play a big role for centuries after that, and is still a dominant presence because, unlike other former abbeys, it has retained not just its church, but many of its other monastic buildings. Its courtyards, cloisters and gardens are spread over a wide area.

The most original feature is the building containing its kitchens which, like the abbey church, dates from the twelfth century. It is a complex octagonal structure with a sharply pointed roof and tiny turrets that mark the outlets of its many chimneys. It is the only one of its sort that survives from the Romanesque period.

Abbey church of Fontevraud: the 'chevet'

The church has been much restored, and makes a rather cold impression, not having the intimate atmosphere of most Romanesque churches. But it is an outstanding example of a domed church that is similar to Angoulême cathedral (see page 200) and others in south-western France. Its nave is covered by a line of four domes, supported by clusters of columns, and has well-carved column capitals. There is also a tall and handsome choir which, like the transept, was built earlier in a different style.

One point of great interest is the four royal tombs that lie prominently at the head of the nave. They are of Henry II, King of England (and Count of Anjou), Eleanor of Aquitaine, his wife, King

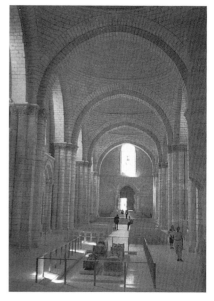

Fontevraud: royal tombs in the nave

Richard I Lionheart, their son, and Isabella of Angoulême, wife of King John. Full-length statues of all four lie in state over their respective tombs, repainted in the nineteenth century.

The abbey buildings owe their survival to the decision of Napoleon in 1804 to use them as a prison. Like other church buildings they had been declared national property after the French Revolution in 1789. This saved them from total destruction, but they were still much damaged over the years, and although it was decided to close the prison in 1963, the last prisoners only left the abbey complex in 1985.

Restoration has removed most of the traces of the long years as a prison, and the buildings are now in immaculate condition. The process has also brought out the austere character of the original abbey. In particular, the church has little surface decoration apart from the capitals in the nave, and this reflects the ideals of its founder, Robert d'Arbrissel.

Robert was a well-known travelling preacher and hermit who like many religious leaders of his time aspired to return to the asceticism of early monastic life. He established himself with his followers at Fontevraud, then a remote spot in a wooded valley, in or about 1100.

He had the backing of the Bishop of Poitiers, and the new abbey quickly attracted support from the great families of the region, who donated money and land. In time it became the centre of an order, with over a hundred daughter houses in western and central France. Robert himself had differences with his benefactors, and took to the road again in 1104, returning but occasionally to the abbey.

The exceptional feature of Fontevraud was that it was a mixed community of both monks and nuns, and the head was always a woman, the abbess. There were in fact more nuns than monks, and the community was divided into four parts: the Grand-Moutier at the centre for 'virgins', the Madeleine convent for married women or those who had 'repented', the St-Lazare priory for lepers and others who were sick, and the monastery of St-Jean-de-l'Habit, outside the abbey walls, for monks – who said mass and performed the sacraments for the whole community.

The church of the Grand-Moutier is still the central building, and had to be large to accommodate the many nuns and monks. Though it is plain and austere, especially on the outside, it has some of the characteristic features of Romanesque churches of its time: round arches on the west front and over the windows of the nave, and a *chevet*, or east end, made up of apse, ambulatory and radiating chapels. The top of the crossing tower, and the two turrets on the west front, were added later.

Inside, the system of domes allowed good-sized windows, which light the nave – and the capitals. These have biblical themes as well as carvings of animals and plants entwined. Like the nave as a whole, they reflect the influence of south-west France; and the same is true of the arches supporting the domes, which are slightly pointed.

The choir and the transept were built between 1106 and 1119, and are similar in style to those of St-Benoît-sur-Loire (see page 154) and St-Etienne in Nevers (see page 71), both of them further up the Loire, except that in Fontevraud the choir is much loftier, with tall columns. The nave was built later, between 1130 and 1150, and it seems that when the time came to construct it, there was a change of plan, and that the system of domes was introduced instead of a continuation of the earlier style.

Outside the church, most of the abbey buildings were rebuilt after the Romanesque period, if often on Romanesque foundations. That is true of the large and fine cloister, for instance, of the refectory, and of a number of other buildings.

But the kitchens survive, and with their complex system of ventilation are one of the most fascinating creations of the Romanesque period. The building is octagonal at its base, and is ringed by a number of small apses, each containing a cooking space and each topped by a turret with a chimney in it. Other outlets for smoke and smells were formed when, higher up, the cross-section became square and then, higher up still, octagonal again.

Altogether there were twenty chimneys, revealing not just the ingenuity of the architect, but the number of mouths to be fed.

Montoire-sur-le-Loir and St-Jacques-des-Guérets

The river Loir is smaller and less well known than the majestic Loire, into which its waters eventually flow, but its valley is an alluring one, dotted with small towns and villages and the occasional ruined castle. And there are several small churches in which remarkable Romanesque paintings have been preserved.

Two in particular are well worth visiting: the tiny chapel of St-Gilles in Montoire-sur-le-Loir and the slightly larger church of St-Jacques-des-Guérets, across the river from the troglodyte village of Trôo. Both have frescoes of the twelfth century, and St-Gilles has one of the most enchanting compositions of the Romanesque period, in which Christ is sitting in Majesty, and the double mandorla that surrounds him is borne by four angels who seem to be dancing.

St-Jacques, too, has a magnificent Christ in Majesty, painted later in the twelfth century in a wider range of colours, as well as a Crucifixion and several other scenes from the Bible and the lives of saints.

In both cases, the paintings were only rediscovered in the nineteenth century, when the plaster – and in some cases the later paintings – that covered them were removed.

The Loir valley lay on one of the pilgrim routes that led to Tours, where the church with the tomb of St Martin was for centuries an important shrine, and then on via Poitiers and the Pyrenees to Santiago de Compostela in north-western Spain (see page 39). So that was an incentive to build and decorate these little churches, and many pilgrims must have stopped at them as they headed south.

The chapel of St-Gilles in **Montoire** belonged to a priory founded towards the end of the eleventh century by monks from St-Calais, a few miles away to the north. Only part of it survives since most of the short nave has collapsed over the centuries, but it stands in a beautiful spot near the river, flanked by a clump of cypresses, and its *chevet* is intact, with some lively and irreverent corbels.

The chapel has three apses, one behind the altar and one at each end of the transept. As elsewhere, not more than a small part of the painting that must once have covered all the walls remains, but the paintings in the apses were high up, out of reach of the damp, and each of them has a painting of Christ in Majesty.

Mural painting in chapel of Montoire-sur-le-Loir: angel dancing

The eastern one, probably painted in the first quarter of the twelfth century, is the most powerful and expressive. The face of Christ is no longer clear, but he is an imposing figure who is giving a blessing with his right hand and holding a book with his left. Above all, he is surrounded by the dancing angels and by the figures that represent the four evangelists – the lion for St Mark, the eagle for St John, the winged man for St Matthew and the bull for St Luke (see page 263) – although the bull can no longer be made out.

They are all painted in a limited range of colours, predominantly red and yellow ochre, but with a lightness and verve that are irresistible. A wind seems to be gusting through the scene.

The paintings in the other two apses are of a later date, probably towards the end of the twelfth century, and are more sophisticated in style and colouring, including the use of lapis lazuli for blue. In both, Christ is an impressive figure with fine robes, reflecting Byzantine influence. In the north apse he has strong, piercing eyes, and six red lines extend out from his left hand to the foreheads of a line of six Apostles: possibly a reference to Pentecost.

There are also paintings in the four arches that support the little cupola: the Lamb of God flanked by two seraphim to the east; the hand of God and the two fish of the zodiac to the south; three heads of angels to the north; and in the west a more ambitious scene in which Christ crowns two warriors, representing Chastity and Patience, who are crushing Lust and Anger respectively.

The church of **St-Jacques-des-Guérets** was also part of a priory, belonging to the nearby abbey of St-Georges-des-Bois. It is better preserved, and it still has a memorable array of paintings most of which date from the middle of the twelfth century.

The most striking are on either side of the window in the centre of the apse: on the left, the Crucifixion and, beneath it, the Resurrection of the Dead; on the right, Christ in Majesty, with the Last Supper below. By this time the painters had a wide range of colours at their disposal, including not just red and yellow ochre but blue, emerald and violet, and that, together with some skilful draughtsmanship, gives these frescoes their great appeal.

In the Crucifixion the Virgin Mary and St John stand poignantly on either side of the Cross while up above are engaging human representations of the sun and the moon, who look down on the scene with surprising equanimity. The Resurrection of the Dead is less well preserved, but the angel who is announcing the Day of Judgment stands out strongly, while the dead can be seen raising the lids of their coffins.

On the other side of the window, Christ in Majesty is a masterly composition in

Mural painting in St-Jacques-des-Guérets: eagle symbolizing St John

which Christ is, once again, a powerful figure seated in a mandorla, and is surrounded by the figures representing the evangelists, all of them vigorously drawn. The lion and the bull are muscular beasts that twist round to gaze at Christ; the eagle and the winged man look down with greater serenity. Down below, the Last Supper is an incomplete but telling scene.

There are paintings of St George and St Augustine in the embrasure of the window, and there are more twelfth-century frescoes along the south wall of the church. In them, St James is beheaded by an insouciant executioner in front of Herod; St Nicholas gives coins to the father of three girls in order to save them from prostitution; Christ raises Lazarus from the dead, watched by Martha and Mary; and, in a monumental scene, Christ descends into Hell to rescue Adam and Eve, while elsewhere the devils continue their tortures of the damned.

It is a superb collection of frescoes. St Jacques also has fragments of some later paintings – an engaging Nativity, for example, on the south wall – but the twelfth-century works make it a gallery of Romanesque art.

St-Benoît-sur-Loire and Germigny-des-Prés

Close to a bend in the Loire, a few miles upstream from Orléans, is the imposing and beautiful basilica of **St-Benoît-sur-Loire**, once part of one of the most important abbeys in France. The basilica has been little changed since it was built, largely in the eleventh and twelfth centuries, and it towers over the surrounding fields, the riverbank half a mile away, and the pleasant small town of St-Benoît.

The abbey was founded in the middle of the seventh century, and used to be known as Fleury. But after about 672, when a group of monks brought back the bones of St Benedict and of St Scholastica, his sister, from Monte Cassino (see page 30), the abbey came to be known as St-Benoît, and throve through possessing the relics of a saint who was widely revered at the time, as we have seen. St Benedict's tomb is still in the basilica, in the eleventh-century crypt.

Having such relics meant that St-Benoît became a leading pilgrimage centre. It also lay conveniently near a much-used pilgrim route to Santiago de Compostela, which began in the Paris region and passed through Orléans on its way to Tours, Poitiers, Saintes, Bordeaux and the Roncesvalles pass over the Pyrenees (see page 39).

Then as now the basilica had a complex and elegantly composed *chevet*, with an ambulatory, radiating chapels, an apse and, topping it all, a tall tower over the transept crossing – all of which the pilgrims saw from a distance as they approached

across the fields. But its most immediately impressive feature was perhaps
the large tower at its western end, the
Tour de Gauzlin, named after the abbot
who built it, which was, and is, a great
achievement of early eleventh-century
Romanesque architecture.

Today, visitors need to walk through
the town to get the best view of the
chevet, which can be seen across the
jumble of backyards and a children's
playground; but the Tour de Gauzlin
has a wide open square in front of it,
planted with trees, which it dominates.

The tower's original topmost level is
said to have been removed in the sixteenth century on the orders of François I
as a punishment for the monks' refusal
to accept an abbot he had appointed;

Abbey church of St-Benoît-sur-Loire: the 'chevet'

and the strangely shaped top that it now has was put up in the following century.
But the two levels that remain are still eye-catching. The ground level is open, and
its arcades of solidly built round arches, resting on engaged columns topped by
capitals, all in different shades of yellowish stone, provide a grand approach to the
west door of the basilica.

The level above is taller, and its high, narrow windows, topped by round
Romanesque arches (with a little Gothic detail in some of them), give a sense
of lightness to the whole tower. The upper level is dedicated as a chapel to St
Michael, and is not normally accessible. But it is possible to see into it from below
and pick out some of the capitals on the engaged columns that flank the windows.
There are also some carvings in low relief set into the north façade, including a
powerful depiction of the martyrdom of St Stephen.

The capitals at ground level are outstanding: they are varied in subject-matter
and have great charm. Some are of biblical scenes, including the Annunciation and
the Flight into Egypt, some are apocalyptic, and many simply have variations on
the basic design of acanthus leaves, with an occasional human figure in their midst.
One capital shows the Four Horsemen of the Apocalypse, another an allegorical
scene of lions and human heads, and another an angel and a devil struggling to
win a human soul, presented as a small baby-like figure. There is also a capital

devoted to St Martin, showing the links
between St-Benoît and Tours.

Inside the basilica the clean lines and
the proportions of the nave and, beyond it, the choir and the apse are
of great beauty. The nave is topped
with Gothic vaulting, put in when the
church was completed in the early
thirteenth century, but its basic design
is Romanesque of the late twelfth century, and it retains the intimacy and
stately quality of that style. There are
solid, square pillars between slightly
pointed arches, and a decorative touch
is added by engaged columns and more
carved capitals.

The choir, which was built earlier,
in the late eleventh and early twelfth
century, is a harmonious composition
on two levels, and one of the most distinguished features of St-Benoît. It has

*St-Benoît-sur-Loire: capital in Tour de Gauzlin
showing the Four Horsemen of the Apocalypse
(book of Revelation, chapter 6)*

a colonnade of arches on each side, a line of smaller, blind arches set into a stretch
of plain wall above that, and at the top carefully spaced windows, framed by round
arches and small columns. Barrel vaulting leads to the rounded forms of the apse
and the colonnade below it, which are divided from the rest of the choir by a small
transept.

Like many other churches, St-Benoît was built over a long period, from the early
eleventh to the early thirteenth century. The Tour de Gauzlin is the oldest part,
followed by the choir, crypt and transept and, finally, the nave. But the differences
in style have not prevented its emergence as a perfectly balanced whole.

One example of its diversity is the recently restored portal on the north side,
built in Gothic style in the thirteenth century. Its tympanum shows Christ in
Majesty surrounded by the four evangelists (see page 263) and, under it, scenes of
the discovery of the bones of St Benedict and their removal to Fleury. On either
side of the doorway are statue-columns.

There is also a reminder of the abbey's long history in the endearing little
church of **Germigny-des-Prés**, only about three miles away. It was originally
built as an oratory by Theodulf, one of Charlemagne's chief advisers, who was

Carolingian church of Germigny-des-Prés

both Abbot of St-Benoît and Bishop of Orléans, and was completed in 805, making it one of the oldest churches in France.

Apart from its great charm, the church shows how the architecture of the Carolingian period was in many ways a precursor of Romanesque, in the way that it drew both on Roman models and on other, more contemporary styles from around the Christian world. Most of Theodulf's oratory is still there, including its original square plan, the central lantern tower and three of its four principal apses, and it has a three-dimensional pattern of robust, rounded arches grouped around the tower.

Most dramatically, it still has one of the original mosaics in the main, eastern apse, rediscovered by chance in the nineteenth century when a layer of plaster was being removed. It is a vivid design in which two large angels and two smaller ones lean over, and point towards, the Ark of the Covenant, a symbol of Christ.

Like other Carolingian churches, Germigny shows some exotic influences. Its square plan, with a large apse protruding from each side and the eastern one flanked by two smaller ones, was derived from Armenian churches. And the influence of Visigothic Spain shows in the keyhole arches high up inside the lantern tower. The fact that Theodulf is thought to have been a Visigoth may well explain this.

The western apse was removed in the thirteenth century to make way for a Latin-style nave, which is still there. But most of the rest of the original church remains, and there is a foretaste of an architectural feature found centuries later in the Romanesque churches of Auvergne (see page 162) in the flying screens, the lines of tiny, open arches built into the stonework above each of the four principal arches supporting the lantern tower. They give a sense of lightness to a complex architectural structure.

Tavant

Some of the best frescoes of the Romanesque period are in a small and shapely church in Tavant, a village on the banks of the Vienne river not far from its junction with the Loire. They are simply and strongly painted, in yellow ochre, dark red, green and white, and some of them are almost stark in their appeal.

The most unusual paintings are in the crypt, which has massive columns and low vaulted ceilings. They enliven it with their colour, and it must have been atmospheric when lit only by candles. Tall elongated figures painted onto a white background stand out from the concave vaulting that reaches over the heads of visitors.

But there are also lively frescoes in the main body of the church – in the apse over the altar and in the round barrel vault which precedes it. And there are carved capitals which, while lacking the sophistication of some in southern France, have an impact and a beauty of their own.

Tavant is about thirty miles south-west of Tours, and was the site of a priory which was founded by the Count of Tours in 987. It was burnt down in the course of a local dispute in 1070, and subsequently rebuilt. The church which survives appears to have belonged to the priory, although the monks did not themselves use it, and to have been built over a period of time between the late eleventh century and the early twelfth.

Sadly, it has lost its two side-aisles; but apart from that it has the distinctive lines of the Romanesque period, with a round barrel vault supported by transverse arches over the nave, a transept, a bell-tower resting on an octagonal cupola over the crossing, and an apse. The west portal is particularly appealing, with carvings of formalized fruit in the archivolts over the large central doorway, which is flanked by two narrow blind arches, and some pretty capitals.

Inside, the rounded vault of the nave and the succession of transverse arches lead the eye to the transept crossing and, beyond it, to the fresco in the apse.

Mural painting in Tavant: the Annunciation

The stonework has been carefully restored, and while the effect is rather clinical, it brings out the pleasing proportions of the church, with its dominance of round forms.

The best of the capitals are in the transept crossing and the choir, and they make a strong impact. There is a naive depiction of Adam and Eve in the Garden of Eden, with the serpent entwined round the tree, but most are not biblical: a mermaid with a double tail, a human head surrounded by a stylized octopus, and a fine assortment of monsters. Even two birds sipping peacefully from a chalice – a common motif in Romanesque art – have shrieking faces at the end of long necks growing out of their tails.

In one capital two intricately plumed birds have their necks entwined as they struggle with each other. In another, there are vividly carved human faces which stare fixedly out on the world.

The most dramatically placed of the frescoes, a huge Christ in Majesty, which fills the apse itself, is not in fact the best. Christ is sitting on an ornate throne inside a mandorla, and is wrapped in a dark red robe, but his head and upper body are small and unimpressive. He is, however, surrounded by vigorous figures which give a sense of movement to the whole scene: angels dancing and, at each corner of the mandorla, the symbols of the four evangelists, all winged (see page 263).

The paintings on the vault of the choir are badly damaged – having been covered over in the past – but those that remain are very moving. There is an Annunciation, a Visitation – reminiscent of a similar scene in the cathedral of St-Lizier, in the foothills of the Pyrenees (see page 366) – and a fragmentary but engaging Nativity. Here, as elsewhere in the church, there is a gracefulness in the figures, and a richness in the colours: to be seen even in a row of feet, which is all that is left of a scene of the Massacre of the Innocents.

As so often in Romanesque times, the crypt was one of the most important and evocative parts of the church. At Tavant, this is partly a matter of the crypt's numinous quality, barely lit as it is by a few small windows at ground level, and partly of its frescoes, which cover a wide range of subjects, all in the same forceful style.

The figures fill the vaults of the nave and the two aisles, and are presented in bold strokes in an almost impressionistic way, painted on to the uneven whitish background which follows the hollow curves of the vaulting. Not all can be identified for certain, but there is a man fighting a lion, who may be either David or Samson; another sitting enthroned, who is thought to be Saul (though he has no crown); and an attractive painting of a crowned figure playing a harp, generally accepted as being David.

Elsewhere a dramatic scene shows Christ drawing Adam and Eve out of Hell while a spear held by a celestial hand transfixes the Devil; and coupled with it is a moving Deposition from the Cross.

There has been much discussion about the identity of some of the figures. Who, for instance, are the two richly dressed women, each carrying what look like a pair of sceptres, who are sitting on thrones on either side of the first arch? Who are the two men who seem to be straining to hold up a beam over their heads, and what are they doing? And why do two angels carrying candelabra have their backs to the east, which is unconventional, with their candles unlit?

Again, who is the man who is apparently dancing: is it David, as often thought, and is he about to throw a stone at Goliath? And why is a man apparently carrying a sort of pennant and waving goodbye to a man carrying what look like branches of a tree? There is some doubt about this last figure, but an ingenious suggestion has been made: that the first man is in fact carrying birds that he has killed and represents winter, while the second is carrying young shoots that represent spring.

Most important, however, is that whoever they are, all these figures are vividly and unforgettably painted.

About some of the subjects there is no doubt. At the east end of the crypt Christ is seated in a mandorla, and St Peter is being crucified to one side. Another scene shows Adam digging and Eve spinning after their expulsion from the Garden of Eden. And there is little question of the significance of two of the most memorable figures in the crypt.

On one side is a curvaceous woman with long hair whose breasts are being devoured by two serpents and who has been run through by a lance. She represents Lust and at the same time, according to an inscription, Anger – because her wound has been self-inflicted. Opposite her is a woman with a halo, possibly the Virgin Mary, who stands for everything that is in contrast to such a woman.

There are even reflections of contemporary life. One fresco shows a knight in armour, similar to those who went on the Crusades, who is transfixing a devil at his feet – probably reflecting the common theme of a battle between the virtues and the vices. Another has an endearing portrait of a pilgrim with his staff and palm branch.

The crypt at Tavant is one of the most fascinating Romanesque survivals. Much about it is mysterious. But it preserves the vision of an extraordinarily talented artist who can still move us today.

Massif Central

The Massif Central is a remote part of France, much of it rural, whose landscape is dominated by the round green shapes of its many extinct volcanoes. So it is an unexpected pleasure to find that it also has some outstanding Romanesque churches, and in particular a school of its own.

The school consists of some exceptionally ornate churches, which combine complex architectural form with eye-catching external decoration, including mosaic patterning that uses the colours of the local volcanic stone.

Five of these churches, all very similar in style, are in the fertile area around

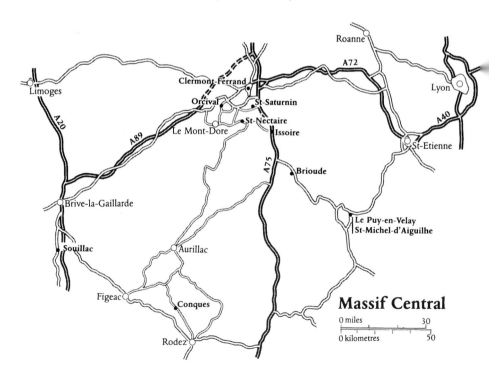

Massif Central

0 miles   30

0 kilometres   50

Clermont-Ferrand, known as the Limagne, through which the river Allier flows. Another, Brioude, is further to the south, also on the Allier, and is closely related to them, although some of its features show the influence of other regions.

Further south again is Le Puy-en-Velay, which was a significant centre in Romanesque times, and the starting point for one of the main routes to Santiago de Compostela. Its cathedral has some original features of its own, marked by influence from Islamic Spain; and the same is true of a small chapel on the outskirts of the city, St-Michel-d'Aiguilhe.

Away to the south-west, along the rugged route followed by the pilgrims after they left Le Puy, is the secluded village of Conques, which has one of the three original 'pilgrimage churches' that still stand – together with St-Sernin in Toulouse and the cathedral of Santiago itself (see page 12). Conques has a superb tympanum over its west door, showing the Last Judgment, and its church is one of the high points of the Romanesque period.

Each of these churches was a pilgrimage centre in its own right, and the five Limagne churches also lay on or near the pilgrim route that led from Clermont, as it then was, to Le Puy.

One of the five, Notre-Dame-du-Port, is in the heart of Clermont-Ferrand, the industrialized capital of the Auvergne region – which has had that name since the seventeenth century, when two rival towns, Clermont and Montferrand, were merged. The others, in Orcival, St-Saturnin, St-Nectaire and Issoire, dominate towns and villages in the surrounding area.

All have tall bell-towers, ornate east ends and high side-walls decorated with blind arcading. They are built in local stone, and this can sometimes be grey and forbidding. But there is both elegance and strength in these churches because the solidity of the walls and their often rough texture are offset by their harmonious lines and by the decorative features they have, both inside and out.

All have carved capitals inside, some of them still painted, as they would have been in medieval times, and they are a notable feature of the school. The capitals are often simple, even naive, but this naivety can be very moving. The subject-matter varies, from foliage to biblical and mythological scenes, including some vividly carved monsters; and since the capitals are sometimes difficult to see from the ground, there is a lot to be said for bringing binoculars, which will help to pick out the details.

A characteristic feature of these five churches is the 'lantern transept', in which a four-sided structure, with windows on three of its sides, rises above the transept crossing proper and supports the bell-tower. It looks rather box-like from the outside, but it lets more light into the crossing, and inside it there is a complex arrangement in which 'flying screens', rows of small, open arches, are set into the stonework above three of the main arches of the crossing.

Each church had its own attraction for pilgrims. Orcival, for instance, had and still has a cult of the Virgin Mary, while the churches of St-Austremoine in Issoire and of St-Nectaire in the village of the same name were dedicated to two missionaries who first brought Christianity to Auvergne, probably at the beginning of the fourth century. Brioude had the tomb of an early Christian martyr of the same period, St Julien.

The five Limagne churches are thought to have been built between the late eleventh century and the middle of the twelfth, but beyond that little is known about the context, or who was responsible for them. Architectural historians have identified a number of archaic features in the school – including the lantern transepts and flying screens – which are thought to go back to Carolingian times. It seems that Auvergne, which because of its remoteness was spared the worst of the barbarian raids of the ninth and tenth centuries, and was often used by monks and others as a place of refuge, early developed a distinctive style of its own.

One feature of the group is that not only are all the five churches similar in style but each of them is itself homogeneous, having apparently been built in a single exercise without the protracted construction periods and changing styles often seen in other churches. And there were more of them. Historians have identified at least two other churches, in Mozat and Ennezat, which were originally in the same style but were rebuilt in later years. One theory is that they were all modelled on a church that no longer exists, the cathedral built in Clermont in the tenth century.

The churches are not big, at least in ground plan, but they seem larger than they really are because of their height and the dramatic quality of their architecture. Most of the bell-towers have been rebuilt since the Romanesque period – only that of St-Saturnin is original – but they are the feature that immediately strikes the visitor to any of them today. They would have been similarly impressive in the twelfth century for the pilgrims making their way towards them.

These bell-towers are octagonal, with two stories of twin arches topped by a more or less blunt spire, and they rest on the lantern transept. The superstructure of this feature extends north and south above the two arms of the transept, and its effect is usually lightened by decorative blind arcading around its windows.

Beneath it is the jewel of these and many other Romanesque churches: the complex *chevet* in which the principal apse is encircled by the ambulatory and, in most cases, a ring of semi-circular chapels that radiate out from it. This creates a waterfall effect in which the rounded forms of the apses, their roofs and the arches above the windows appear to cascade down from the central bell-tower.

The *chevets* are all full of decorative detail: string courses that run over the arches of the windows, largely stylized corbels under the cornices, roof-combs, tiny blind colonnades and, most unusually, simple but striking mosaic patterns, often based on star shapes. The details vary from church to church, some being more ornate than others; but the *chevets* all have a complexity of form and richness of decoration that are the mark of the school. They contrast with the relative simplicity of the churches' side-walls and the plainness of their western façades, which were left largely undecorated because they took the brunt of the bad weather.

The lantern transept was, it seems, derived from the buildings of the Carolingian period, and the mosaic patterns from early Christian or Gallo-Roman originals – although some have seen Arab influence in the mosaics, and particularly in the use of stones of alternating colours in the arches. There were originally other archaic features inside the churches, among them a narthex at the west end. They still have plain barrel vaulting in their soaring but generally dark naves, which are lit only by small windows in the aisles and in the galleries above them.

But while this darkness gives an austerity to the body of the church, the distribution of light was carefully planned by the architects so that as you approach the transept and, beyond it, the choir, the light becomes stronger. Over the crossing there are the massive arches that support the superstructure of the lantern transept and the bell-tower above it, and there is a wonderfully complex structure to be seen as you peer up, with the flying screens built into the arches and the light coming in through the windows.

The arrangement of the arches, and especially the flying screens, is reminiscent of the little Carolingian church of Germigny-des-Prés (see page 156), in the Loire country, which was built early in the ninth century.

The choir of these churches has a design similar to those in Romanesque churches elsewhere, particularly on the pilgrim routes. It is slightly raised above the level of the nave, to give it greater prominence, and is surrounded in the east by a semi-circle of columns, divided by tall, rounded arches, all with large, finely carved capitals. Above is the apse, while light comes in from a ring of windows immediately above the columns and, less directly, from the radiating chapels that most but not all of the Limagne churches have.

Most of the churches also have crypts under the choir in which the relics of saints were kept. They are simple structures with low ceilings and solid columns to support the weight above.

Brioude

The tall and craggy church of St-Julien, which towers over the small town of Brioude, is one of the oldest Christian sanctuaries in Auvergne, and one of the finest. St Julien was a Roman legionary who was martyred for his faith, according to tradition, in 304, and it is thought that the small crypt-like structure that lies under the choir of the existing church contains what is left of a shrine built over his tomb soon after his death.

The present church is predominantly Romanesque, and its scale reflects the importance of the cult of St Julien, which drew pilgrims to Brioude from all over France, and from further afield. For centuries St Julien's relics were themselves attraction enough, but as the pilgrimage to Santiago de Compostela became increasingly popular, Brioude served also as a staging-point on the route between Clermont, as it then was, and Le Puy-en-Velay (see page 185), where pilgrims set off on one of the main routes to Santiago.

The Romanesque church was built between the middle of the eleventh century and the closing years of the twelfth, over a fifth-century basilica which had itself taken the place of the original shrine. With its tall bell-tower and decorative east end, and the internal design of its narthex, nave, choir and ambulatory, it is similar to the five churches of the Limagne (see page 162) in and around Clermont-Ferrand. But it also has its differences, due partly to influences from elsewhere, including Burgundy, and partly to the fact that unlike them it was built over a period of more than a century, so that it is not homogeneous in style.

It stands in the middle of a maze of narrow streets at the heart of the modern town. But there is an open space to the east from which it is possible to see the eye-catching *chevet*, with its radiating chapels and richly decorated apse; and above it the two-storey bell-tower – although its blunt spire, with coloured tiles, was designed in the nineteenth century. There is also a pleasant little square to the south which gives a good view of the fine porch on that side, one of the oldest parts of the church. There is a similar porch on the northern side, but like the Limagne churches, St-Julien has a plain western façade, though it was given a tower and Romanesque-style doors in the nineteenth century.

Brioude and its church were for several centuries under the rule of a chapter of canons, founded by Béranger, Count of the Brivadois, the surrounding area, at the beginning of the ninth century. The canons, who lived in monastic style, came exclusively from the best aristocratic families and, as canon-counts of Brioude, exercised a considerable degree of secular power until the French Revolution, subject only to the King and the Pope.

Collegiate church of Brioude: the 'chevet'

The east end that they had erected in the second half of the twelfth century differs from those of the Limagne churches in a number of ways. Brioude does not have the lantern transept that is typical of them. The *chevet* itself is also simpler in that it essentially has only two levels, those of the five radial chapels and, above them, the apse; and the east end as a whole is more disjointed because the *chevet* was built up against a pre-existing structure, the plain fortress-like wall, and not wholly integrated with it.

On the other hand the windows of the chapels are more ornate than those of the Limagne, in the Burgundian style, since they have moulded arches flanked by small columns that are themselves topped by capitals containing an array of sirens, dragons and other such lively creatures. And there is a meticulous arrangement of the apse, with each window framed by a round arch and flanked on either side by a smaller blind one. But there is also an Auvergnat feature, a strong band of mosaic decoration made up of stars and other patterns in black and white stone that runs round the apse under the cornice.

The interior of the church makes a rugged but majestic impression. The Romanesque columns of the nave are formed of stone of several different colours, part volcanic, part sandstone, which gives them a distinctive appeal, and they are topped by very slightly pointed arches dividing the nave from the side-aisles. But high above them is more sharply pointed Gothic vaulting, which replaced the original vaulting in the thirteenth and fourteenth centuries, and below it windows of the same period. So the nave is tall and full of light, while on either side of it are Romanesque side-aisles with their round arches and groin vaulting.

At the western end is a beautifully proportioned Romanesque narthex, one of the oldest parts of the church and one of the most accomplished, with chapels on its upper level from which it is possible to look out over the length of the nave and the side-aisles – and, what is hardly ever possible, see some of the capitals from close to. The floor of the church is covered by a patterned pavement of coloured pebbles which dates from the sixteenth century but was only recently rediscovered.

St-Julien only has short transepts, which do not extend beyond the line of the side-aisles. The transept crossing, and the bell-tower high above it, are supported on four tall, pointed arches that bear the great weight with ease and style.

East of that the choir has a traditional Romanesque plan in which a semi-circle of four columns, with a ring of windows above it, supports the apse, and an ambulatory runs around the outside, with chapels radiating off it. But the pointed arches between the columns are an indication of its late date, and the growing influence of the Gothic.

There are good capitals scattered throughout the church, and also some freshly-

Brioude: mural painting of Christ in Glory, in chapel of St Michael

coloured wall paintings from the Romanesque period, particularly in the chapel dedicated to St Michael in the gallery above the narthex – although many of them consist only of tiny fragments, recently discovered when the walls and the columns were being cleaned. Much of the church would have been painted in medieval times, in spite of the care taken to use multicoloured stone in its construction, and the capitals and the paintings are an indication of the attention that was paid to its decoration.

In the choir, the capitals of the four columns of the semi-circle consist mainly of foliage; but there is one capital under the crossing that gives a touching version of a typical Auvergnat theme, the visit of the holy women to the empty tomb of Christ after the Resurrection.

Elsewhere, it is interesting that none of the original Romanesque capitals has a biblical theme. There are scenes of a devil exulting over the misdeeds of a miser, of soldiers in medieval armour doing battle, and of donkeys playing musical instruments. There are griffins, centaurs and a minotaur. There are a pair of tritons, and another of sirens, that are almost Renaissance in style. There is great variety in subject-matter as well as in quality, and a great deal of vigour. Art historians have identified the work of at least six workshops.

Of the Romanesque paintings, the best-preserved are in St Michael's chapel. They date from the twelfth century, and show Byzantine influence. One on the vault presents Christ in Glory, surrounded by the angel, lion, bull and winged man who symbolize the four evangelists (see page 263), as well as choirs of angels. Below is a dramatic version of the punishment of the rebel angels, presided over by the archangels Michael and Gabriel, with a bestial Satan being devoured by the flames of Hell and, at the same time, one of the damned being dragged in. Another painting, much calmer in style, shows the battle between the virtues and the vices, suitably personified.

Down below, in the western bays of the nave, there are tantalizing patches of painting: the archangel Michael appears again; a cavalryman is thrown off his horse; a human face has been painted almost in caricature. In its great days, St-Julien would have been a mass of colour.

Clermont-Ferrand: Notre-Dame-du-Port

The industrial city of Clermont-Ferrand is an unlikely setting for one of the finest Romanesque churches of Auvergne. But there Notre-Dame-du-Port stands, in a commercial district in what was once the separate city of Clermont, a church that

Collegiate church of Notre-Dame-du-Port, Clermont-Ferrand, from the south-west

was mostly built between the late eleventh and the early twelfth century, and has only been superficially changed since then.

It is largely built of arkose, a local sandstone, and has the combination of ruggedness and style that is the mark of the Limagne group of churches. On the outside it has some immaculate decoration, particularly on the *chevet*. Inside, it has both height and harmony, a subtle use of limited light, and one of the best collections of carved capitals on the pillars that form a semi-circle round the choir.

There have been some changes over the centuries. The bell-tower over the transept crossing is a nineteenth-century reconstruction – the original was the victim of an earthquake in the fifteenth century – and the unprepossessing tower over the narthex, at the western end of the church, is from earlier in the same century. The plain west front was remodelled in the twentieth century.

But the greater part of the outside of the church is Romanesque at its best. The south side, in particular, recently cleaned, has a pleasing arrangement of round arches – larger ones over the windows of the aisle and sets of three smaller ones up above under the corbels of the cornice – and the façade of the south transept has a delightful design, with a similar arrangement of arches, a mosaic pattern on the pediment, and a carved capital showing Abraham's sacrifice of Isaac on the central column.

There is a twelfth-century carved tympanum over the south door which was badly damaged during the French Revolution but has much left of what must have been a compelling work. In the upper part, in a shape that is slightly more than a semi-circle, Christ sits in majesty, flanked by two seraphim and the surviving symbols of the evangelists, the winged bull representing St Luke and the lion of St Mark (see page 263). Below, in a pediment shape, are the Adoration of the Magi, the Presentation in the Temple and the Baptism of Christ, all carved with a sense of drama and movement.

The *chevet* is hard to see as a whole because the surrounding houses are so close. It is an exquisitely complex three-dimensional design, however, made up of the apse, the ambulatory and the radiating chapels, with the lantern transept and the bell-tower up above to form the climax. The basic pattern is that of most pilgrimage churches of the Romanesque period, but the meticulous decoration – black and white mosaics, tiny blind arcades, roof-combs and small pediments – is typical of Auvergne, as is the lantern transept, with the string course running over its round-topped windows. There are also some lively and well-carved capitals under the cornices of the chapels.

Inside, Notre-Dame-du-Port has simple lines, like other Auvergne churches, and is dark. The only natural light comes from windows in the aisles and from the galleries above them – which have rare trefoil arches, perhaps as a result of Islamic influence. But the eye is drawn along the length of the nave, with its high barrel vault, to the choir, where the light is stronger and where the semi-circle of columns, divided by round arches, supports the apse. It is a dramatic effect, which is further enhanced when the choir is lit artificially.

Looking back, one sees the reconstructed narthex at the west end, which has an array of arches dividing it from the nave: a wide one at ground level, above that a trio of smaller ones topped by a larger arch that open onto a tribune, and two tiny ones at the top. Most of the Limagne churches originally had a narthex like this, but the one in Notre-Dame-du-Port was demolished, and this one is modelled on the surviving narthex in St-Nectaire (see page 192).

The transept crossing is another characteristic feature of the Limagne churches, set as it is inside the lantern transept. In Notre-Dame-du-Port, as elsewhere, there are flying screens on three sides of the crossing, and light comes in through the many small windows.

There are carved capitals in all parts of the church, many of them with formal designs of acanthus and other plant motifs, all beautifully worked. There are also a number of historiated capitals, including one in the nave of the Temptation of Christ and another of a man holding a monkey with a rope round its neck, a common theme in Romanesque times. Others show centaurs and a pair of birds surrounded by foliage, also frequent subjects.

But the most arresting set of capitals is on the columns that surround the choir, which are each carved on all four sides and each devoted to a particular theme. One capital is signed 'Rotbertus me fecit', and it is believed that Rotbertus, or Robert, was the stonemason who carved all or most of them.

The overriding theme is that, though mankind fell from grace because of the disobedience of Eve, it has been redeemed through the obedience of the Virgin Mary. So one capital focuses on the events in the Garden of Eden, and there are two which are mainly devoted to Mary. The fourth capital illustrates the more general theme, again often found in Romanesque art, of the struggle between the vices and the virtues.

This shows an armed human figure representing Charity locked in battle with Avarice, shield to shield, a half-naked Anger killing herself with the head of a lance, two warriors representing Generosity and Charity triumphing over unnamed vices and, unusually, an unknown donor, Stefanus, presenting a capital to an angel.

Some of the most vivid scenes are on the capital illustrating the events of the Garden of Eden. We see a voluptuous and half-naked Eve presenting the apple to Adam, God in the form of Christ passing judgment on Adam, Adam and Eve being expelled from Paradise, and finally a picturesque but enigmatic carving in which a winged figure, possibly Satan, pulls apart the stems of a plant growing between his legs.

The first of the capitals devoted to Mary centres on the events surrounding the Incarnation. It shows Zacharias being told that his wife will have a son, the Annunciation made to Mary, the Visitation of Mary to Elizabeth, and the dream of Joseph, in which an angel tells him that he must not repudiate Mary.

The second is the climax. Mary is taken up to Heaven to rest in the arms of Christ, a winged figure blows a trumpet to proclaim victory, the gates of Paradise are reopened by two angels, and another angel opens the Book of Life, which features Mary in capital letters.

Like most Romanesque sculpture, these capitals have a naive quality, but they also have a simple power which makes its appeal across the centuries, and across the deep cultural divide between then and now.

Conques

The village of Conques is one of the most enchanting survivals of the Romanesque period. It lies in a thickly wooded valley, halfway up one of the slopes, and still has narrow, cobbled streets that wind up and down, flanked by part-timbered houses, as well as some of its old town gates. There are views from the hills all around of the cluster of houses, their roofs and turrets covered in slabs of the local silvery-grey schist.

At the centre is the magnificent church of Ste-Foy, dedicated to the fourth-century girl martyr (see page 36), which was once the focal point of a powerful abbey and an important stop for pilgrims on their way to Santiago de Compostela. The church still towers over the village, a harmonious building of the eleventh and twelfth centuries; and the tympanum on the west front, with its detailed presentation of the Last Judgment, is an outstanding work. It also has one of the best surviving medieval treasuries, containing the bejewelled statue of St Foy.

The church's two pyramid-shaped towers were added to the west façade in the nineteenth century when the whole church was restored (and only just saved from dereliction), and the bell-tower over the transept crossing dates from the four-teenth century. But the bell-tower was built in Romanesque style, and the greater part of the church is still as it was in Romanesque times.

Its interior in particular, tall, elegant and yet intimate, is as inspiring now as it must have been for the twelfth-century pilgrims.

Tympanum of the abbey church of Conques: Christ dominant in scene of the Last Judgment

Ste-Foy has marked similarities to the other two surviving 'pilgrimage churches' (see page 12): St-Sernin in Toulouse (see page 274) and the cathedral in Santiago de Compostela. Like them, it gives an impression of height, with round arches in a barrel vault high above the nave, aisles divided from the nave by more round arches, and galleries that open above the aisles through pairs of smaller arches. At the east end, a semi-circle of columns is topped by rings of arches and an apse.

There is a range of carved capitals, some with formalized vegetation, some with simple but moving religious scenes, which provide a decorative touch; and there are some larger sculptures, of the Annunciation, Isaiah and St John the Baptist, in the north arm of the transept and the central cupola. Light is filtered in through small windows in the aisles and the galleries, and in the tower over the transept crossing.

A key feature is the space provided for pilgrims to circulate round the church. Ste-Foy is not a large church because of the constraints of the site on which it is built, but both the nave and the transept are broad, and have aisles to provide extra room. There are chapels off the transept, at which pilgrims could stop and pray, and more off the ambulatory that runs round the back of the choir.

The church's most dramatic feature, however, is the tympanum, which is the focal point of the pretty little square in front of the church. It was carved in the first half of the twelfth century, and is remarkably well preserved. It still has some traces of paint, blue, red, yellow and black, that are similar to what must

Conques: the 'chevet'

originally have covered the stonework – as would have been the case with the other tympana of the period.

At the centre is the forceful figure of Christ seated inside a mandorla in a firmament of stars and surrounded by angels. His right arm is raised, and his left points downwards, with the palm open. Above him are more angels, sounding trumpets and holding a large cross, while on either side are scenes of the joys of Heaven and the horrors of Hell.

Below the feet of Christ souls are being weighed on a pair of scales by the archangel Michael and a grinning devil who is trying to tilt the balance his way: a scene derived from ancient Egyptian art and often shown in Romanesque depictions of the Last Judgment – in the tympanum of Autun cathedral in Burgundy, for instance (see page 51).

As is often the case, the scenes of Hell are the more arresting. A grotesque, grimacing figure of Satan sits with his legs entwined by snakes and his feet resting on a man who is being burnt while a toad crawls over his feet – the punishment for spiritual sloth. To one side of him is the large head of a monster, representing the mouth of Hell, into which sinners are being forced by a devil with a large club, while all around him unfortunates are being hanged, skewered, burnt and otherwise tortured by gleeful devils.

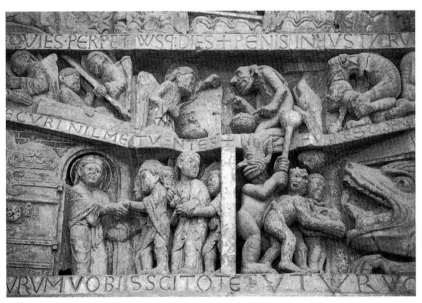

Tympanum of Conques: Heaven and Hell in scene of Last Judgment

There is a comprehensive collection of sinners, including kings, monks, knights, adulterers, heretics, forgers, gluttons, misers, slanderers, poachers and even musicians: these last regarded as leading people astray by, for instance, drinking songs. No pilgrim can have missed the stark message being conveyed.

On the other side of the tympanum, by contrast, all is calm and serenity. The Virgin Mary and St Peter head a procession of the Blessed who include Bego III, abbot of Conques at its zenith, and also Charlemagne with a crown and sceptre, representing the Carolingian benefactors of the abbey. St Foy is shown in an angle praying to an outstretched divine hand, with the manacles of prisoners released through her intervention hung up behind her. Below is the Heavenly Jerusalem, with Abraham sitting at the centre.

Jerusalem is the antithesis of the scene of Hell presided over by Satan. To one side, the Blessed are being welcomed through the door by an angel, while Abraham sits peacefully surrounded by saints and prophets, male and female, under a row of round arches. At the far end there are two pairs of women, one pair carrying funeral ointments, the symbol of the Passion, the other an open Bible.

The whole tympanum is very powerful, both visually and as a depiction of the Christian teaching of the time. And it has one easily missed feature which exemplifies the humanity, and humour, that is found in so much of the best Romanesque art.

Round the outer edge of the arch that encloses the tympanum can be seen the eyes, noses and foreheads of fourteen tiny faces, all identical, of people who are apparently trying to pull aside a roll of material, or parchment, with their fingers and peer into the dramatic scene being played out below. At the top one of them has succeeded, and peers out triumphantly. Just who these little people are is not known for sure. But they add an extra dimension to the Conques tympanum.

The origins of Conques as a Christian centre go far back into the Dark Ages when the whole of Gaul had been occupied by the Franks and Christianity was spreading to distant country areas. It seems that the area was raided by the Arabs in the eighth century, and that a certain Dadon, or Datus, later chose Conques as the site for a hermitage and built a new church there. He was attracted by its sheltered position in a hollow (the name of Conques is said to derive from *concha*, a shell), and by the excellent spring, the Plô, which still flows below the west façade of the church.

Dadon's hermitage became a monastery which adopted the Benedictine rule, and it flourished with the support of, among others, the Carolingian rulers of the eighth and ninth centuries. But in an age when the possession of saintly relics was all-important for the attraction of pilgrims, it felt the lack of any of its own.

So, according to a well-publicized account, one of its monks was despatched in the middle of the ninth century to the monastery in Agen which possessed the remains of St Foy, who had been martyred in 303. He spent ten years in Agen and, one fine day in about 866, broke open the sarcophagus and carried off the relics to Conques. Conques immediately became a leading pilgrimage centre, with the prosperity that went with it, and never showed any shame over the way it had acquired its relics.

The story is a good one, and typical of the period. But there is no record, on the other hand, of any complaint by the monastery of Agen, and it has been suggested that the truth may in fact have been less discreditable: that the relics of St Foy may have been deliberately moved to Conques for their protection in the 860s, when the whole region was suffering from devastating raids by the Vikings, and simply never returned.

Whatever the truth of it, the abbey of Conques came to attract more and more pilgrims on the strength of its possession of the relics, and the miracles for which they were said to be responsible. It extended its influence across Europe, with other monasteries that were dependent on it, and became a notable stopping place on the pilgrim route that began at Le Puy-en-Velay (see page 39), in the Massif Central, and crossed the desolate Aubrac plateau before reaching Conques.

The narrow stone bridge by which the pilgrims crossed the river Dourdou, just below Conques, on their way on to Figeac, still stands, and is still in use: a very picturesque site, with wooded hills all round. Misleadingly, it is called the 'Roman' bridge, although it is in fact medieval, and that is possibly because at one time all pilgrims were known as *Roumis*, from the fact that Rome was long the main pilgrimage centre in Europe.

Construction of the existing church began in the middle of the eleventh century, and the lower parts of the attractive *chevet*, with its characteristic Romanesque pattern of apse, ambulatory and chapels, were built in reddish sandstone at that time. Later builders, particularly in the time of Bego III (1087-1107), used a honey-coloured limestone together with the local schist for the rest of the building.

Little of the other abbey buildings survives today, but one side of the cloister has been restored, and even in its incomplete state it is a beautifully peaceful place, with a range of round arches and several lively capitals – one of which shows a group of stonemasons with their tools peering over a wall of cut stone. In the centre of the cloister space, the elegant round fountain, carved of green serpentine and ringed by tiny columns, has also been restored.

Off the cloister is one of the high points of a visit to Conques, the treasury. In the Middle Ages, most abbeys had rich treasuries. But Conques is special because the people of the village succeeded in saving the splendid pieces it had acquired over the centuries. Some were buried in the church during the Wars of Religion in the sixteenth century and only rediscovered by chance in 1875. Others were hidden in people's homes in 1792 to avoid requisition in the aftermath of the French Revolution.

The showpiece of the collection is the enthroned statue of St Foy, an ornate and fascinating work, covered in gold and jewels, which was designed to hold her relics. St Foy's face is a mask in embossed gold dating from the late Roman period, the fourth or fifth century. The rest of the statue was crafted from the ninth century on, with gold ornamentation and jewels being added over several centuries.

There are many other sumptuous pieces in the Conques treasury, particularly reliquaries and portable altars. They are decorated with gold and jewels and exquisitely worked. Several of them date back, at least in parts, to the tenth century or earlier.

These gorgeous objects reveal a significant aspect of the religious life of the times. They were the rich gifts that an important abbey like Conques could expect to receive from wealthy benefactors, including emperors and kings, and they were some of the wonders that pilgrims would travel hundreds of miles to see.

Issoire

The church of St-Austremoine in Issoire is the largest of the Limagne group, and its richly patterned *chevet*, which dominates an expanse of open ground that is part gardens and part car park, is one of the most astonishing sights in the region.

The *chevet* has recently been cleaned, revealing the soft colours and texture of the sandstone, arkose, in which it is mainly built; and while its various elements – radial chapels, main apse, blind arcades and bell-tower – are similar to those of the other churches, they are even more extensively decorated than the others. The frequent black-and-white mosaic patterns stand out vividly against the stone.

There is also another contrast, between the rounded forms of the arches and apses and the angular shape of the various pediments, making this a complex and balanced three-dimensional design. (See page 13.)

The range of decorative features is phenomenal: chequerwork patterns and stylized corbels under the cornices, a string-course running over the windows of the chapels, tiny blind colonnades, and roof-combs above the rounded tiles. The main apse has a mosaic band of stars running round it. There is even, unusually, a carving in relief of each of the signs of the Zodiac above the chapel windows.

The church was originally part of a Benedictine abbey dedicated to St Austremoine, a shadowy figure who, as Stremonius, is said to have been one of the first Christian missionaries in Auvergne at the beginning of the fourth century, and to have been martyred. It is known that the abbey was an old one, having traditionally been founded by St Austremoine himself and having been for some time the guardian of his relics. But all that is known about the present church is that it was probably built in the middle of the twelfth century.

Issoire: detail of the 'chevet'

It was badly damaged in the French Wars of Religion in the sixteenth century, when Protestant troops occupied Issoire, and it was damaged again at the time of the French Revolution. It was extensively restored in the nineteenth century, and much of the restoration is criticized by art historians. In particular, the bell-tower which is the culminating point of the *chevet* was completely new, and it is now generally regarded as mediocre. The same is true of the very plain western façade and the tower above that.

Even more critical is what was done inside the church, because the nineteenth-century architects decided that St-Austremoine should be entirely painted, walls, columns, vaults and all; and the result was garish, with strong colours and patterns everywhere. In their defence, it is argued that medieval churches *were* painted, and that the taste for bare stone walls and columns is a modern one. But the critics reply that though the church may indeed have been painted originally, it would not have been in the bold and distracting style used by the nineteenth-century restorers.

That said, St-Austremoine is an impressive building, both outside and in. It stands in the centre of Issoire, which used to be a small town – and still has a maze of narrow streets around it – but has in recent years become an industrial centre, with aeronautical and other factories on the outskirts as well as new housing.

The ground around the church which in the past was taken up by the many buildings of the abbey is now largely clear, so that it is possible to admire the strong
lines of the church's design.

Like the other Auvergne churches, it has a lantern transept, with the distinctive
box-like structure that supports the bell-tower and extends over part of the arms
of the transept; and the effect of that is lightened by rows of blind arches on each
side, some of them enclosing windows. The ends of the transept are also decorated
with rows of arches, as are the outside walls of the long nave.

Inside, in spite of the painting, it is possible to appreciate the same solid, but
elegant structure as in the other Limagne churches, with a barrel-vaulted nave,
vaulted side-aisles and galleries above them, separated from the nave by small
arches. Above the crossing is the lantern transept, the structure which supports the
bell-tower, complete with flying screens built into the stonework above the arches.
The choir, raised slightly above the nave and less high than it is, has a semi-circle
of eight columns, all with capitals, topped by an apse; while around its edge runs
an ambulatory from which five chapels radiate out.

As in the other churches of the area, the capitals are one of the high points,
although in Issoire they too are controversial. It is known that they were badly
damaged like the rest of the church when the Protestants occupied Issoire, and
have been restored several times since. They were repainted in strong colours in
the nineteenth century. So there is considerable doubt as to whether they have
survived in their original form.

There are, however, several skilfully carved capitals, both in the choir and elsewhere in the church. The principal ones are in the choir, where four of the eight
are of foliage and four of scenes before and after the Crucifixion. The outstanding
one is perhaps the one that shows the Last Supper, with Christ and the disciples,
including Judas Iscariot, occupying all four sides of the capital, a table and table-
cloth implausibly but tellingly suspended in front of them.

The others show scenes from the Passion, the visit of the three holy women to
the empty tomb and the appearances of Christ after the Resurrection, and all are
vivid and immediate, if naive. There are scenes of the Apostles deep in grief as
Christ carries the cross to Calvary, of medieval-looking Roman soldiers fast asleep
near their shields by the empty tomb, and of Christ greeting Mary Magdalene and
reassuring the doubting Thomas.

The other capitals are scattered around the church, and many of them are less
overtly religious. They have flowers, birds, griffins, centaurs and other creations of
the medieval imagination. One shows a devil dragging off two sinners, another a
peasant straining under the weight of a sheep, a third a man apparently presenting

two chained monkeys. There is life and vigour in all of them, even if they are not wholly in their original form.

Orcival

The church of Notre-Dame in Orcival is different from the other churches of Auvergne in that not only has it always been a pilgrimage centre in its own right but it continues to be one. It still has a touching Romanesque statue of the Virgin and Child enthroned, decorated in silver and gilt, which dates back to the first half of the twelfth century, when the church itself was built; and there is a pilgrimage there in honour of the Virgin Mary on Ascension Day every year.

The statue, dignified and moving, is one of the few to survive from that time, and the only one with its silver and gilt decoration, having been saved from destruction at the time of the French Revolution by being walled up in the narthex of the church. It stands on a tall plinth in the most prominent part of the church, in the choir behind the high altar, where the light is strongest.

The church is as impressive as the others in the group, with its tall bell-tower, *chevet* and lantern transept, although there is a roughness and austerity in the grey andesite in which it is built, most noticeably inside. It also has a perfect setting, soaring above the steep slate roofs of the village of Orcival, which itself lies in a wooded hollow between two hills. The village has kept much of its charm, even if its many restaurants and souvenir shops are an indication of the crowds that pour in during religious and other holidays. (See page 36.)

As elsewhere in the Limagne, there is some uncertainty about the origins of Orcival. But it is known that in the middle of the twelfth century Guillaume VII, Count of Auvergne, made a gift of one-fifth of the church to the monks of the Benedictine monastery of La Chaise-Dieu, and that they founded a small priory there, with two monks. The builders, whoever they were, had to dig into the hillside at the west end in order to achieve the proper east-west orientation, and build out the foundations at the east end.

Today the body of the bell-tower, octagonal with two levels of rounded arches, is in its original form, but the two-part spire above it is a product of the nineteenth century, because the original was knocked down during the Revolution.

The church's three doors have a feature not often found: they still have their original hinges and ironwork, on which various designs have been worked. The south door, for instance, has convoluted tendrils and even tiny human heads.

Inside the church the nave is dark, but there is a majestic quality to its columns,

Orcival, from the east

topped by the twin arches of the galleries; and the two side-aisles complement it with their round transverse arches and groin vaulting. Finely carved capitals stand out in the light that filters in from the side-windows. Most of them are of foliage, but one, inscribed 'FOLDIVES', shows a rich man with a bag of money being tormented by devils, and another twin eagles together with smaller human figures.

The choir and the ambulatory have more capitals. There, too, they are mainly of foliage, finely carved, but there is also a range of other subjects, many of them both fantastic and picturesque: among them, angels guarding the celestial city of Jerusalem, a peasant carrying a sheep, a devil astride a goat, a mermaid, and a pair of griffins sipping from a sacred vase. They give their own distinctive touch to a very individual church.

Le Puy-en-Velay

Tucked away among the débris of ancient volcanic eruptions is one of the most extraordinary cities in France, Le Puy-en-Velay. Its cathedral, chiefly built during the eleventh and twelfth centuries, stands on an outcrop of volcanic rock that rises above the modern town, while towering behind that is a higher mass of sheer black rock, circled by trees and crowned, since the nineteenth century, by a statue of the Virgin Mary. (See page 22.)

Not far away is an even more dramatic sight: a black, needle-like outcrop on the outskirts of the town which is sheer on every side and has an ancient Romanesque chapel, St-Michel-d'Aiguilhe, perched high on its peak.

Not everyone appreciates the nineteenth-century statue, but the view of the town as a whole, which appears laid out in a hollow between volcanic hills when you arrive from the direction of Clermont-Ferrand, is another spectacular one.

Le Puy has always been remote. But in the Middle Ages it was an important religious and political centre that was in active contact with other towns in southern France and even Spain. Mont-Anis, on which the cathedral is built, seems to have been the site of a Celtic religious cult in pagan times, and it remained pagan for a time after the arrival of Christianity in the region in, perhaps, the fourth century. A Christian shrine was built there in the sixth century, and over the years it became a significant pilgrimage centre in its own right because of the attraction of its cult, and statue, of the Black Virgin.

By the eleventh century the city had acquired added prestige as one of the four main starting points in France for pilgrims setting off on the long march to Santiago de Compostela (see page 39). From Le Puy they made their way across some desolate landscape, including the rocky Aubrac plateau, to Conques (see page 174). They then passed through Cahors (see page 254) and Moissac (see page 262) on their way to the Roncesvalles pass over the Pyrenees.

The narrow paved streets in the old town, which wind up and down the slopes around the cathedral, retain much of the atmosphere of the past, when they would have been thronged with pilgrims – many of them from far afield, including Germany. They are still lined with old stone townhouses of character, mostly built by local aristocratic families, some of which go back to medieval times.

The bishops of Le Puy were powerful secular rulers in the turbulence of the Middle Ages, and engaged in constant struggles with the local nobility. They often received the support of the kings of France whose influence over the secular aristocracy of distant Auvergne was limited. They also received papal support, especially as the growing popularity of the heretical Cathars, which led eventually to the Albigensian Crusade in the thirteenth century, presented a growing threat to the Church. Both popes and kings made gifts and paid frequent visits.

It was a bishop of Le Puy, Godescalc, who did much to popularize the pilgrim-age to Santiago by travelling there with his entourage in 950 or 951. In 990, one of his successors, Guy of Anjou, proclaimed at a council of the Church, held in Le Puy, the establishment of a Truce of God on certain days of the week in an attempt to reduce the fighting taking place at the time. And in 1095 Adhémar of Monteil, another bishop of Le Puy, became papal legate for the First Crusade after being the first to respond to Pope Urban II's call to arms, made that year at Clermont.

Today, it is part of the charm of Le Puy that it still has not just the cathedral but several other buildings that surrounded it in medieval times, with narrow streets running between them. They include the lovely little cloister, the chapterhouse that opens off it, and the baptistery of St John, as well as some of an overtly military character, reflecting the temporal power of the bishops: the guard-room through which one now reaches the cloister, for instance, and the massive machi-colated building to the north of the nave, which houses the chapel of relics and the treasury of religious art.

The most evocative street is the steep little Rue des Tables, complete with steps, which climbs up from a pretty square, the Place des Tables, to the cathedral's west front. The street and the square both take their name from the stalls that were set out with goods to entice pilgrims, and they are still surrounded by houses that date back to those times.

The west front is one of the most dramatic in France, primarily because of the extreme ornateness of its decoration. Rows of arches in stone of alternating colours are piled one on top of another, and the whole façade, with its use of different-coloured stones arranged in formal patterns, is like a vast mosaic. It has an exotic quality, with influences both from the Islamic world south of the Pyrenees and from Byzantium.

This exotic character is one of the unique features of Le Puy. It is not only in evidence on the west front. The cloister and, not far away, the little chapel of St-Michel-d'Aiguilhe are two other notable examples. Both of them show the clear influence of Islamic Spain. And it is thought that the original form of the cathedral, and the subject-matter of the paintings and the column capitals, also show the influence of the Byzantine world, particularly of Coptic Egypt.

The Islamic influence must have come from the contacts Le Puy had with Spain as a result of the pilgrimage to Santiago, and also from the presence in the city of a community of Mozarabs, the Christians who came from the Muslim-ruled parts of Spain. The Byzantine and Coptic influence is thought to derive from the monastic community that had been founded in the fifth century on the Lérins islands (see page 29), off the south coast of France. This community always had close links with the eastern world, particularly Coptic Egypt, and it is noticeable that several of the early bishops of Le Puy had Greek-sounding names.

The west front of the cathedral, however, also has another peculiarity, and that becomes immediately obvious to the visitor. There was always very little room at the top of Mont-Anis, the hill on which the cathedral is built, and so, when plans were made in the twelfth century to extend the nave to the west, the whole western end of the cathedral including the façade had in effect to be built out over a void, and supported by columns.

The result of this is that there are three tall arches at the foot of the west front that lead visitors into a cavernous inner space, within which flights of stairs take them up into the cathedral. The original stairs emerge in the centre of the nave, not far from the high altar, so that, as one seventeenth-century French writer, Odo de Gissey, put it, you enter the church 'through its navel'. There is also another flight, built in the eighteenth century, which goes off to the right and comes out on the south side of the nave.

The entrance area is still as imposing as it would have been for pilgrims in the Middle Ages. Much of it is now in Gothic style, having been rebuilt in the four-teenth century, but there are still two Romanesque doors on which biblical scenes have been carved in low relief. Remarkably, one of them has an inscription in Arab *kufic* script, saying that the work was done according to the will of God.

The interior of the cathedral is much restored and, although the way it was done has been criticized by art historians, it is both original and impressive. A line of huge arches, built in grey stone and almost Islamic in outline, leads the eye the

Le Puy-en-Velay: nave of cathedral

length of the nave to the high altar, where a statue of the Black Virgin, replacing the original one that was destroyed during the French Revolution, sits in state. The earlier, easternmost arches are rounded, those at the western end of the nave pointed.

Between them, in another indication of Byzantine influence, there are octagonal domes over the bays, and they are fully decorated. Within the domes each of the eight sides rests on an arch with stones of alternating colours, and the arches are supported by pairs of small columns topped with capitals.

The pillars of the nave are angular and massive, and topped by quite shallow capitals. But the capitals are finely carved, and have an arrangement of human and animal subjects, often set in luxuriant vegetation, whose themes are thought to be linked to the teaching of the Eastern Church; and the pillars have an elegance that belies their girth.

There is a further sign of Byzantine influence in the recently restored frescoes, thought to be contemporary with the cathedral, in the north transept, which represent the Holy Women at the Tomb and the martyrdom of St Catherine of Alexandria; and in the striking frescoes of St Michael and other saints and apocalyptic figures in the tribune above.

Having come in near the 'navel' of the cathedral, today's visitors can leave it through one of what the same writer called the 'ears' – the porches at the two sides of the choir. The more inspiring of the two is the Porche du For, an ambitious structure built at the end of the twelfth century (though the upper floor was added later). Its two arches are like the segments of huge wheels, complete with spokes, and they rest on ornate columns, complete with some intricately carved capitals.

The Porche du For leads to an open space shaded by trees – the town's original forum – which has the bishop's residence on one side and is one of the best viewpoints in Le Puy. Down below is the modern town. Above are the porch and, alongside it, the south end of the transept, topped by a pediment and decorated with mosaic patterns and two rows of blind arches.

Soaring above the whole scene is the distinctive bell-tower, originally built in the middle of the twelfth century and rebuilt in the nineteenth century after being damaged by lightning. It is made up of a number of cubes, all in the local reddish stone and each of a different design, that have been constructed one on top of another, with a small pyramid at the top. Much of the detail is most attractive. The overall design is, if not immediately appealing, certainly striking.

The cloister, on the other hand, is indisputably one of the high points of a visit to Le Puy. Rectangular and relatively small, it was built, like the cathedral itself, in

Le Puy-en-Velay: cloister of cathedral

the course of the eleventh and twelfth centuries, and its patterned stonework and rich, harmonious colours are an outstanding example of the influence of Islamic Spain. There are echoes of the great mosque of Córdoba in the arches, in which alternating black and white stones seem to radiate upwards and outwards, and in the mosaic of black, red and white diamond shapes above them.

The cloister is also, however, clearly a Christian building. It has some lively capitals in which human figures, animals and vegetation illustrate the temptations of earthly life and the rewards for those who resist them. In one of the most vivid of them, a female centaur evades the attentions of a male; in another, an abbot removes a crozier from an abbess. Above is a finely carved frieze showing animals and monsters, an illustration, it seems, of the fate awaiting sinners.

Off the cloister, through a formal stone doorway, is the chapterhouse, a long, vaulted room with a thirteenth-century fresco of the Crucifixion at one end. It was used for some years as a burial place for canons of the cathedral.

Another high point of Le Puy, in both senses of the word, is the chapel of **St-Michel**, built on the tip of a shaft of basalt in what used to be the neighbouring village of **Aiguilhe** and is now part of greater Le Puy. The cult of St Michael was frequently linked with high places, as at Monte Gargano in southern Italy and Mont-St-Michel in Normandy (see page 134), and this chapel has as dramatic a

Le Puy-en-Velay: chapel of St-Michel-d'Aiguilhe

setting as any. Like the site of the cathedral, it is likely to have been a pagan shrine before it was Christian.

There is a flight of 268 steps winding up to the top of the rock, so that it is not for those who are short of breath or upset by heights. But the reward is the sight of the exquisite twelfth-century doorway, with its exotic design of trefoil arch, carved stonework and multicoloured tiles arranged in mosaic patterns. The themes of the stonework are profoundly Christian: Christ as a judge flanked by the Virgin Mary, St Peter, St Michael and St John at the top, and the Elders of the Apocalypse (see page 263) venerating the Lamb of God within the arch. But the architects have not hesitated to draw on pagan imagery or Islamic design to convey their teaching. The lintel has two sirens to illustrate temptation, one with a serpent's tail and one with a fish's. (See page 20.)

Inside, the arrangement of the chapel shows how use could be made of very limited space. An early shrine, constructed at the end of the tenth century, is largely intact, with two small apses and some barely preserved frescoes, including scenes of the Last Judgment. Leading to it are a narrow ambulatory and a tiny nave, added when the chapel was enlarged in the twelfth century, and marked out by columns with plain, mostly stylized capitals.

Like the cathedral, St-Michel-d'Aiguilhe has received pilgrims for hundreds of years and, simple though it is, it still conveys the atmosphere of its long history. Excavations were carried out in 1955, and a treasury of religious objects was found under the altar, including a small wooden crucifix of the eleventh century and several pieces of Byzantine origin, which are now on display.

The bell-tower, also built in the twelfth century, is best seen from below. It dominates both the little chapel and the rock on which it stands. It is similar in style to the bell-tower of the cathedral, with a pyramid shape at the top, but smaller and more satisfying, with several stories of rounded arches in stone of alternating colours.

There is also another decorative little building of the twelfth century in a small square at the foot of the rock – the chapel of St-Clair. It is octagonal with a small apse, and it too is ringed by blind arches in two colours, with mosaic patterning.

St-Nectaire

The church of St-Nectaire, named after one of the first Christian missionaries in Auvergne, has the most picturesque and dramatic site of all the churches in the Limagne group. It stands on a hill above the village of St-Nectaire-le-Haut, and its

Priory church of St-Nectaire, from the east

tall, shapely outline, topped by the characteristic bell-tower and by two lower towers at the west end, is visible for miles around, surrounded by wooded hills.

The hill, Mont-Cornadore, is itself an ancient site that was settled in the first millennium BC and later used by the Romans as a setting for public baths. The lower part of the village, St-Nectaire-le-Bas, is still a flourishing spa, with hotels and other facilities to match, and the village as a whole has given its name to one of France's better-known cheeses, widely produced in the surrounding country-side.

Just what connection the village had with St Nectaire himself, who is thought to have arrived in Auvergne with St Austremoine (see page 180) in the fourth century, is uncertain, as are the circumstances in which was church was built. But the presence of his relics made it a centre for pilgrims, and it is known that the monks of La Chaise-Dieu, an important Benedictine monastery in the region, received the land as a gift from Guillaume VII, Count of Auvergne, in the mid-twelfth century and established a priory there. The church must have been built soon before or after their arrival.

It is in any case a breathtaking sight. It was badly damaged during the French Revolution, and thoroughly restored in the nineteenth century, in a way not appre-ciated by art historians. The central bell-tower was completely remade, having lost its upper storey, and the two western towers were added. But the varying shades of

St-Nectaire: detail of the 'chevet'

the church's light-grey trachyte stone, together with the golden patches of lichen, give a colourful, and homogeneous, appearance to its complex architectural forms.

In the *chevet* the different shades of the trachyte have been used to make a mosaic pattern of stars that circles the central apse. They form the central feature of a harmonious cascade, topped by the bell-tower, with three chapels leading off the ambulatory and one off each arm of the characteristic lantern transept. And there are similarly decorative mosaics at the end of each arm.

There is also much to see inside the church of St-Nectaire. The nave has the solidly based but soaring elegance of all the churches of the Limagne group, with the difference that it is lined by round columns rather than the more robust-looking pillars that the other churches have. It also has some vigorous column capitals, many of which still retain some of their original colouring, and a treasury which includes some rare works that have been saved from theft or destruction over the centuries.

These include a powerful twelfth-century bust, in gilded copper, of St Baudime, another of the companions of St Nectaire in the fourth century, in which the Roman-looking saint stares fixedly ahead into the distance; a painted wooden statue, also of the twelfth century, of the Virgin and Child enthroned; two twelfth-century gold binding plates decorated with Limoges enamelwork; and an embossed silver reliquary arm of St Nectaire from the fifteenth century.

St-Nectaire is the only church of the group to have retained its original narthex, and a tall gallery above it which is separated from the nave by a three-bay arcade. It also has a rare decorative detail on the wall at the end of each arm of the transept: a triangular 'mitred' arch between two round arches representing the Trinity.

The finest capitals, as in all the Limagne churches, are on the columns surrounding the choir, six of them in this case. Each capital carries a wealth of detail on each of its four sides, and it is well worth taking time to study them. They are all historiated, and they are vividly carved, with some remaining traces of colour.

There are biblical themes on five of the capitals: the Transfiguration and the multiplication of the loaves; the events of the Passion; the Resurrection and Descent into Hell; the Apocalypse; and the Last Judgment. The sixth capital is devoted to St Nectaire himself and the miracles he carried out. It has a representation of the church itself on one of the faces, surrounded by the wall that protected it during the barbarian raids of the ninth and tenth centuries.

The capitals are all in a naive style that is deeply moving. Christ, surrounded by the Apostles, multiplies the loaves and the fishes. He is shown as a small, bent figure carrying the cross to Calvary. The three holy women are met by an angel at the empty tomb. Angels announce the Last Judgment.

One of the mysteries is the presence on the capital containing the scenes of the Transfiguration of someone named as Ranulfo, holding on to a column and being pulled in different directions by an angel and a devil. One theory is that he was the founder, or one of the founders, of the church and that his gift is represented by the column; and the scene symbolizes the basic struggle between good and evil.

There are also other good capitals in St-Nectaire. On the north side of the ambulatory one has the story of Zachaeus, the tax-collector, who climbed a tree to see Christ pass and was greeted by him. Others show a miser being tortured, shepherds carrying lambs and symbolic fights between animals. In the nave are Christ being tempted by Satan; Moses being saved from the water by Pharaoh's daughter (where there are some voracious crocodiles with pig-like ears); a donkey playing a lyre confronted by a man riding a goat; and St Baudime slaying a wild beast.

In some, the message is clear; in others, allegorical. But they all have vigour, and an appeal that reaches over the centuries.

St-Saturnin

St-Saturnin is the smallest of the Limagne churches, and one that has a distinctive charm. It stands on a hill in a historic village full of old houses, and has as its

St-Saturnin: the 'chevet'

neighbour a castle that used to belong to one of the great families of France, the barons of La Tour d'Auvergne, from which Catherine de' Medici, wife of Henri II, was descended.

As with the other churches in the Limagne group, little is known about its origins, except that St Saturnin, also known as St Sernin, was the first Bishop of Toulouse, who was martyred in the third century (see page 276). But it is thought that the church, which may have been built later than the others, was complete by the middle of the twelfth century.

It is similar in style to the others, with its octagonal bell-tower, elaborate *chevet*, lantern transept and mosaic patterning. Seen from the outside, the ambulatory at the east end is plainer than those of the other churches because it has no chapels radiating off it. But the cornices of the ambulatory, the apse and the two transept chapels are as ornate as those of the others, with chequerboard patterns and corbels, and there is a ring of mosaic stars round the apse.

Most striking of all are the bell-tower above, which is exceptional in having survived intact from the twelfth century, and the lantern transept that supports it. The twin rounded arches on each face of the tower are precisely proportioned, with the lower story very slightly larger than the upper, and a stonework course that runs over the lower arches, with a sharp point at each corner. The stone structure beneath is especially ornate, with dark basalt and light-coloured arkose alternating in the arches that run round it, lightening its effect.

St-Saturnin has original ironwork on its main door like some of the other churches, with contorted shapes and the heads of humans, snakes and lions.

Inside, the church has an intimate feel to it because of the arkose, a sandstone, in which it was built and the subtle distribution of the light. Its architectural form is similar to those of the rest of the Limagne group, with its barrel vault over the nave, the tall rounded arches lining the nave and, above them, smaller arches linking it with the galleries. The church has no narthex, but it has the wonderfully complex structure of flying screens over the transept crossing, all lit by the windows, that is a distinctive feature of the Auvergne school.

The choir is slightly raised, and has a semi-circular ring of six columns to the east. As elsewhere in the Limagne, the columns have prominent capitals, but these are much simpler than the capitals elsewhere, and that is true of the church as a whole. The capitals, which are carved in a darker, volcanic stone, are stylized, and include representations of birds and plants. They lack the vigour of historiated capitals, and are thought to be later in date; but they have an appeal of their own.

Western France

Western France was an exceptionally inventive region in the Romanesque period, and there is great variety in its churches, which include some of the finest of the time. The west front of Notre-Dame-la-Grande in Poitiers, the mural paintings of St-Savin-sur-Gartempe, a few miles east of Poitiers, and the crypt of St-Eutrope in Saintes all figure among the great achievements of Romanesque.

There are two main architectural styles in the region. Notre-Dame-la-Grande is an example of a hall church, in which the side-aisles are as high, or almost as high, as the nave – which has a barrel vault. Angoulême cathedral, by contrast, is a domed church, in which the nave is covered by a line of three domes, and there are no side-aisles.

Significantly, both churches have magnificent west fronts that are covered with sculptured figures, and such fronts are another feature of the region. St-Jouin-de-Marnes, north-west of Poitiers, is another outstanding example, and there are many others – St-Hilaire in Melle, for instance, and Airvault.

Western France was not alone in Romanesque times in giving sculptural decoration a prominent place in the architecture of its churches. But its sculpture has a special vigour. The Abbaye aux Dames in Saintes and Aulnay-de-Saintonge, a few miles to the north, both have porches that are covered with intricate and often exquisite carving, and it is noticeable that, unlike many churches in other parts of France, neither has a carved tympanum over the door. Instead, it is the archivolts which are filled with decorative stonework – human figures, mythological creatures and entwined tendrils.

The Saintonge as a whole – as the region around Saintes is known – is notable for the way that doors and windows are brought to life by the figures that swarm over and round them, often surrounded by formal decoration.

Sometimes the decoration is so lavish as to be classifiable as 'baroque' – in Rioux, for example, south-west of Saintes, and Rétaud a few miles away – and purists find this hard to accept. But it has a richness that is all its own.

Painting must once have covered the inside of most churches, of course, and

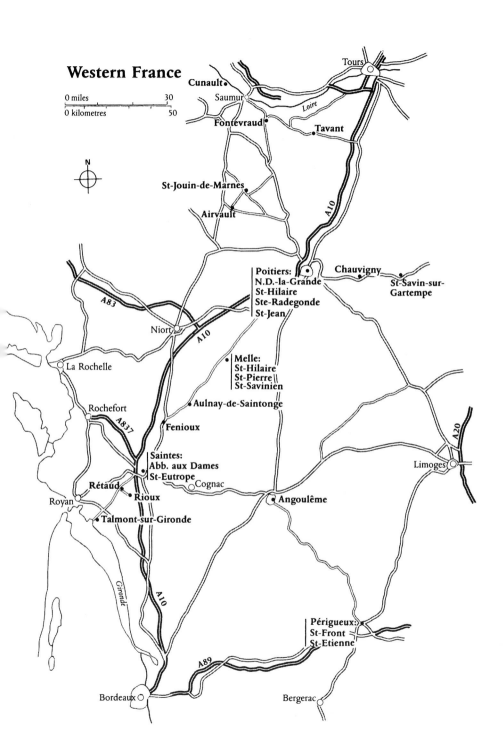

Western France

0 miles 30

0 kilometres 50

N

Tours

Cunault

Saumur

Loire

Fontevraud

Tavant

St-Jouin-de-Marnes

Airvault

A10

Poitiers:
N.D.-la-Grande
St-Hilaire
Ste-Radegonde
St-Jean

Chauvigny

St-Savin-sur-
Gartempe

A83

Niort

A10

Melle:
St-Hilaire
St-Pierre
St-Savinien

La Rochelle

Rochefort

A837

Aulnay-de-Saintonge

Fenioux

A20

Saintes:
Abb. aux Dames
St-Eutrope

Cognac

Limoges

Rétaud

Rioux

Royan

A10

Talmont-sur-Gironde

Angoulême

Gironde

A10

Périgueux:
St-Front
St-Etienne

A89

Bordeaux

Bergerac

now hardly survives. But St-Savin-sur-Gartempe has one of the most splendid arrays of Romanesque murals that are still to be seen – and is, besides, a beautiful hall church in a grand setting overlooking the river Gartempe.

A few miles to the west is Chauvigny, which has another hall church, this one with some of the most original column capitals of the period.

The two cities of Poitiers and Saintes were each leading centres in Romanesque times, and even before, and that can be seen in the churches that they still have. As well as Notre-Dame-la-Grande, Poitiers has the pilgrim church of St-Hilaire-le-Grand, the smaller church of Ste-Radegonde, and several others that are still partly Romanesque, including the cathedral. The baptistery of St-Jean is a rare example of a church building that dates back to the fourth century, and Roman times.

Saintes, too, was a flourishing city in the days of the Romans, and it has two churches from the Romanesque period, when it was a pilgrimage centre. St-Eutrope has a wonderful crypt, with heavy, round arches and superb carved capitals, as well as other delightful capitals in the upper church. The Abbaye aux Dames has the porch on its west front and, over the transept, one of the most beautiful Romanesque bell-towers.

Angoulême and Périgueux, too, were significant centres, and they are both interesting for their domed churches. They were much restored in the nineteenth century, particularly St-Front cathedral in Périgueux, but the former cathedral of St-Etienne, also in Périgueux, is more as it used to be. Angoulême cathedral, in addition to its magnificent west front, is one of the most majestic of the domed churches of western and south-western France.

But it is worth getting out into the country, for the churches that are to be found in small villages. The church at Talmont, for example, has a glorious setting overlooking the waters of the Gironde; and at Fenioux, north of Saintes, there is a *lanterne aux morts*, one of the tall thin towers built to stand over the graves in a cemetery.

Angoulême

Angoulême cathedral has one of the stupendous west fronts created during the Romanesque period. It has suffered badly over the centuries, and much of what can be seen today, both on the west front and elsewhere in the cathedral, was put there during extensive restoration in the nineteenth century. But enough is left of the original twelfth-century building to convey the grandeur and originality of its architects' conceptions.

Angoulême cathedral: the west front

The top level of the west front, including the two turrets, dates from the nineteenth century, but the rest of the façade is a grand twelfth-century composition, with some finely carved sculpture set in a harmonious arrangement of round arches. Christ stands in the centre in a mandorla, arms outstretched, in a scene which is partly the Ascension and partly the Second Coming. Down below are dancing angels, the jubilant Elect, the Virgin Mary and eleven Apostles and, to give a proper balance, two grim scenes of malefactors being tortured by devils. All over the façade plants, birds and animals provide decorative detail.

Inside the cathedral, the nave's three domes make a splendid sequence, giving the nave both height and a sense of spaciousness. They are supported by slightly pointed arches, and the eye is led the length of the church, past the crossing to the choir and the semi-circle of round arches that surrounds the east window. It is only unfortunate that the nineteenth-century restoration has, by cleaning up the stonework, had a rather clinical effect.

Angoulême did not lie on one of the main pilgrim routes through France to Santiago de Compostela, but it was not far from Poitiers (see page 223), which did, and it was an ancient centre in its own right. Built in a strategic position on a spur of rock above the river Charente, it is thought to have had a cathedral since the fourth century, and was a focal point on one of the lesser pilgrim routes.

The cathedral is still in a commanding position today, near the line of the ramparts which once used to surround the upper city. From it there are views out over the lower town and the countryside beyond, and there are some pleasant narrow streets, lined with old houses, in the surrounding area.

The building of the Romanesque cathedral was largely inspired by an activist bishop of Angoulême, Girard II, who was elected in 1101 and who also played a prominent part in wider Church affairs. He was papal legate for Aquitaine until the schism of 1130, when two popes were elected in Rome by different cardinals on the same day. Girard backed Anacletus II, the eventual loser, and ended his life discredited six years later. He was buried in his cathedral, but Innocent II, who had emerged the winner, had his body exhumed and buried anonymously elsewhere.

By the time of Girard's death the cathedral was nearly complete, with its ornate west front and the succession of domes in the nave. The architects had drawn on the experience acquired in the building of other domed churches, among them the cathedral of Cahors (see page 254) and the abbey church of Souillac (see page 270), and they had themselves made innovations which were taken up elsewhere, at Fontevraud abbey (see page 147) in the Loire valley, for example.

Angoulême also had at least the makings of two tall bell-towers, one over each arm of the transept, which would have made an eye-catching east end, combined with the lantern over the transept crossing and the apse with its radiating chapels. But the southern tower was never completed, and today there is only one bell-tower, over the northern arm of the transept, which was rebuilt in the nineteenth century.

Fortunately, the rebuilding was faithful to the original, and the tower is a memorable sight, with its tiers of arcades built one above the other; and it is visible for miles around.

Its internal structure, too, is most attractive. Looking up from inside the transept, one sees the four tall arches that support the tower, complete with some finely carved capitals, and above them an octagonal cupola lit by four windows.

The lantern that now covers the transept crossing is a nineteenth-century construction that replaced the original dome. But the choir and the chapels are mainly original, and from outside there is a good view of the cathedral's *chevet* and bell-tower across the little garden at the east end. On the outside wall above the east window is a small frieze, thought to be the work of sculptors from the basilica of St-Sernin in Toulouse (see page 274), which shows two hounds converging on a deer in the midst of foliage, while a pair of lions look on – a symbol of spiritual quest.

The nineteenth-century reconstruction was the work of Paul Abadie, an architect who also carried out some radical alterations to Périgueux cathedral (see page 220), and is perhaps best known for having made the plans for the Sacré Coeur basilica in Paris. In Angoulême, the most obvious change he made, apart from building the lantern, was to add the extra level at the top of the west front. The two flanking turrets that it now has were pure invention on his part, and so was the gable, with its five blind arches, between them.

These additions altered the proportions of the façade, giving it a vertical emphasis that it did not originally have. But at least they left in place the superb carvings that it carried, in a decorative style derived from Poitou to the north, and it is possible to imagine how it would all have looked without Abadie's super-structure.

When building first began, it seems, the intention of Girard and his advisers was to confine the outside sculptural decoration to the row of five arches at the lowest level of the façade, and leave the five tall arches up above them plain. But subsequently it was decided, first to fill the upper arches with statuary, and later to add a new tier of smaller arches above them, with the larger arch over the central section.

That central section is certainly the most effective on the façade, with a well-balanced and dramatic composition. Angels reach down to Christ through

West front of Angoulême cathedral: the Ascension and the Last Judgment

billowing clouds over his head, and he is surrounded by the symbols of the four evangelists – the eagle of St John, the winged man of St Matthew, the bull of St Luke and the lion of St Mark (see page 263). In the archivolt above him are massed angels, while below his feet others are announcing the Second Coming, celebrating the Tree of Life, or simply dancing.

It is thought that the original idea was to depict the Ascension but that it was then decided to link that theme with the Second Coming and the Day of Judgment. So the arches on either side of Christ have tiny medallions, each of which contains one of the Blest, and lower down there are complete figures of people dancing for joy. Lower still are arches which contain the statues of eleven Apostles and the Virgin Mary and, at either end, the scenes of the malefactors being tortured.

The two horsemen further down are nineteenth-century works representing St George and St Martin, although the figure of a woman on the left, behind St George, is original apart from her head, and represents the Church. There were once two quite different statues there, which represented, it is thought, the Emperors Constantine and Charlemagne.

At the lowest level of the west front, the original tympanum above the entrance door has mostly been lost, and it has been replaced by an unappealing nineteenth-century work. But the decoration of the arch above it, with its meticulous carvings of animals and, in particular, birds drinking from a cup, is original. So are the tympana and the similar carvings on the four smaller, blind arches. The tympana show the Twelve Apostles setting off, book in hand, to evangelize the world, and are also thought to be the work of the sculptors from St-Sernin in Toulouse.

One lintel, under the figure of St Peter and two other Apostles, is especially interesting. It shows a battle between Christian and Muslim knights, and is thought to represent scenes from the *Song of Roland*, in which Archbishop Turpin fells the giant Abime and Roland kills King Marsile. The belief is that this theme was introduced to celebrate the capture of Saragossa from the Moors in 1118, when French knights from Aquitaine and Poitou fought alongside the Aragonese.

Aulnay-de-Saintonge

The stylish, twelfth-century church of Aulnay-de-Saintonge, on the pilgrim route between Poitiers and Saintes, has survived more or less in its original form, and is one of the best examples of late Romanesque architecture in what used to be Aquitaine. It has a tall, narrow nave topped by a pointed barrel vault, which is in

Aulnay-de-Saintonge, from the east

the style of Poitou, and wonderful stone carving, both inside and out, that has many similarities to that of the Saintonge, further to the south.

The church has a picturesque setting in the middle of an old cemetery where it is surrounded by a handful of cypresses and numerous grey stone sarcophagi and tombstones that stand up out of the grass. As you walk round it, you can see the clear lines of the architecture, and also its range of decorative devices, harmoniously placed – the tall arches over the windows, the rows of corbels, the clusters of engaged columns, and the carved capitals.

Some parts were added later. The tall spire and the top stage of the bell-tower immediately below it date from the Gothic period, either the late thirteenth or early fourteenth century. So do the plain upper section of the west façade and the heavy buttresses built onto that façade, which were put up in the fifteenth century, when repair work had to be carried out; but not the dainty conical turrets on either side, which were part of the original twelfth-century church.

These modifications do not detract seriously from the overall effect, however. Aulnay is a harmonious and distinctive church which is even in places – in the inside of the choir, for instance, and in the side-aisles – deliberately austere. And within this framework it has some very rich decoration.

The high point of the church, as it stands today, is the south porch, a well-balanced composition that has an unforgettable carved doorway, full of detail, and above it, a row of three blind arches, also carved. But there is also some vigorous carving on the three arches of the west façade, which must have been as compelling as the south porch before it was reshaped in the fifteenth century; and there is more round the windows below the apse in the *chevet* of the church.

Architectural historians insist that Aulnay is incorrectly named. In the first place, they say, it should be called Aunay, from its Latin name Aunedonacum, as it was until the French Revolution. Second, the link with the Saintonge is wrong because before the Revolution Aunay had always been part of Poitou, and its church was in the diocese of Poitiers.

However that may be, the little town was on the old Roman road between Poitiers and Saintes, two prominent cities in those days, and this road continued to be used in the Middle Ages, not least by pilgrims heading for Santiago de Compostela (see page 39). The pilgrim route started in Paris, and after Saintes headed further south to Bordeaux and the Pyrenees.

There was an earlier church on the site known as St-Pierre-de-la-Tour, and in the eleventh century this came into the possession of the Benedictine monastery of St-Cyprien in Poitiers. In the following century the monks handed it over to the chapter of Poitiers cathedral, and it was the canons of the cathedral, it is thought, who were responsible for building the existing church, probably between 1140 and 1170.

The doorway of the south porch is one of the masterpieces of Romanesque sculpture in western France: highly ornate but, like the church as a whole, carefully formed. As elsewhere in western France, there is no tympanum over the door. But the porch has four round archivolts, set one within the other, and they have a band of human or animal figures on each outer face, as well as more carving on their undersides.

The innermost archivolt has a low relief of mythical animals in a thicket of tendrils, and the next one pairs of haloed figures thought to be Apostles and Old Testament prophets respectively. The third archivolt has an array of Elders of the Apocalypse, each wearing a crown and carrying a stringed instrument and a cup of perfume (see page 263). The outermost one has a parade of animals and monsters taken from a bestiary of the time.

The stonework was designed to give an overall effect of radiating outwards from the doorway. Each figure in each band is meticulously carved, and the impression they make, both from a distance and from close to, is most endearing.

Aulnay-de-Saintonge: detail of the south porch

The carving on the undersides of the archivolts is only properly visible from below, but it includes one of the most engaging features. There is a sequence of tiny human figures on the undersides of two of the archivolts who appear to be holding up the whole structure. One set have a knee on the ground and one hand raised to support the stone above them; the others are squatting, and stretching both arms above their heads.

There is other decorative stonework on the porch, including carved capitals and friezes, and it is a great pleasure to linger over each point of detail. A line of corbels runs along a cornice above the doorway, and the porch as a whole is framed on either side by a cluster of tall engaged columns, a device which gives it its sense of unity.

Above the cornice are the three blind arches and, though they are less ornate than the doorway, they too are distinctive. The central one has a pointed arch, and on one of the archivolts is a theme often found in the Saintonge churches: armed men with tall shields trampling monsters, taken to represent the combat of the virtues and the vices. The only jarring note is struck by the round window that has been cut into the arch.

The west façade has suffered badly from the repair work of the fifteenth century. It is not just that it has lost the decoration of the upper level – which is known to have included a statue of a horseman representing Constantine or, as was often said, Charlemagne. It is also that the fifteenth-century buttresses have obtruded on the three richly decorated arches, obliterating part of them.

What is left is enough, however, to show how grand they once were. The central round arch, over the doorway, has four carved archivolts, divided by plant-patterns. They show, starting from the innermost one, the Lamb of God surrounded by angels, another version of the combat of the virtues and the vices, the Wise and the Foolish Virgins and, on the outermost archivolt, the signs of the Zodiac and the tasks of the various seasons.

The two side arches are blind, with no door below them, and unlike the central one are quite sharply pointed. They are also more decorated, and better preserved. The tympanum of the left-hand one shows St Peter, to whom the church is dedicated, being crucified upside down; the other has Christ enthroned in the middle of two saints. Both have vivid carving, mainly of semi-abstract, plant-like motifs, as well as some lively capitals that are full of action.

The other part that was paid attention in any Romanesque church was the *chevet*, and that is certainly true of Aulnay. Its *chevet* is beautifully composed, with three apsidal chapels, and with the bell-tower over the crossing marking the culminating point.

Each of the chapels has tall engaged columns running up to a line of lively carved corbels, showing humans and animals, and the large central one has two more clusters of columns, framing it on each side.

It also has some original sculpture in the arches that surround the windows. The stonework round the east window, including low-relief carvings of men apparently struggling in thickets of tendrils, is one of the many glories of the church.

In its interior, Aulnay has the same strong but harmonious lines as on the outside, and also some excellent capitals. The pointed barrel vault gives an upward *élan* to the nave, in anticipation of Gothic style, but this effect is carefully limited by the elevations on either side: sizeable capitals, each intricately carved, on top of the pillars, smaller pairs of columns above them, and a horizontal line running along the base of the vault. These break the upward movement and help to provide a characteristically Romanesque sense of space.

As in other churches built in Poitou style, the nave is not directly lit but receives light from the smallish windows in the aisles. This serves to focus attention, as so often elsewhere, on the choir and, above it, the apse. These are strongly lit by the windows of the *chevet* and are, in contrast with the rest of the church, largely bare of decoration.

In front of them, the crossing has a cupola with a rare design, divided by insubstantial ribs into eight segments and resting on pendentives.

The capitals are, as always, an integral part of the architectural plan, and in Aulnay they are full of vitality and beautifully worked. There are mythical animals and monsters, entwined vegetation, masks and, mixed in with them, biblical scenes.

One of them is a trio of elephants – who must have seemed almost mythical to Europeans at that time. Others show Samson having his hair cut off while a forceful Delilah ties his arms, a happier scene of him fighting a lion, Cain felling Abel with a club, and St George, or some other warrior, confronting a dragon while a servant holds his horse for him. They are one of the most decorative features of a very decorative church.

Chauvigny

Chauvigny is only a small town, some fifteen miles east of Poitiers (see page 223). But it lies on a bend in the river Vienne, a tributary of the Loire, and dominating the bend is a strategically placed outcrop of rock. On this can be seen, from across the valley as one approaches from the south-east, the ruins of several castles and, at their centre, the collegiate church of St-Pierre.

So the setting itself is idyllic, but the church is also worth visiting for the very original series of column capitals in its choir. They are apparently the work of one Gofridus, who is otherwise unknown, and are a mixture of images, all in a naive and unforgettable style: biblical and apocalyptic scenes, voracious monsters with tiny humans in their jaws, and other figments of Gofridus's imagination.

One of the strangest has a dancing human figure with a single head and two arms, but divided from the chest down, so that he has two waists and two pairs of legs – while biting into his shoulders as he dances are two lions. No one has yet found a satisfactory explanation of what this figure represents.

Chauvigny is no more than a short distance from one of the main pilgrim routes to Santiago de Compostela that went through Poitiers. But it owed its early

Capital in Chauvigny: monster devouring a sinner

Capital in Chauvigny: dancer with two waists and four legs

importance to its strategic position, and one of the ruined castles – of which there are five – was erected in the eleventh century by the bishops of Poitiers, who were then lords of the town, and at the same time controlled the chapter of canons at St-Pierre.

Just when the church was built is, as so often, a matter of controversy, but one view is that the work was carried out over a century, approximately from 1130 to 1230. Certainly much of it is late Romanesque, and some of it is already Gothic. That goes for the topmost cornice of the bell-tower, and it is noticeable that while the easternmost parts of the church and even the eastern end of the nave have rounded arches, the arches over the western end of the nave are quite sharply pointed.

Full as it is of medieval buildings of one sort and another, the upper town of Chauvigny is very pleasant to walk through. The *chevet* of the church has radiating chapels that have decorated arches over the windows; and, set into parapets above them, some archaic sculptures apparently taken from an earlier church. A picturesque little turret has a conical top covered with a scale-like design like those at Notre-Dame-la-Grande in Poitiers.

Inside, the first impression is of the painted décor applied in the nineteenth century and recently restored. But architecturally, it is a fine example of the hall churches often found in Poitou. This means that, as elsewhere, the side-aisles are almost as tall as the nave, and windows set high in the aisles light the nave. The transept crossing is topped by a cupola, but the eye is drawn to the choir beyond, with its tiers of arches topped by the apse.

If the crossing has some excellent carvings, including lions and a mermaid, it is the choir capitals that are exceptional. We know the name of Gofridus because he had it clearly inscribed in the most prominent place, on a capital behind the altar, above a scene of the Adoration of the Magi in which the Virgin Mary holds the new-born Jesus and the Hand of God appears from above. The inscription says simply: 'Gofridus me fecit' (Gofridus made me).

That capital is the only one wholly devoted to biblical events: the Annunciation, the visit of the Three Wise Men, the Presentation in the Temple, and the Temptation of Jesus, all of them depicted with a simple directness and power.

Elsewhere, Gofridus has ranged widely: from a gruesome portrait of Satan surrounded by lesser devils to sphinxes apparently drawn from Near Eastern mythology. Human beings, presumably sinners, are being devoured by monsters with wings and long twisted tails, and tortured by huge, long-beaked birds. Tormented faces, trapped between winged lions, cry out in agony.

One fascinating capital focuses on the Last Judgment. On one side it shows the

Capital in Chauvigny: infant Jesus presented in the temple

Capital in Chauvigny: the Temptation of Christ

Capital in Chauvigny: Joseph pensive, and devil pulling on scales

archangel Gabriel announcing the birth of Jesus to the shepherds, while directly opposite the archangel Michael in similar style announces the end of the world, flanked by a tiny, suppliant human and a devil pulling at the scales of justice. In between is 'Babylon, the Great Whore', an evocative and telling portrait of a woman with large eyes, long hair and elaborate dress; and on the opposite side, 'Babylon Deserted', in which an unnamed prophet sits and meditates.

The mysterious Gofridus and his work have been dismissed by some critics as merely naive and maladroit. Naive they certainly are. But they have an imagery and a power that make the Chauvigny capitals one of the most memorable achievements of Romanesque art.

Fenioux

Fenioux is a tiny hamlet that looks out over the countryside in a valley north-east of Saintes, and its *lanterne des morts* (lantern of the dead) is a rare survival from the Romanesque period. The church also has a stately west front, covered with the sculpture that was typical of the Saintonge region in Romanesque times. So it is among the most interesting of the many small country churches in the region.

Fenioux: detail of west doorway

The *lanterne* stands in the middle of what used to be the cemetery, with an open space near the top where a fire was lit, symbolizing the eternal life of the soul. It is a stylish structure, not unlike a minaret. The shaft is ringed by eleven engaged columns, each of them with a base and a capital, while above them is an open circle of twelve shorter columns, that surround the place where the fire was lit. At the top is a tall pyramid with the scaly effect often found in the west of France, surrounded by four small tapering columns.

Today, the medieval cemetery has gone, and the *lanterne* stands almost alone, apart from a small crypt at its foot that was used as an ossuary, surrounded by a lawn and a few trees, with the valley down below. It is a stirring sight, and a reminder of the exoticism of much Romanesque architecture.

It is still possible to climb the thirty-seven steps that spiral up in the dark inside the *lanterne*, and to emerge high up in the middle of the circle of short columns, through which there are views all round.

The Fenioux *lanterne* is not the only one in France, but it is an outstanding example of a distinctive architectural form. It stands some distance away from the church, which is a relatively old one, with parts that date back at least to the early eleventh century, when its builders used materials from a structure of the Roman period.

Like other small Saintonge churches, Fenioux has a simple floor plan with just a nave and no transept – and a choir that was built in the sixteenth century. But towards the end of the twelfth century it was given its west front, as well as a tall bell-tower, and the west front makes up with its detailed stonework for the simplicity of the rest of the church.

As you approach, the first impression is of its massiveness, because there is an array of engaged columns that rise almost to roof level on either side, framing the round arch of the central doorway and giving the effect of a pair of buttresses. But the doorway is deeply recessed, with its own arch and four archivolts each filled with sculpture, and the richness of the decoration, combined with the robust proportions, means that the little hamlet of Fenioux has one of the most imposing entrances of the period, reminiscent of a Roman triumphal arch.

In addition to the carving over the doorway, there is a gallery above it, also recessed, which has more sculpture. Christ sits in the centre, surrounded by tiny symbols of the four evangelists (see page 263), with three standing figures of saints on either side. Above them is a cornice carved with formal patterns and with a row of grotesque heads as corbels, and above that is a window, also surrounded by flower patterns.

It is the carving on the archivolts over the doorway, however, that stands out, and that was designed to convey the essence of the Christian message. The outermost rim has the signs of the Zodiac alternating with people engaged in the labours appropriate to the various months of the year. Inside it are the wise and the foolish virgins, the wise ones on the left with their flasks held high and the foolish ones on the right with their flasks held upside down, and the celestial bridegroom in the centre at the top.

Next are angels flying up towards the Lamb of God, holding censers in their hands, and, further in again, the triumph of the virtues over the vices. This was a common theme in the west of France, and in Fenioux the virtues are represented by women holding shields and spears, with which they are transfixing the vices, represented by devils lying at their feet.

The arch of the doorway itself has some skilful carvings of formal plant patterns, and so have the capitals, along with a few monsters.

There is more fine carving on a doorway on the north side of the church, which also has formal plant patterns and two capitals with monsters. And on the south side there is an engaging latticework window from an earlier period, in which the stonework has been carved to look like a woven pattern.

Towering over the whole church is Fenioux's tall and ambitious bell-tower. This has suffered from being too thoroughly rebuilt in the nineteenth century, but with its open arcades and tiny turrets it shows the finesse that was achieved by architects towards the end of the Romanesque period.

Melle

The small town of Melle, south-west of Poitiers, is unusual in having no fewer than three Romanesque churches, all built in the course of the twelfth century and all very largely preserved. The one that makes the greatest impact is St-Hilaire, a decorative and well-proportioned former priory church which stands on the bank of the little river Béronne. But both the others, St-Pierre and St-Savinien, have attractions to offer, in style and decoration.

The importance of Melle stemmed partly from the fact that, like Aulnay-de-Saintonge (see page 205), it lay on the pilgrim route between Poitiers and Saintes. But another factor was the existence of a silver mine to the south of the town, which was much worked from the fifth century on and brought prosperity to the town, although it was more or less abandoned after the tenth century.

The monastery of St-Hilaire, dedicated to St Hilary, the fourth-century bishop of Poitiers, stood on an ancient Christian site by the river. It was a dependency of

Priory church of St-Hilaire, Melle, from the south-east

the influential abbey of St-Jean-d'Angély, some miles to the south-west, which was itself linked, like many others, to the great Burgundian abbey of Cluny (see page 61). The church is a good example of the Poitou regional style, with decoration on the outside – particularly on the west façade and the north side – and a tall nave, topped by pointed barrel vaulting, inside.

One of the best views of it is from the road on the far side of the Béronne, where you can see how well the various parts of a Romanesque church combine to form a three-dimensional whole – the tiered *chevet* with its ambulatory and radiating chapels, the square bell-tower, with decorative arches set between engaged columns, the two arms of the transept, each ending in a pediment, and the long nave, with its line of rounded windows punctuated by buttresses and a pediment at the west end.

The west façade can be seen from the town side where a little square looks down on the church. It is an unspoilt version of the tripartite pattern found on many Poitevin churches, corresponding to the nave and aisles: three arches at the lower level, of which the central one frames the entrance door, and the other two are blind; three more arches over the windows at the level above; and a plain triangular pediment at the top.

At the corners on either side, and giving a sense of unity to the whole design, is a cluster of tall columns, and above each of them a small turret whose conical top has tiles shaped to create the scale-like effect typical of the region.

The decoration is noticeably restrained, and mostly confined to the window level. The receding archivolts of the central doorway have been left plain, apart from the carved capitals, and so have the two blind arches. But the upper level has some very fine detail. There is carving round the windows, on the two cornices, each supported by a line of corbels, and on the little turrets, and this adds distinction to a harmonious design.

Another uncommon feature of St-Hilaire is that, whereas most Romanesque churches have such external decoration as there is on the south side, where it is lit by the sun, and the north side is relatively plain, this church has the opposite arrangement. This was because in Romanesque times the road used by pilgrims and other travellers ran along the north side. So the north door was fully carved for them to see as they arrived, as were the column capitals and the corbels along the whole length of the church.

Sadly, the doorway has been badly mutilated over the years, and the tall horseman in the arch above it, with a small figure apparently being trampled under the horse's hoof, is a stiff modern reconstruction. A horseman like this was a common feature on churches in western France, and is generally thought to have represented the Roman Emperor Constantine, possibly trampling paganism, though he is also often said to be Charlemagne, or even Jesus Christ.

The carving in the arch over the horseman's head, however, and the remains of the carved figures on the archivolts over the door, show that this must once have been a powerful composition.

Once the pilgrim entered the church, presumably through the ornate north door, one of the first things he or she would have seen was another ornate door – the inside of the south door, which is straight ahead across the nave, and has tiny figures of Christ and thirty Apostles and saints in its outer arch. This was no accident.

Turning to the east, the pilgrim would have looked the length of the nave, with its pointed arches, to the rounded arches of the crossing and the choir. As in other Poitevin churches, the nave is relatively dark because there is no direct lighting of the barrel vault, and this focuses attention on the east end, with its ring of columns linked by round arches.

There are capitals in the nave and aisles that are full of movement, and more on the columns of the choir: entwined foliage, animals, monsters, and some human activities such as the playing of musical instruments. One of the most vivid, on the south side of the nave, is a scene of a wild boar hunt, with the hunter wielding a spear in front and two dogs attacking the boar from behind.

The contrast between the round and pointed arches is marked, and indicates that the eastern part of the church, including the transepts, was built first, probably in the first half of the twelfth century, in a relatively low, intimate style. It was followed later by the nave after the new, more lofty style, with pointed arches, had been introduced.

St-Savinien, which stands in a dominant position nearer the centre of Melle, is the least well preserved of the three churches, because it was turned into a prison after the French Revolution, and was used in that way for over a century. But it has been restored, and is an imposing, chunky building which is now used as an exhibition centre.

The west front has an attractive doorway which is much damaged but still has a carving of Christ between two lions on the lintel – a rare feature that is also found at Notre-Dame-du-Port in Clermont-Ferrand (see page 170) – and some carved capitals. The south door is also decorated, and there are more capitals that are worth looking at inside the church.

St-Pierre is in another outlying part of the town, in a little park above the Béronne. It too was originally a priory church, dependent on the abbey of St-Maixent, north of Melle, and is thought to have been the last of the town's three

churches to be built. That would have
been in the middle of the twelfth
century, just before late Romanesque,
which already had pointed arches, gave
way to Gothic.

Like St-Hilaire, St-Pierre has a
pointed barrel vault over the nave, indirectly lit by the windows in the aisles
in the Poitevin style, but it also has
pointed arches in the choir. It has some
good capitals in the nave, including
carvings of birds, beasts and foliage,
all intertwined. There is a capital illustrating the Entombment of Christ, and
another with the endearing subject of a
person extracting a thorn from his foot.

Outside, St-Pierre is generally less
ornate than St-Hilaire. Its west façade
is relatively plain, and its bell-tower,

Priory church of St-Pierre, Melle, from the south

while similar to that of St-Hilaire, is a nineteenth-century reconstruction. But it
has a *chevet* with well-carved decoration round the windows and some lively
corbels, and it is worth walking across the town to see that.

St-Pierre also has a formal portal on the south side, though that too is badly
damaged. It has a mutilated Christ sitting enthroned between two saints on the
upper level, a cornice with carvings of foliage, centaurs, animals, birds and fish,
and a carved doorway with pointed archivolts and an array of plant designs.

Périgueux

The cathedral of St-Front in Périgueux is one of the most dramatic and exotic in
western France. It stands on a hill above the river Isle, and gives an almost eastern
impression, with five domes each topped by a small conical turret, an array of
other, similar turrets, and a soaring bell-tower that carries the biggest turret of
them all.

Turrets like these, with their circle of fine columns and tiles in the cone above
that give the effect of scales, are found on many Romanesque churches in western
France – in Poitiers (see page 223) and Saintes (see page 232), for example. So are

Cathedral of St-Front, Périgueux, from the west

domes, although St-Front is different from the other domed churches of the region in being modelled, like St Mark's in Venice, on the former church of the Holy Apostles in Constantinople. It has its domes in the form of a Greek cross, with four arms of equal length.

What sets St-Front apart is that, while it stands on the site of a Romanesque church, and one that lay on one of the main pilgrim routes through France to Santiago de Compostela (see page 39), the present cathedral is to a great extent a nineteenth-century reconstruction. This is because by the middle of that century the Romanesque church was almost derelict, having suffered principally at the hands of the Protestants during the religious wars of the sixteenth century; and something had to be done.

The task was taken on by Paul Abadie, who also worked at Angoulême cathedral (see page 200). Over the next fifty years or so he and other architects pulled down much of what was left of the old St-Front and rebuilt it – and in the process added embellishments of their own.

So even though Abadie and his colleagues preserved most of the original plan and used the style of Romanesque architecture, and the present cathedral is a most compelling building, purists insist that it is not in fact Romanesque, but a nineteenth-century conception of what it *should* have been.

Among other things, they point to Abadie's turrets, which are more numerous and prominent than those on the twelfth-century church, and also to the fact that whereas the main arches inside the church were originally pointed, when Abadie rebuilt them he made them round.

Today, St-Front has to be taken as it is and, in spite of everything, it is eminently worth a visit. Périgueux is a charming old city, with a few remains of its Roman past, and the cathedral is breathtaking when seen from outside. Its interior is also very fine, even if the new stone makes it seem rather cold. The five great domes create a sense of both space and harmony in what is one of the largest churches in western France.

The church's origins go back to Roman times when Périgueux was an important town known as Vesunna, the main settlement of the Petrocorii, a Gallic tribe. St Front brought Christianity to the region, probably in the fourth century, and was buried at the site of the present cathedral, which was then outside the city. A settlement grew up around his tomb, which attracted a large number of pilgrims, and it came to rival the main city.

As Santiago de Compostela became increasingly important as a pilgrimage centre, St-Front and its monastery were a stop on the pilgrim route that began in Vézelay (see page 93), in Burgundy, passed through Limoges, and after Périgueux headed south towards the Pyrenees. In 1669 St-Front became the cathedral.

The first Romanesque church had been built in the middle of the eleventh century, but it was largely destroyed by a fire in 1120. A few traces of it remain, however, because it stood on the site of the present courtyard at the western end of the cathedral and extended under the present bell-tower. The new domed church, which was completed in the course of the twelfth century, was built as an extension to the east.

Some of the best views of St-Front, including the still magnificent bell-tower, are from the Place de la Clautre, to the west, where a market is held. From there it is also possible to look into the little cloister, with its mixture of Romanesque and Gothic galleries and, in the centre, the original cone-shaped top piece of the bell-tower, taken down and replaced during the nineteenth-century reconstruction.

Further afield, it is worth walking to the original cathedral, St-Etienne, which was supplanted by St-Front in 1669. St-Etienne is also Romanesque and is another domed church, which was built in the eleventh and twelfth centuries in the local Périgord style, with its four domes in a line. But it too was damaged by the Protestants in the sixteenth century, and of those four domes only the two easternmost are still there, and even they had to be extensively restored after the storm had passed.

What survives is plain and massive but has a certain style. The east end, for instance, is a tall, almost cubical structure with stout pillars at the corners. But its effect is lightened by the blind arcades running from top to bottom, with rounded windows halfway up, and by its dome, which has a small turret, similar to those on St-Front, on top.

Inside, there is again the sense of space that is given by the domes, and a marked contrast between the two surviving bays, each corresponding to one of the domes. The first, which now encompasses the nave, was constructed earlier, in the late eleventh century, and is well proportioned but relatively plain.

The second, eastern bay is now the choir, and was built in the second quarter of the twelfth century. It shows how the building style had evolved. The bay is altogether lighter and more ornate, with triple windows flanked by columns on three sides and clusters of engaged columns at the corners.

Poitiers

Poitiers is an ancient city which has several churches that are wholly or partly Romanesque, and they include one of the glories of the period: the ornate west front of Notre-Dame-la-Grande, in a market square in the centre of the city (see page 2). This magnificent façade is covered with carvings that range from religious scenes to fantastic monsters.

It dates from the early twelfth century, and has been cleaned in recent years to remove the accumulated grime, so that its honey-coloured stone now glows in the afternoon and evening sun, a witness to the vital role played by sculpture in Romanesque architecture. Behind it is a delightful bell-tower built over the eastern end of the nave which until recently was still not cleaned, but has a decorative pattern, with two tiers of open, rounded arches and a scaly cone-shaped top that echoes and complements the two turrets on the west front.

Little is known of the origins of Notre-Dame-la-Grande, or why it has that name. It may be that there was another smaller church nearby also dedicated to the Virgin Mary, or else that its founders were thinking of Santa Maria Maggiore in Rome. But building began in the late eleventh century, and continued into the twelfth, and the church is still mostly Romanesque.

Like others in Poitou, it is a hall church, with aisles that are almost as tall as the nave, the nave divided from the aisles by relatively slender pillars with engaged columns set into them, and light coming in from windows high in the aisles. This creates a broad and lofty hall-like effect, while also leaving the round barrel vault of the nave in relative darkness and focusing the eye on the choir at the east end, with its apse and semi-circle of columns beyond.

The nave and aisles of Notre-Dame-la-Grande suffer from having been oppressively over-painted with geometrical and other patterns in the nineteenth century. But the hall-church effect remains, and so does the ring of columns, topped by some beautifully carved capitals, beyond the choir, while above them in the apse there are traces of Romanesque painting, showing the Virgin Mary in majesty. There are also other murals that depict saints and are better preserved, in the crypt below, but it is often not open to visitors.

It is the decoration of the west front, however, that sets the church apart. Here too, the style is typical of the Poitou region, and the façade of Notre-Dame-la-Grande is the outstanding example of the style, not just for its rich overall design but for the quality and detail of the carving.

The façade is framed by two corner towers, each topped by a turret with one of the distinctive conical roofs. Between them are a tall central window flanked on each side by two rows of smaller round arches, a deep central door below it, which has rounded archivolts and a blind pointed arch on either side, and above all, an astounding array of sculpture set into this complex and perfectly structured composition.

The climax is the ornate mandorla in the upper section of the façade, with Christ at the centre surrounded by the symbols of the four evangelists (see page 263), and little figures above representing the sun and the moon. This is set for maximum effect in the middle of a nearly plain pediment, decorated only by simple patterns of inlaid stone. Below it, statues of saints and the Twelve Apostles fill the arches on either side of the central window, the two outer ones in the upper row being thought to represent St Hilary and St Martin.

Lower still, a series of vivid little scenes, each full of life and movement, shows, from left to right, Adam and Eve in the Garden of Eden, Nebuchadnezzar, the prophets Daniel, Jeremiah, Isaiah and Moses, the Annunciation, Jesse and his family tree, the Visitation, the Nativity, and the bathing of the infant Jesus with Joseph looking on.

One of the notable features of the whole west front is that it is alive with animals, monsters, entwined plants and patterns – in the arches, in the capitals, under the cornices. Every time one looks, one finds more engaging details, and this adds to the impact it makes.

Poitiers has been an influential city since the days of the Romans. It is strategically placed on a promontory between the rivers Clain and Boivre, and lies on what was, and remains, one of the main routes between France and Spain. In the fourth century one of its first bishops was the influential St Hilary, or St Hilaire, who among other things was the teacher and patron of St Martin of Tours; and after his death his shrine became a leading pilgrimage centre.

Notre-Dame-la-Grande, Poitiers: detail of the west front

In Romanesque times the city was also the stronghold of the Counts of Poitiers, who were simultaneously Dukes of Aquitaine, and they gave it an active court life. It became another of the main stopping points on one of the main pilgrim routes to Santiago de Compostela (see page 39). The route began in the Ile de France, passed through Tours, and after Poitiers headed for Saintes (see page 232), Bordeaux and the Pyrenees.

The focal point for pilgrims was the large and imposing church of St-Hilaire-le-Grand, which still stands, a little way out from the centre of the city, although it has been much changed over the centuries. The church is entirely Romanesque but there is a continuing debate among archaeologists about how and when the various parts were built, and whether the extensive rebuilding in the last century was true to the original design.

From the outside its most satisfying feature is the well-proportioned *chevet*, or east end, dating from the twelfth century. There is a broad sweep to the ambulatory and its radiating chapels, which have engaged columns topped by some vigorously carved capitals. One of the best views of it is from the little square alongside the church, from which one can also see the strong lines of the transept and the bell-tower, both of the eleventh century.

It is the nave and the side-aisles that have been most changed over the years. The interior of St-Hilaire has the elegance characteristic of a Poitou church, with rounded arches the length of the nave and a stylish choir. Both the choir and the transept are raised above the

Pilgrimage church of St-Hilaire-le-Grand, Poitiers: detail of the 'chevet'

level of the nave to accommodate the crypt, at the east end. However, St-Hilaire is not a typical Poitou-style hall church since the outer aisles are significantly lower than the nave, and it has a complexity of design that derives from its history as a pilgrimage church.

Originally, it seems, there was a single very broad nave and the bell-tower was a separate structure. As the number of pilgrims soared, an aisle was added on each side to create more space for them, one of which incorporated the bell-tower. This raised the question of the vault. It would originally have been flat and made of wood, but wood was a fire hazard, and when it was decided after a fire to vault the nave and aisles in stone, it was discovered that they were all too wide to bridge.

The solution adopted was to narrow these widths by adding extra rows of pillars so that the vaulting could be supported. One row of pillars was built along each side of the nave, in from the already existing pillars between the nave and the aisle – which in effect created another, quite narrow aisle. Then a further row was built along the middle of each of the aisles. So St-Hilaire can now be said to have a nave and six aisles, and the effect is of a forest of columns.

Even at this point the arguments do not end. The greater part of the nave as it now is, together with the side-aisles, was rebuilt from the ground up in the nineteenth century because the old one had largely collapsed after the French Revolution. The new nave had to be shorter than the old one, and the architects of the time decided to vault it with octagonal cupolas. But it is now argued that St-Hilaire's original nave did not have cupolas but barrel vaulting.

All this adds interest to a visit to St-Hilaire, particularly in view of the church's long history. It also has a handful of historiated capitals, including a touching one that shows the death of St Hilary and angels carrying his soul up to Heaven; and there are some especially good capitals, with foliage and animals, on the ground-floor of the bell-tower. There are Romanesque frescoes in the ambulatory and on the columns at the east end of the nave, showing saints and bishops of Poitiers.

Poitiers' cathedral is a large and monumental building, reflecting the power of the city and its bishops, but it is largely Gothic in style. There are, however, other survivals from Romanesque times, one of them the bell-tower of St-Porchaire, which stands four-square in one of the shopping streets, not far from Notre-Dame-la-Grande. A skilful construction with three tiers of rounded arches, carefully disposed, it is a relic of a Romanesque church dedicated to St Porchaire, a sixth-century abbot of St-Hilaire who later became a hermit and, after his death, an object of veneration for pilgrims.

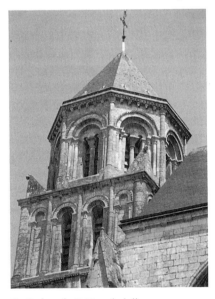

More extensive is the church of Ste-Radegonde, which is in a peaceful setting down by the river Clain, and has a charm of its own. It too has kept its Romanesque bell-tower, one of the most beautiful of the Poitou region, and its austere Romanesque *chevet*, both dating from the late eleventh century, while the nave in between them is Gothic.

St Radegonde, or Radegund, was Queen of the Franks in the sixth cen-

Ste-Radegonde, Poitiers: the bell-tower

tury, as consort of Clotaire I. A devout and active Christian, she founded the convent of Ste-Croix in Poitiers, and also a church outside the city walls on the site of the present church, in which she was eventually buried, and which became a shrine for pilgrims, too.

The choir of Ste-Radegonde still has its well-balanced Romanesque design, which is similar to others in the region, though it too suffers from over-bold nineteenth-century painting. It has a semi-circle of columns with large, strongly-carved capitals depicting humans, animals and vegetation, a tier of round-topped windows above them, and an apse. The choir is raised above the level of the nave, and has a crypt below it.

One of the most intriguing buildings in Poitiers is not far from Ste-Radegonde, and very different: the baptistery of St-Jean. This was founded in the middle of the fourth century, well before the final collapse of the Roman Empire, and is thought to be the earliest surviving example of Christian architecture in what was then Gaul. It is an evocative building, now used as a museum, in which it is still possible to see the walls of the pool in which aspiring Christians of that distant time were given total immersion.

The baptistery itself has been much changed since those days. It was renovated in the seventh century at the time of the Merovingians, for instance. But it main-

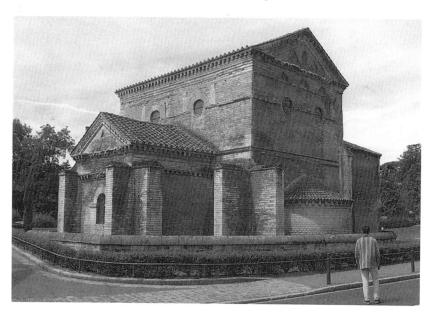

St-Jean, Poitiers: early Christian baptistery

tained its function over the centuries, and a colourful feature is the array of Romanesque paintings which, if incomplete and sometimes covered by later, Gothic work, still decorate the walls of the main chamber.

High on the east wall is the Ascension of Christ, a young-looking figure with the hand of God pointing up at him from below; while on either side are flying angels and, slightly lower, the Twelve Apostles, divided up into two lively groups. The Apostles are walking on uneven ground, representing the Earth, and busily engaged in conversation.

On the two side-walls are saints: to the south St Maurice, whose relics were preserved in Poitiers cathedral, which is near the baptistery, and to the north an unknown figure. Both are accompanied by symbolic creatures, the unknown saint by two peacocks, the symbol of immortality, and St Maurice by a peacock on one side and a dragon on the other. Another man is about to attack the dragon with a sword from the side.

There are some striking paintings of four horsemen, who face each other on the east and west walls. Not all of them are well preserved but one is clearly marked with the name of Constantine, the Roman Emperor who established Christianity, and another, which is more complete but unnamed, also appears to represent a king or emperor. The horses are strongly and vigorously drawn.

The baptistery paintings are predominantly in soft reds, browns and whites, and are all full of life and movement. Like the similar and more numerous paintings in St-Savin-sur-Gartempe (see page 241), not far away, they add an extra dimension to the religious and artistic life of Poitiers and its region in Romanesque times.

Rioux and Rétaud

The Saintonge, the region around Saintes, abounds in Romanesque churches. Most of them are small, but they are often decorated with a lively display of carved stonework, and this ornateness gives the churches in Rioux and Rétaud, with their 'baroque' tendency, a special charm.

The church at Rioux in particular is a feast for anyone who enjoys extremely ornate stonework. Its *chevet* is like a many-faceted piece of jewellery, with decorative features applied, one above another, to the five faces of the apse.

Its west façade also has its appeal. It is simpler, but has a well-structured composition in which a broad central doorway is enclosed within a system of blind arches, each covered in decorative detail; and at its centre there is a full-sized statue of the Virgin Mary carrying the infant Jesus, set in a mandorla.

Rioux: detail of west front

The *chevet* is criticized by architectural historians as going too far, and as being decoration for the sake of decoration. But it can be appreciated for the sheer richness of the stonework, laid lavishly onto a simple form.

Rétaud is similar, if rather less ornate. Its apse has the same form as Rioux's, with five faces, all of them covered with carving, and together the two churches represent a significant trend in Romanesque architecture of the later twelfth century.

They are fairly close together, in villages in the flat agricultural land south-west of Saintes. The Saintonge was something of a crossroads in Romanesque times. It had a long coastline, much used at a time when roads were often poor, and it also lay across one of the main pilgrim routes to Santiago de Compostela (page 39). The route began in the Ile de France, passed through Tours and Poitiers (see page 223), and went on to Bordeaux and the Pyrenees.

As a result the sculpture of the churches, while notable for its exuberance, shows influences from other parts of France. At **Rioux**, the importance of the pilgrimage to Santiago is shown by the presence of cockle shells, symbol of the pilgrim, on the west front, carved on the capitals of the two tall columns that form the outer edge.

The effect of this façade is rather spoilt by the square Gothic bell-tower which was placed on top of it in the fifteenth century, completely altering its overall proportions. But apart from that, the façade has a very fine design. The central doorway, originally inspired, like so many others, by Roman triumphal arches, is deep and broad, with a sequence of archivolts, which have largely geometrical patterns set into them.

On either side, the tall outer columns lead the eye upwards to a line of nine blind arches all with sumptuous carving and, in the middle, the statue of the Virgin and Child. The angels that once supported the mandorla have almost entirely vanished, and the statue has been damaged over the centuries. But the image is a striking one.

The supporting columns have different patterns. Each is topped by a carved capital, and a sort of frieze, with a formal plant design, runs along the tops of the arches. Just above is a cornice with human and animal corbels.

The south side of the church has a twelfth-century chapel added on, and with its arched doorway, surrounded by shrubs, it makes a pretty corner. But the church's most dramatic feature is its *chevet*, with its combination of decorative motifs, which is also set among the shrubs, flowerbeds and trees of the churchyard.

The design is on three levels, covering each of the five faces of the apse. The lowest level is relatively plain, with simple geometrical patterns on a flat surface, and x-shapes carved onto some of the columns. But the level above, where there is a window on each of the five faces, is surrounded by a range of different designs, and is much more elaborate. So is the upper level, which has a line of blind arches similar to those on the west front, and above that a cornice and corbels.

There are some human faces peering out of the stonework, and a few animals on the column capitals; but the decoration is largely abstract, or at least made up of formalized plant designs. The dominant impression is of the sheer profusion of detail, and that, while it is off-putting to some, can be irresistible.

The detailed stonework on the outside contrasts with the relative plainness of the interior of the church. This has been much restored, but the apse, with its five rounded windows, is intact and well proportioned.

Here again, there are those who say that the architects went too far, and many might agree, because the columns supporting the arches over the windows are distinctly 'baroque'. A wobble has been built into them by cutting the blocks that make them up, not vertically, but at a slant to each other.

Rétaud is in general less profusely decorated than Rioux, but this too is an ornate church, at least on the outside, and it has the same form and proportions. The whole of the outside of the apse is covered with patterning, much of it geometrical, and the upper levels are especially ornate, with a cornice that is full of detail and some engaging corbels.

The upper part of the west front is plain. But the lower half is skilfully arranged, with a carved cornice running across it, complete with more corbels. The cornice is supported by four engaged columns, which flank the central doorway and the blind arches on either side of it.

Saintes

Saintes, north of Bordeaux on the banks of the river Charente, was known as Mediolanum Santonum in Roman times, and it still has the remains of its Roman arena, as well as a well-preserved monumental arch from the first century. It continued to be important during the Romanesque period, and since it lay on one of the pilgrim routes to Santiago de Compostela (see page 39) – the one that began in St-Denis, outside Paris – it had a great number of churches, some of them quite large.

None of them has survived intact from that time. But St-Eutrope, a priory church, and the Abbaye aux Dames have enough left to show that they were magnificent buildings in the twelfth century. St-Eutrope's crypt provides one of the

Abbaye aux Dames, Saintes: the bell-tower

Priory church of St-Eutrope, Saintes: the crypt

most powerful and moving evocations of the religious life of Romanesque times, and the Abbaye aux Dames has its eye-catching bell-tower and west front.

Both churches are outside the old city of Saintes, which has picturesque streets clustered around the cathedral. The cathedral was itself once Romanesque, but it has little left from that period apart from the dome over its south transept.

St-Eutrope's attraction was that it possessed the remains of St Eutropius, who was believed to have brought Christianity to Saintes at the end of the third century and to have become its first bishop before being martyred. Its crypt is in fact a lower church in its own right, with a nave, aisles and ambulatory, and an ancient sarcophagus, only recently rediscovered, which is inscribed with the name of Eutropius and is now installed in front of the altar.

With its low barrel vaulting, thick transverse arches and short, massive pillars, the crypt combines strength with a sense of intimacy. At the same time, since it is only partly below ground, light comes in through the windows in the aisles, illuminating the pillars of the nave and, beyond them, the fine vaulting over the semi-circular space behind the altar.

And sturdy though they are, the pillars are lightened in their visual effect by the engaged columns that are set into them, topped by some capitals of great artistry. The capitals are deeply carved into the stone and have formalized plant designs: acanthus, palmettes and other leafy patterns.

The origins of St-Eutrope are lost in the mists and upheavals of the Dark Ages. But the priory stood outside the walls of the Roman city near the road to Bordeaux, where St Eutropius appears to have been buried, and in 1081, like many others, it was brought into the orbit of the great Burgundian abbey of Cluny. The Cluniacs set about building a large and imposing church for the many pilgrims who came to venerate the relics of St Eutrope, very often on their way to Santiago de Compostela.

Both the crypt and the upper church were consecrated in 1096, the crypt by the bishop of Saintes and the upper church by Pope Urban II. The church as a whole had probably not been completed by then, and work continued during the first thirty years or so of the twelfth century.

The completed building must have been quite a sight, with three main parts, each built on a different level: the lower church, the choir and transept immediately above it, and, to the west of them, a nave at an intermediate level from which one could either go up some steps into the choir or down others into the lower church. This meant that pilgrims could come into the nave and go down into the lower church without disturbing the monks above them in the choir.

Since then, parts of the Romanesque church have been pulled down to make way for Gothic additions, not least the great tower. But the severest loss was in the early nineteenth century, when the local prefect ordered the destruction of the Romanesque nave. Today, there is an open space at the western end of the church where the nave once was, and the upper church consists of no more than the transept and choir of what was once a much longer building.

There is still, however, a stretch of the original Romanesque outer wall along the north side of the church, and it is tantalizingly elegant: lavishly decorated in the style of the Saintonge region, with rounded arches over the windows of both the choir and the crypt, and an apsidal chapel on two levels.

The inside of the church, truncated as it is, also retains much from the twelfth century, including the high barrel vault of the choir, with its slightly pointed transverse arches, and the column capitals below them, similar in style to those in the crypt. But the glory of the upper church is the pair of multiple capitals on the eastern edge of the transept crossing, which show the Saintonge style of decoration at its most imaginative and fanciful.

The main scene on one is the weighing of souls at the Last Judgment, with the Archangel Michael confronting a devil (see page 51); and on the other, Daniel in the lions' den. But on both there is also a tumultuous array of entwined foliage, mythical monsters and small human figures, in addition to the edifying themes of the historiated parts.

Lions rear up through the midst of the tendrils. Huge birds perch on the backs of griffins and peck at their necks, while the griffins twist around to bite the tail-feathers of the birds. A line of tiny men crouches under other monsters. Other, larger men seem to be struggling with the foliage. This is Romanesque art at its most engaging – and, as far as its meaning is concerned, most impenetrable.

The Abbaye aux Dames is on the far side of the river, and its church, too, is still a handsome building, with a well-shaped west front and, behind it, its lovely bell-tower. In medieval times the church belonged to a rich and influential Benedictine convent, founded in the middle of the eleventh century, but it has suffered much since then, having been handed over to the army in the aftermath of the French Revolution and then used as a barracks for more than a century.

Much of it is still intact, however, including the bell-tower, and other parts have been restored. The bell-tower is similar in style to the one at Notre-Dame-la-Grande in Poitiers (see page 224), and like that one, has a number of stages. Square as it rises from the church, it has a polygonal level above that, and is conical on top, with tiles that give the effect of scales.

The whole tower is ornate, with an exotic flavour. Three decorative arches rest on tall engaged columns, all topped by capitals, on each side of the square section – some of them with windows, some blind. Above that are four little turrets, one at each corner, which mark the transition to the polygonal stage, and that is a shapely, open structure, with pairs of tiny arches, each topped by a larger, decorative one, on each face, and daylight visible through them.

The west front of the church was badly damaged by the long military occupation, and had to be restored in the twentieth century. But much of the carved stonework is still intact, though worn, not least the masterly carving over the central doorway and the similar but less ambitious designs on the blind arches on either side.

The whole façade still has an almost Roman grandeur to it, with three round arches at ground level and three more above them. At the same time, it is also typical of the Romanesque architecture of the Saintonge region in the richness of its decoration.

The central doorway is one of those pieces of Romanesque sculptured design with an infinite wealth of detail – humans, animals, birds, monsters, plants – every part of which has its own fascination. There is no tympanum over the door. But the archivolts form arches within arches, all covered by carving, with four principal bands of figured sculpture and other ornamental bands between them. The overall effect is of a rich, and characteristic, mix of the figurative and the decorative.

In the innermost archivolt is the hand of God, surrounded by angels; above that the Lamb of God, together with the symbols of the four evangelists (see page 263), all framed by entwined tendrils; then a band in which small human figures, presumably Christian martyrs, are being killed by other small figures; and finally, a row of elderly men, crowned and seated with stringed instruments and cups of perfume, who may be the Elders of the Apocalypse.

There is a similar combination of narrative and decoration in the blind arches on either side. One shows the Last Supper, and the other Christ surrounded by angels, possibly representing the Ascension, although that is disputed.

The inside of the Abbaye aux Dames is less impressive than it used to be because it once had a domed nave, similar to those in the cathedrals of Cahors (see page 254) and Angoulême (see page 200), and elsewhere in the west of France. The two domes replaced an earlier arrangement of a narrower nave and two side-aisles. Sadly, the domes were destroyed in a fire in the seventeenth century, and the empty circular space that each of them filled is now covered by a plain wooden ceiling.

But the huge pointed arches that supported the domes are still there, and they give an idea of the past grandeur. And beyond them the choir, with its barrel vault and rounded arches, has the proportions and harmony of twelfth-century Romanesque, Saintonge style.

St-Jouin-de-Marnes and Airvault

Two tall and imposing churches built in the distinctive Romanesque style of Poitou are only a few miles apart in the flat farming country north-west of Poitiers: St-Jouin-de-Marnes and Airvault. Both were later given Gothic vaulting, and Airvault has a Gothic spire. But both still have the decorative west front, the majestic nave flanked by high side-aisles, and the elegant semi-circle of columns and round arches in the choir that were characteristic of the Romanesque period.

St-Jouin-de-Marnes has the better preserved west front, and it is one of the most accomplished examples of the Poitevin style, while Airvault's west front is built over a rare feature, a narthex set below street level. Both have excellent carving, on the arches that frame the windows on the outside and on the capitals inside the church.

St-Jouin-de-Marnes is an especially impressive sight. It stands on high ground, with fields to the south and east, and there are good views of it both from across the fields and from the village side. Its *chevet* has an apse, ambulatory and chapels built in a yellow stone that glows in the sunlight, and the engaged columns

Abbey church of St-Jouin-de-Marnes: the 'chevet'

give it a marked sense of height – although the effect is marred by some ungainly flying buttresses added in the Gothic period.

The *chevet* is dominated by a fine bell-tower with ranges of round arches on two levels, and it has some good carving, much damaged over the centuries, on the blind arches that run round the base of the ambulatory and chapels. The strange machicolated gangway high up on the façade of the south transept was built for defence during the Hundred Years War (1337-1453), and has never been dismantled.

The outstanding feature of the church, however, is the west front, the building of which began between 1120 and 1150. If it is less ornate than the façades of Notre-Dame-la-Grande in Poitiers (see page 224) or the cathedral of Angoulême (see page 200), it is a complex and beautifully constructed design which illustrates the decorative achievements of later Romanesque architecture – and in its bold use of columns and round arches appears to anticipate the Renaissance.

The sculptured figures set into the façade, surrounded by clear or patterned spaces, are a purely Romanesque feature, and so is the intricate and lively carving in the arches over the windows and on the capitals. But the architects have also created a three-dimensional effect. The wide central doorway with its receding archivolts stands out boldly from the rest of the façade, and the relief effect is enhanced by the pairs of engaged columns set on either side of the central window, as well as the clusters of columns, topped by two typical Poitevin turrets, which frame the façade on either side.

The sculptured figures are damaged, but not badly enough to spoil the impact that they still have. On the pediment is a powerful figure of Christ seated in front of a large cross and flanked by two angels. Below him is the Virgin Mary with two praying figures at her feet and, on either side, a long line of pilgrims marching staff in hand towards her.

Below them, around and above the windows, are figures of saints, a symbolic representation of the Church, and a touching scene of the Annunciation. A man who perhaps represents Constantine gallops over a prostrate figure, cloak flying, Samson struggles with a lion, and one of the figures is the frequently used symbol of lust, a naked women whose breasts are being devoured by snakes.

Inside the church, the nave and aisles have been much restored. However, they make an impressive sight as one looks the length of the long nave to the semi-circle of the choir at the east end. They also provide an interesting example of the evolution of style through the different phases of Romanesque as it led to Gothic. The first three bays of the nave are late Romanesque, with a barrel vault and pointed arches, but the succeeding bays are Gothic, having replaced, it is thought, a barrel vault with round arches put there in an earlier phase of Romanesque.

This earlier phase can still be seen at the transept crossing and in the choir, which were the first parts of the church to be built, beginning in the second half of the eleventh century. There, apart from the vault of the choir, which is Gothic, the arches are round, as they are in the vaulting of the easternmost bays of the aisles. The choir has a pleasing arrangement, with substantial composite pillars linked by wide arches and, above them, an arcade of blind arches.

The capitals in the choir are simple and formal. There are also good capitals the length of the nave and at the crossing. They, too, are relatively simple – symmetrical arrangements of animals, plants and some human figures – but they have a naive charm.

St-Jouin-de-Marnes was an abbey church, built by Benedictine monks on the site of the tomb of St Jovinus, a fourth-century hermit. **Airvault** was a monastic creation as well, whose name is derived from *aurea vallis*, or 'golden valley', and whose church was inspired by a reforming abbot, Pierre de Saine Fontaine. Both profited from being near one of the main pilgrim routes to Santiago de Compostela (see page 39), and flourished in the twelfth century.

Airvault has suffered more damage than St-Jouin-de-Marnes over the centuries. Its west front dominates a market square in the centre of the small town, and

Abbey church of Airvault: detail of west front, showing the Elders of the Apocalypse

although it is asymmetrical, which is rare, with windows and doorways of different form and size, it has an attraction of its own, with enough left of its carving to show how decorative it must once have been.

A surviving handful of Elders of the Apocalypse (see page 263) still sit, crown in one hand, cup of perfume in the other, in the lower parts of the pointed arch over the main door. What is left of a horse, presumably once ridden by Constantine, stands forlornly under another pointed arch, which is exquisitely decorated with formal plant patterns. And there is more carving, of plants and animals, on column capitals and in the various arches.

It is worth going round the south side of the church to see what is left of the cloister and, above it, some decorative windows. Later additions have somewhat spoilt the lines of the *chevet*, but there is more meticulous carving there, in the yellowish stone of the region.

The entrance to the church is through the narthex, several steps down from the square. It is a strange, almost claustrophobic, area, with two bays divided by two rather rough columns, which support an ornamental arch. Up above, but not normally accessible, is a chapel dedicated, as such higher chapels usually were, to St Michael.

Once you are through the elaborate doorway into the main church, however, your view opens up and you see the tall, typically Poitevin nave leading to the semi-circle of the choir. The whole nave is vaulted in Gothic style, and so is the choir. But as in St-Jouin-de-Marnes the lower parts are still Romanesque, and there are carved capitals the length of the nave as well as in the choir.

Airvault is a church that becomes more alluring as one spends more time in it. There is a wide range of subjects on the capitals – biblical scenes, animals, formal vegetation. Those in the nave are, once again, quite simple, but there is a rarely found design high up on either side: the capitals are flanked by large figures standing on masks. Those in the choir are more complex, with the subject-matter intricately entwined to form some immaculate designs.

The church also has two special features: in the north transept, the twelfth-century tomb of the founder, Pierre de Saine Fontaine (*Petrus a Fonte Salubri* in the Latin inscription), in which a sculptured sarcophagus rests in an arch, borne by two crouching figures; and at the western end of the north aisle, a Romanesque altar front which has Christ seated in a mandorla in the centre, surrounded by the symbols of the four evangelists (see page 263), and on either side standing saints.

St-Savin-sur-Gartempe

Not many Romanesque paintings have survived the passage of centuries of war, revolution, dilapidation – and restoration. But a few have. One of the best collections of murals, and certainly the biggest, is at St-Savin-sur-Gartempe, a small town twenty-five miles east of Poitiers (see page 223). St-Savin was once the setting of an important abbey of the same name, and the abbey church is an inspiring sight, dominating as it does the town and the banks of the Gartempe.

The best view is from the west, across the gentle, slow-flowing river. There is an ancient stone bridge from the thirteenth and fourteenth centuries, now used mainly by pedestrians, and from it, or from further upstream, there is a full view of the church with its characteristic Romanesque *chevet,* its little crossing tower and transept, and its single Gothic feature, the tall spire built onto the Romanesque tower at the west end. (See page 15.) Seen from outside, St-Savin is a lofty, well-proportioned church, with a touch of austerity in the clear lines of the nave and transept, and even in the little apsidal chapels with their rounded windows that cluster round the outer edge of the ambulatory. From the bridge it is only a short walk up through the town to the main square, and as one goes one has a closer view, above all of the magnificent western tower which, even before the spire was added on, dominated the church and its surroundings.

*West porch of St-Savin-sur-Gartempe: mural painting in which a dragon tries to devour
a new-born baby boy – scene from book of Revelation (chapter 12)*

It is, however, its beautiful interior that puts St-Savin among the outstanding
Romanesque churches. The greater part of the nave is lined by stylish single
columns, topped by some immaculate capitals with intricately carved foliage; and
above them, for almost the whole length of the nave, the barrel-vaulted ceiling is
covered with mural paintings. There are four rows of Old Testament scenes, taken
from the books of Genesis and Exodus, and with their delicate colours and fluent
brushwork they are a vivid depiction of some dramatic stories.

There are also some powerful murals in other parts of the church: scenes from
Revelation in the west porch; from the Passion and Resurrection of Christ in the
tribune above it; and from the martyrdom of St Savin and St Cyprien in the main
crypt – although this is normally closed to visitors. But it is the paintings of the
nave, incomplete and damaged in places though they are, which make St-Savin
what it is.

The story starts with the Creation, and God is shown putting the sun and the
moon in place. Another scene shows the creation of Eve and her presentation to
Adam – even if the effect is spoilt by the beard given to Eve in some medieval
retouching. Then follow the stories of Cain and Abel, Enoch, Noah, the tower of
Babel, Abraham, Jacob, Joseph and Moses.

The order is often hard to follow – and since the paintings are so high, it helps to have binoculars. But one theory is that in placing the various scenes the artists were following certain doctrinal principles: 'evil' characters had to face westwards, for instance, with their backs to the altar; the stories of Adam and Abraham, and of Joseph and Moses, had to be in parallel; and scenes involving bread and wine had to be at the east end, near the altar.

Throughout, however, there is the same range of light, warm colours – yellow and red ochre, green, white and black – and a light, fluent touch in the artists' draughtsmanship. The scenes of Noah's Ark, of the building of the Tower of Babel, and of the Egyptian cavalry plunging into the Red Sea in pursuit of the Israelites are unforgettable. So are some of the less dramatic scenes, as when, for instance, God in billowing robes receives the lamb offered to him by Abel, or welcomes Noah and his family as they come ashore from the Ark.

There are some stylistic differences, which are perhaps the result of three or four artists from one workshop being involved. In some places they used fresco technique, painting onto a mixture of fine sand and slaked lime while it was still wet, whereas in others they painted onto a layer of whitewash, laid either on dry or re-wetted mortar. But the consensus is that all the painting was done at one time, without interruptions, over a period of some three or four years, and was completed, like the rest of the Romanesque church, before the end of the eleventh century.

Just what the origins of the abbey of St-Savin were is uncertain. There is some suspicion that the story of St Savinus and St Cyprianus, two brothers from 'Brixia', probably Brescia, who are said to have been martyred on the banks of the Gartempe in the fifth century, and whose bodies were allegedly discovered around 800, was mainly, if not wholly, a fabrication, designed to attract pilgrims in search of saintly relics.

On the other hand, it is known that a certain Baidilus, who is said to have built a church to house the relics of the two brothers after they had been found, was a real person, and a prominent one. He was Abbot of Marmoutier, an influential abbey in Touraine, and an official at the court of Charlemagne. So it is likely to be true that the abbey at St-Savin was founded in the late eighth or early ninth century, inside a Carolingian fort.

It then went on to play an influential part in the monastic reforms introduced by Charlemagne and continued by his son, Louis the Pious, who succeeded him in 814. Charlemagne ruled that all the monasteries in his domains had to observe the Benedictine Rule, drawn up by St Benedict of Nursia in the sixth century. But this was not achieved in his time, and the process was taken further by Louis, with the help of the second St Benedict from Aniane in southern Gaul.

At Benedict's instigation St-Savin was reformed in the ninth century under a new abbot, and its influence spread, not only in Poitou, where it became a place of refuge for monks fleeing from the Viking raids, but also in Burgundy. The monks of St-Savin were asked to reform the abbey of St-Martin in Autun, and that, too, became a centre of reform along Benedictine principles.

In 910 Hugh of Poitiers, later St Hugh, who had been one of the most prominent members of the monastic community of St-Savin, and the first prior of Anzy-le-Duc in Burgundy (see page 43), played a role in the decision by William the Pious, Duke of Aquitaine, to found the abbey of Cluny (see page 61), which subsequently became the most important of all the medieval monasteries.

Just when the present church of St-Savin was built, and what the sequence of construction of its different parts was, are matters of controversy. Recent opinion is that the whole church, apart from the spire, was built in a relatively short period, between 1040 and 1090, and that the transept and choir are the oldest parts. It is also accepted that there was initially a western façade, and that the great western tower was built onto that.

There is one especially interesting aspect to all this. There is a clear difference in style, and in alignment, between the western end of the nave, made up of three bays, and the eastern end, which has six. The vaulting is different, and so are the columns that support it. And significantly, the two sections of the nave are four degrees out of alignment with each other. So it is clear that when the builders came to the nave they must have found that the two parts of the church that had already been built, the transept at one end and the western façade and tower at the other, were not properly aligned.

This does nothing to detract from the beauty of the building. Like other churches in Poitou, St-Savin is a hall church: it has aisles with groin vaults which are only slightly less high than the nave, and the aisle windows cast an indirect, subdued light on the paintings on the ceiling of the nave. There are also similarities in the style of its capitals and, like the others, it has a choir surrounded by columns, with an ambulatory runnning round them, and chapels leading off that – the only difference being that the choir is polygonal, rather than semi-circular. But St-Savin has a harmony and a style in its proportions which, added to its paintings, make it distinctive.

Like many others, the church has had a hard life since Romanesque times, being damaged during the Hundred Years War, the Wars of Religion and the French Revolution. Its exceptional quality was recognized in the nineteenth century, and restoration has been under way ever since.

Talmont-sur-Gironde

The little church of Talmont-sur-Gironde is worth visiting for itself and its splendid setting, on a headland overlooking the Gironde estuary, and also for the village
which lies beside it. The church is not large, but it is tall for its size, with a well-
formed *chevet*, and it is a unique sight as it rises from its rock high above the waters
of the estuary.

It towers over the village, which has narrow winding streets lined with stone
walls, houses with round-tiled roofs and a distinctive feature: a mass of hollyhocks
which seem to have taken root everywhere.

The church has been much restored. It was largely built in the second half of the
twelfth century in the style of the Saintonge region. Its *chevet* has a similar form to
those of Rioux and Rétaud (see page 229), and the façade of the north arm of the
transept is also typical of the Saintonge. The church is less ornate than some of the
others of the region, but like them it has some lively carving, including scenes of
human activity and mythical beasts and birds, both outside and in.

Sadly, most of the stonework on the outside has been badly damaged by wind,
rain and sea air over the centuries. But there has been some restoration, both of the
façade of the north transept and of the corbels of the *chevet*, which gives an idea
of what must once have been there. And the carved capitals inside the church have
survived more or less intact.

Not much is known about the origins of the church, or exactly when it was
built. But it is known that a smaller church that stood on the site earlier was
donated at the end of the eleventh century to the influential abbey of St-Jean-
d'Angély, north-east of Saintes, and that like the older church, the new one was
dedicated to St Radegonde, the sixth-century Frankish Queen who founded an
abbey in Poitiers (see page 227) and eventually became a simple nun there herself.

It seems that Talmont was just a small village attached to a coastal fortress overlooking the Gironde – some of whose fortifications still exist on the cliff – and
that the monks of St-Jean-d'Angély built such an inspiring church largely to
impress, and to be used by, the many pilgrims passing through on their way to
Santiago de Compostela (see page 39).

The precariousness of the church's position and the audacity of its builders are
shown by the fact that the west end simply fell away in the fifteenth century, so
that the westernmost bay of the nave and the original west front are no longer
there. A new undistinguished west front was built, and the crypt that was under the
vanished bay fell into disuse. This makes the church shorter than it once was, and

Talmont-sur-Gironde, from the east

even today there is a danger that the rock on which it stands could be worn away further by erosion, so that it needs to be shored up.

But the *chevet* is still there, with its high apse, two chapels and, behind them, the transept, and it has a successful arrangement of engaged columns, arches and cornices. The apse is divided into three tiers: at the lowest level it is plain, above that is a semi-circle of five arches, three of which enclose windows, and above them is a ring of smaller, blind arches. The corbels are not all original, but many of them are engagingly grotesque.

Some of the liveliest carving is, or was, on the façade of the north arm of the transept, which is also on three levels, the lowest of which, a doorway flanked by two blind arches, was profusely decorated. Like other churches in western France, Talmont has no tympanum over the doorway, but it has figures moving up and round within the narrow semi-circular strips of the archivolts, and a similar but simpler arrangement in the two blind arches. The capitals on either side of the doorway are also carved.

Much of the detail of the sculpture is now hard to make out, but the restored sections around the central doorway have some vigorous scenes, with formal decoration in between: lines of men pulling a huge lion with a rope, acrobats standing on each other's shoulders, and angels worshipping the Lamb of God.

In the left-hand arch it is still possible to make out a dramatic confrontation between two monsters, as well as a third monster which is threatening a prostrate woman. In the right-hand arch the small seated figure of Christ in the centre is modern, but much of the original vine pattern over his head is still there.

In spite of being shortened, the inside of the church retains much of its twelfth-century style, particularly in the choir and apse. The dome over the transept crossing is modern, but the surviving bay of the nave, the choir and the transept all have the original pointed barrel vaulting. And the capitals in the crossing and under the apse are well preserved.

Those in the crossing are particularly telling, with men and monsters, lions and birds facing each other in formal poses, against a background of twisted tendrils. One capital has St George on foot confronting a formidable dragon, with a distressed damsel standing behind him and his horse tethered to a nearby tree.

The capitals under the apse are less ambitious, but they form part of a skilful ensemble of choir and apse, similar again to those in Rioux and Rétaud. The ring of round arches at the east end of the church, with light coming in through the windows in three of them, still makes a focal point, just as it did for pilgrims in the twelfth century.

South-West France

South-west France lay across the pilgrim routes heading for Santiago de Compostela, and most of the churches of the Romanesque period were built and decorated with pilgrims in mind. The architectural styles vary, but they generally have some unsurpassed sculpture designed both to inspire and educate the pilgrims as they passed through.

The great basilica of St-Sernin in Toulouse is one of the surviving examples of an early pilgrimage church, with barrel vaulting over the nave, double side-aisles and a lofty ambulatory with radiating chapels. By contrast the abbey church of Souillac, to the north on the river Dordogne, is a delightful example of a domed church, with a line of three cupolas over the nave and transept, and no side aisles.

There is superb sculpture in both. St-Sernin has two outside porches that both have decorative stonework, while inside there are some beautifully carved capitals and an unexpected feature: full-length figures of Christ and various Apostles and angels, carved in low relief. At Souillac the original porch has been dismantled, but its parts have been set up inside the church, and they include some unforgettable images – the figure of Isaiah, for instance, and a column covered with a unique, seething mass of animals and humans.

The outstanding church, however, is at Moissac, between Toulouse and Souillac on the river Tarn. The south porch of Moissac, with its scene of the Apocalypse on the tympanum, is a major work of Romanesque art, and the church's cloister has an array of carvings on its capitals that make it one of the most beautiful in France.

Other churches were built on the rivers that flow through south-western France to the Atlantic. The cathedral of Cahors, on the Lot, is another domed church, which also has an elaborate porch, and inside it a lovely tympanum that combines the scene of the Ascension with the martyrdom of St Stephen.

On the Dordogne upstream from Souillac are two other churches with splendid porches, and tympana inside them. Carennac has a tympanum depicting Christ in Majesty, and Beaulieu-sur-Dordogne has one of the most dramatic tympana of the period, which shows the Second Coming of Christ.

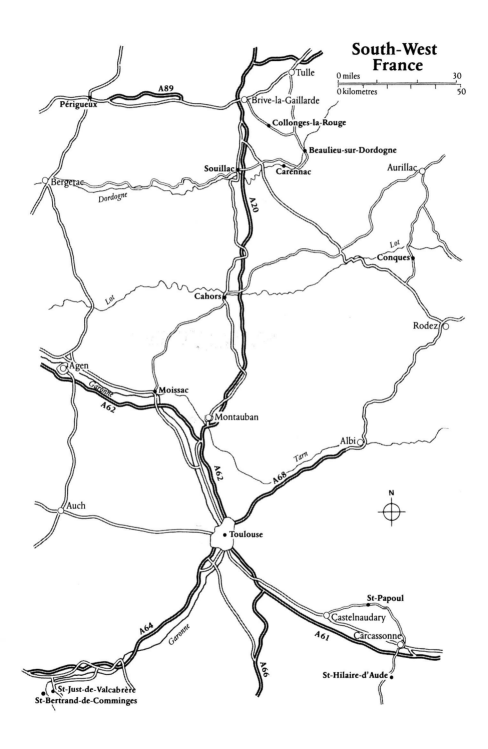

South-West France

0 miles · 30
0 kilometres · 50

Tulle

A89

Périgueux

Brive-la-Gaillarde

Collonges-la-Rouge

Beaulieu-sur-Dordogne

Souillac

Carennac

Aurillac

Bergerac

Dordogne

A20

Lot

Conques

Lot

Cahors

Rodez

Agen

Garonne

Moissac

A62

Montauban

Albi

Tarn

A62

A68

Auch

Toulouse

N

St-Papoul

Castelnaudary

A64

Garonne

A61

Carcassonne

A66

St-Hilaire-d'Aude

St-Just-de-Valcabrère

St-Bertrand-de-Comminges

Tympanum of priory church of Carennac: Christ in Majesty

A fascinating village in the region is Collonges-la-Rouge, which lies between the Dordogne and the Corrèze, and is almost entirely built in the local red sandstone. Its church, too, has an original tympanum, which shows either the Ascension or the Second Coming of Christ – the experts disagree – and is thought to be the work of sculptors of the Toulouse school.

Beaulieu-sur-Dordogne

Beaulieu means 'beautiful place', and that is a good description of Beaulieu-sur-Dordogne, an atmospheric small town on the banks of the river Dordogne which was once the setting of an important abbey. The abbey church is still there, a towering building surrounded by old houses and narrow streets, and its great tympanum covers the doorway in its south porch.

Beaulieu did not lie on any of the main pilgrim routes to Santiago de Compostela, but it was a pilgrimage centre in its own right because of the many relics that it possessed, mostly of saints from south-western France. And like Carennac (see page 257) and Souillac (see page 270), both further downstream, it

Tympanum of abbey church of Beaulieu-sur-Dordogne: the Second Coming of Christ

was not far from two of the main routes. So there were many pilgrims from near and far who travelled along the lesser routes to see the abbey and its church.

Today Beaulieu has become a market town that has long outgrown the walls which used to surround it – and which are still marked by a circular boulevard. It is only a short walk to the riverbank, where there are sweeping views of the Dordogne and the hills opposite, and also of the twelfth-century parish church, now known as The Penitents, which stands in an eye-catching position on the edge of the water.

The abbey church was itself built mainly during the first thirty years or so of the twelfth century, and apart from some later additions, such as the tall bell-tower at its western end, is a well-proportioned building in the style of the Limousin region that surrounds Limoges.

The *chevet* was always an important part of Romanesque churches, and Beaulieu has five semi-circular chapels, three of them radiating out from the ambulatory and two from the transept, all of which have the tall and elegant windows of the region. Above the ambulatory is the apse, and to either side of that are two little turrets. They make up a well-balanced complex, topped by a simple, but rather engaging octagonal bell-tower with a pointed roof, set on a square base.

While Beaulieu is squarely in the Limousin, however, it is in the south of the region, near the border with Quercy, and the tympanum in its porch clearly shows the influence of the porches of that region such as those of Moissac (see page 262) and Cahors (see page 254), to which it is similar in style.

The theme is the Second Coming of Christ, and it is treated with a rare sense of drama. A large seated figure of Christ dominates the scene, holding his arms outstretched in the form of a cross, while behind him, over his right shoulder, is the cross itself, carried by two angels and giving a powerful echo of his gesture.

The choice of this theme was exceptional for the period. It shows Christ enthroned and triumphant, proudly displaying the signs of his crucifixion, and surrounded by angels and Apostles. Though there are two rows of grisly monsters at his feet, who are devouring sinners and who represent the evil that he has conquered, the time for the Last Judgment, depicted in other tympana, such as those of Conques (see page 174) and Autun (see page 49), has not yet come.

Two angels blow trumpets, standing on either side of Christ, while two others hold the great cross, and two more fly out of the clouds at the top, carrying a nail from the crucifixion and a royal crown. On either side the Apostles sit in pairs, with St Peter clutching his keys and looking dumbstruck; while a tiny figure, perhaps representing an Old Testament prophet, sits and watches from the side.

Tympanum of Beaulieu-sur-Dordogne: the fate of sinners

Down at the bottom, the dead are pushing up the lids of their coffins, and there are also two lively little groups of exotically dressed people. One group of three is walking towards the central scene, while four others are pointing up at it and apparently discussing it. One theory is that they represent the peoples of the outside world in general. But it has also been suggested that they are Jews arguing with Christians about the meaning of it all.

Altogether it is a vivid scene, packed with people and monsters, but without any sense of clutter. Christ, the angels and the human figures are all graphically carved, with individual gestures and expressions and flowing draperies, while the various monsters down below are convincingly gruesome.

The two beasts immediately below Christ's feet, a griffin and a lion, have wings, while two others have sinners in their jaws. The trio in the lower row are a corpulent bear, a plump monster with seven heads, and a long serpent-like creature with a human head, a snake's head on its tail, and ferocious monkey-like creatures emerging from its coils – all designed to terrify pilgrims into mending their ways.

As at Moissac, the tympanum is set within a very slightly pointed arch; and it is also like the Moissac tympanum in being supported by a decorative *trumeau*, or central pier. The Beaulieu *trumeau* has a compelling image: three straining human figures – a boy standing on someone else's shoulders, a full-grown man and a bearded old man (perhaps representing the three ages of man) – brace themselves to support the lintel on their shoulders, one on each face.

On either side of the two doors are worn, but lovingly poised figures of St Peter and St Paul, also like figures in a similar position in the Moissac porch.

Just what sort of covering the porch would originally have had is not known since the present structure over it is modern. But it is likely that there was some such covering, because there are carved scenes on the walls on either side. They too are badly worn, but they are still recognizable depictions of, on one side, Daniel in the lions' den, and on the other, the Temptation of Christ.

The story of Beaulieu goes back to the middle of the ninth century, when Raoul de Turenne, an aristocratic Archbishop of Bourges, was taken with the site and decided to build a Benedictine monastery there. It was he who gave it the name of 'bellus locus', which evolved into 'Beaulieu'. Over the next two centuries the monastery became rich and powerful; but it was badly in need of reform, and in 1076, like many others, it was put under the authority of the abbey of Cluny (see page 61).

It was under its Cluniac abbots that most of the present church, including the south porch, was built. Inside, it has a tall nave topped by a barrel vault, two side-aisles with groin vaulting, transepts with chapels on their eastern sides, and a dome over the transept crossing. The great arches supporting the dome are slightly pointed, and there are also some pointed arches in the rather irregular aisles.

The apse is characteristic of the period and, like other pilgrimage churches, Beaulieu has a pleasing arrangement of colonnades and windows below it which encircle the choir. Three small chapels radiate off the ambulatory.

Interestingly, three of the doors have lintels with archaic carvings on them, clearly taken from some earlier building – two in the transept and one in the north aisle. One shows Daniel with two lions, another an unidentified person with two bears, and the third a Tree of Life, of Persian origin, with a lion on either side.

The church has only a few, quite simple capitals, with formalized foliage and some human figures on them. But it has a majestic quality to it, and that, combined with the soft, diffused light and the rugged-looking stone in which it is built, gives it a typically Romanesque mixture of style and intimacy.

Cahors

Cahors lies on a big loop in the river Lot, and has taken advantage since pre-Roman times of its strategic position. The Pont Valentré on its western side, built in the fourteenth century, is its most dramatic sight today, but there are also good views of the old town, with its stone walls, towers and partly timbered houses with tiled roofs, from across the Lot to the east – and particularly from the hills on that side of the river.

In the Romanesque period Cahors was a stopping point on the pilgrim route (see page 39) that began in Le Puy-en-Velay (see page 185), passed through Conques (see page 174), and then wound its way over some rugged countryside between Figeac and Cahors. Its bishop was a powerful man, on the political as well as the religious scene, and in the eleventh century he was formally granted the ex-officio titles of count and baron of Cahors, as we have seen.

The cathedral still towers over the old town, and its massive, mostly plain western façade, added on in the fourteenth century, reflects its military role. But building had begun about 1100, and there is still much left of the original Romanesque structure.

Most prominently, there are the two large domes, which give it an exotic, Byzantine character, visible against the lines of the rooftops from many parts of the town. The cathedral is dedicated to St Etienne, or Stephen, and is thought to have been not only the first of the many churches built with domes in Aquitaine in the twelfth century, but the one with the largest domes. Only those of Aghia Sophia in Constantinople (now Istanbul) had a greater span, it is said.

The other survival from Romanesque times is the ornate, sculptured north porch, similar in style to those of Moissac (see page 262) and Beaulieu-sur-Dordogne (see page 250), though less well preserved than either of them. The porch was originally part of the west façade of the cathedral, and was the main entrance to it; but it was moved to its present site on the north side during restoration work in the thirteenth century. Its two doorways, long blocked up, have recently been reopened.

The porch is a building of great beauty, which can be seen well from the little square on the north side of the cathedral, with the two domes high above it. It is solidly built, with echoes of a Roman triumphal arch, but the arch at its centre is larger than a Roman one and slightly pointed. It is also covered with decorative carving, and inside the arch is a tympanum over the two doors which depicts the Ascension, with scenes of the life and martyrdom of St Stephen on either side.

Rosettes run up and down on either side of the arch, and the engaged columns that stand between them have meticulous capitals, with formalized plants, mythical animals, and a mixture of the two. A cornice that marks the beginning of the arch has a graphically carved hunting scene, with horsemen and dogs in full cry,

Tympanum of Cahors cathedral: the Ascension of Christ

and it evolves into a slender archivolt which has tiny elongated figures that are hunting, fighting or, in one case, so it seems, shoeing a horse.

Up above, under the ornate cornice, heads and shoulders, and sometimes whole bodies, emerge from the stonework, most of them grimacing at the world – as do other faces along the side of the cathedral.

If the tympanum has been damaged over the centuries, it still has lightness and grace. At the centre is Christ standing in a mandorla, being borne aloft in the company of angels. The two on either side are in ecstatic poses, with swirling drapery, and give a sense of movement to the whole scene, while others reach down from the clouds above. Down below, under a row of trefoiled arches topped by tiny buildings, are the Virgin Mary and a row of sensitively carved Apostles, each of them in a different pose, some talking and some gazing up.

The four scenes of the martyrdom of St Stephen strike a very different note. Simply but strongly carved, the two on the left show him being arrested and then preaching to his captors, one of whom has the conical hat that marks him out as a Jew, while two others block their ears. On the right, in a vivid final section, Stephen is being stoned to death by two young men, while a seated figure, presumably Saul, the future St Paul, holds their clothes for them.

Stephen raises his hands to God, who sits enthroned above him with Christ at his side, and a hand reaches down to him through the clouds. At the top are tiny faces representing the sun and the moon.

Tympanum of Cahors cathedral: the martyrdom of St Stephen

The porch as a whole is a mixture of powerfully realistic sculpture and exuberant formal decoration. The tympanum has a border of entwined vegetation, probably derived from an illuminated manuscript, and it is interesting that in the part next to the scene of the stoning of St Stephen there is a human figure entangled in the foliage who is also flexing his arm to throw a stone at the martyr.

Inside the cathedral, much has been changed since Romanesque times, and the profuse decoration is all later. But the grand scale of the two great domes, supported on pendentives, shows how spacious it would have been in those days, with no need for side aisles.

It is also worth going out to the cloister on the south side of the cathedral. It is in a much later style, with Renaissance touches. It is a charming and peaceful place, in spite of the damage it suffered from the Protestants in 1580 during the Wars of Religion. One of the capitals shows a fight between two *coquillards*, as the pilgrims who had been to Santiago de Compostela were known.

From the cloister one can see the original south wall of the Romanesque cathedral, with the windows covered by round arches and, above them, more grimacing faces under the cornice. Even more arresting, one sees once again the two great domes.

The old part of Cahors is generally well worth walking round because it is full of narrow streets and old houses, many of them well restored, which reflect the great days of the city. And the square in front of the cathedral is a lively place on market days.

From it one can see another doorway, on the south side of the cathedral, whose innermost arch has a trefoil form. It shows that Cahors, like other towns and cities in southern France, was influenced by the Islamic world south of the Pyrenees.

Carennac

Perched above the river Dordogne, with wooded slopes all round, the picturesque village of Carennac seems far removed from any centres of activity, whether medieval or modern. But like Beaulieu-sur-Dordogne (see page 250), a few miles upstream, and Souillac (see page 270), a few miles further down, it lay near two of the main pilgrim routes to Santiago de Compostela, and it had a significant role in the Romanesque period as one of the priories dependent on the great Burgundian abbey of Cluny (see page 61).

The priory church, built in the first half of the twelfth century after Carennac had been incorporated into the Cluniac system, still stands, and it has a very decorative tympanum over its west door, depicting Christ in Majesty. Inside, the church is a good example of the way in which Romanesque architects used carefully judged proportions and limited light, coming in through small windows, to create an intimate and uplifting setting.

The village of Carennac has not changed much in recent centuries, and the main approach to the church is through an arch in the fifteenth-century wall

Tympanum of Carennac: Christ in Majesty

surrounding the priory. The arch provides a frame for one's first view of the west door and its tympanum, covered in a yellowish patina, a short way up a narrow paved road.

The tympanum does not have the dramatic force of Moissac (see page 262), Cahors (see page 254) or Beaulieu, but it is an appealing, well-balanced composition, with lively figures and carved decoration round the edge, including vegetation, animals, birds and fish. The tympanum appears to have been modelled on the intricately worked gold altar-fronts of the period, even to the extent of having holes in the stonework for coloured glass or stone.

Christ sits enthroned in the centre of a mandorla, his right hand raised, his left on the Bible, while the sun shines down on him from above and the four Beasts of the Apocalypse, representing the evangelists – the lion for St Mark, the bull for St Luke, the winged human figure for St Matthew, and the eagle for St John (see page 263) – gaze in at him.

On either side are the Apostles, engagingly naive and individual figures who are grouped in pairs and appear quite detached from the dramatic event that is unfolding. An angel approaches from either side, bowing deeply, and in the bottom corners are two tiny, monk-like figures each displaying a book.

Beyond the tympanum are a small narthex and, on the door into the church, some naive but notable capitals, including two entwined animals apparently breathing fire and a beast with two heads. These capitals, like other similar ones inside the church, are thought to be of a much earlier date than the tympanum.

The inside of the church was much added to after the Romanesque period, and was restored more recently. But the charm of the original twelfth-century design has been preserved, with the barrel vaulting over a tall, relatively narrow nave, the rounded arches between the nave and the side-aisles, the cupola over the transept crossing, and the soft light.

As so frequently the capitals, all of them in the same naive style, add a colourful touch: stylized birds, abstract patterns, contorted monsters, and even the occasional human figure. In one capital, a couple are locked in an embrace, with a gesticulating human figure on one side and a monster on the other, apparently representing lust.

The cloister was one of the parts of the church that was rebuilt in later years, and was badly damaged during the French Revolution. But a small part of the Romanesque cloister survives on the side running along the church, and it is worth going into the cloister to see one of the showpieces of Carennac, a sixteenth-century sculptured group of the Entombment.

Collonges-la-Rouge

Collonges-la-Rouge, in the Limousin region south-east of Brive, is another scenic old village, and one of the most striking in France because the red sandstone gives its colour to the whole village.

The narrow streets and squares have a number of once-aristocratic houses, several of them with little turrets, that date from the distant days when the village was a good deal more prosperous than it is now – and life was less peaceful. At their heart is the small priory church, which has been much rebuilt over the centuries, but has kept two features from the Romanesque period: a tall and complex bell-tower over the crossing and a carved tympanum over its west door.

The tympanum is in a white limestone that contrasts with the sandstone that surrounds it. It was only pieced together again in 1923, and the doorway as a whole is obviously restored. But it has been well done, and the carved figures are full of life, with the power and grace of those elsewhere in south-western France. It is thought that they date from the end of the first half of the twelfth century.

The bell-tower is also from the twelfth century, or even the late eleventh century, and is in any case earlier than the tympanum. It is built in a typical Limousin style, in stages, with two levels of open rounded arches, a level of pointed gables above them and, at the top, an octagonal section, now topped by a conical roof. As elsewhere, the gables mark the transition from square to octagon.

Priory church of Collonges-la-Rouge, from the south-east

The church as a whole is in a jumble of styles without much sense of unity. It belonged to a priory that was originally founded in Collonges in the eighth century by the influential Benedictine abbey of Charroux, in Poitou, and the monks, after building the Romanesque church in the eleventh and twelfth centuries, reshaped it with a number of Gothic features in succeeding centuries.

They also, like monks elsewhere, became involved in the power struggles of the surrounding region, and so the church had to be fortified. The result is that, small as it is, the church has no less than three large towers, each of a different shape and design. The two later ones were built in the fourteenth and sixteenth centuries respectively, and came to have a largely military function as watchtowers. These were needed, it seems, in the village's factional fighting.

Today, all three towers rise high above the roofs of the village and give it an unmistakable profile, visible from far away.

The church's jewel, however, is the tympanum. The scene it depicts is generally taken to be the Ascension, although it has also been suggested that it might be the Second Coming of Christ. Whichever it is, Christ stands at its centre under a slightly pointed arch holding a book in his left hand, while two angels hold a

Tympanum of Collonges-la-Rouge: the Ascension of Christ, or the Second Coming

piece of drapery under his feet and two others gesture vigorously in his direction. For once, Christ is not surrounded by a mandorla, which suggests a relatively late date. Below are full-length sculptures of the Virgin Mary and eleven of the Apostles, standing under a row of rounded arches.

The figures are beautifully poised, with flowing draperies and the engagingly wide-eyed, innocent expressions of the sculpture of the time. The two gesturing angels convey a strong sense of movement, and Mary and the Apostles are each given their own identity and pose. At either end of the line of arches a lively group of three Apostles is clustered together, deep in conversation. The scene as a whole is surrounded by a decorative frieze of interwoven fronds, with heads, apparently of angels, peering down out of the middle of them.

The double doorway below has been rebuilt, but the ornate trefoil arches and leafy capitals are similar to those that it is thought to have had originally. There is one endearing detail. The right-hand doorway has an original capital with a formal leaf design and, above it, a small carving in relief of a bear-trainer and his large, shaggy bear, held by a rope round its neck.

Inside, it is possible to make out the shape of the Romanesque church, and there is one notable survival from that period: the transept crossing that bears the weight of the bell-tower. A plain cupola rises over the crossing from four engaged columns, each topped by a carved capital with a plant design and set into a massive pillar. At its centre is a large circular hole through which one looks up inside the tower, where the light pours in through the windows. It is a simple but dramatic effect.

Moissac

You might not expect to find one of the masterpieces of western art in a small market town on the banks of the river Tarn, north of Toulouse. Moissac today is a pleasant but unremarkable shopping centre in a mainly agricultural area known for its dessert grapes, the Chasselas.

But in its great days, which began in the mid-eleventh century and lasted well beyond the Romanesque period, its abbey of St-Pierre was one of the wealthiest and most influential in southern France, and a substantial property-owner which controlled other monastic institutions both in France and across the Pyrenees in Catalonia.

It was also a high point for pilgrims on one of the main routes to Santiago de Compostela (see page 39). So the narrow streets of what was then a walled town would have been crowded on religious festival days with travellers from all over France and further afield, all heading for, or returning from, Spain.

Before reaching Moissac, the outgoing pilgrims would have collected in Le Puy-en-Velay (see page 185), in the Massif Central, made their way over the rugged Aubrac plateau to reach Conques (see page 174), and travelled across more rough country to Cahors (see page 254), down the river Lot. From there they progressed to Moissac, and then went on to cross the western Pyrenees at the Roncesvalles pass.

The splendid church porch that the pilgrims would have seen when they arrived in Moissac has survived through the centuries, and it is extraordinarily compelling. Behind it, on the far side of the church, is one of the most enchanting cloisters of the period, with a wealth of carved capitals and several full-length figures carved in low relief.

The church as a whole is in a mix of styles. The nave and the east end were rebuilt later when Gothic had taken over, replacing, it is thought, a line of domes similar to those found elsewhere in south-western France; and so was the brick bell-tower above the porch. But the sculptures in the porch and the narthex that opens out of it, and those in the cloister, convey the supreme artistry of Romanesque Moissac.

The central feature of the porch is the superb tympanum over the doors, which dates from the first half of the twelfth century and depicts the Vision of the Apocalypse as described in the book of Revelation, beginning in the fourth chapter. It has Christ enthroned majestically in the centre, and around him the four Beasts of the Apocalypse, which, as we have seen, are always taken as representing the four evangelists: the lion for St Mark, the bull for St Luke, the winged man for St Matthew, and the eagle for St John. A tall angel stands on either side of them, and the Twenty-Four Elders sit in rows, each holding a cup of perfume and a stringed musical instrument.

Tympanum of the abbey church of Moissac: the Vision of the Apocalypse

There is a sense of drama in the scene, and a plastic quality in the carving of the figures. Christ is stern and masterful, and the four Beasts, which twist around to gaze at him, give the scene contrast and movement. The winged bull and lion are especially vigorous creations. Each of the Twenty-Four Elders is treated individually and almost humorously as they too crane their necks to look at the central figure of Christ. It is a perfect example of the way a deep sense of devotion is combined with humanity in the best Romanesque art.

It should perhaps be noted that in the Authorized Version of the Bible the second Beast is said to have been a calf, but that at Moissac, as elsewhere in Romanesque art, St Luke is represented by a fully-grown bull.

Like many others, the scene on the tympanum is generally agreed to have been inspired by an illumination in a contemporary manuscript. But there are those who see it as also being an example of the influence of Islamic art on the art of the Christian church in Romanesque times. John Beckwith writes in *Early Medieval Art*: 'The scene on the tympanum at Moissac is a *diwan* of Divinity, Christ holding court like an Umayyad or Buwaiyid prince, crowned like a Spanish king, and surrounded by elders playing lutes and viols, themselves derived from illustrations of Islamic musicians.'

Beckwith sees much else in the doorway that suggests the influence of Islam: the scalloped sides of the two doors, the row of rosettes on the lintel immediately below the tympanum, which are being disgorged by a monster at each end, and the three dramatically placed pairs of lions, one male and one female, on the central pillar, or *trumeau*. The whole doorway, with its slightly pointed arch, has an exotic quality that does reflect the influence of the Islamic world beyond the Pyrenees.

Whatever the cultural influence of Islam, however, the dominant themes are strongly Christian. On either side of the *trumeau* are exquisite, elongated figures of Jeremiah and St Paul, while St Peter and Isaiah stand in relief on the outer edges of the doorway. And the two side-walls are a showcase for Christian teaching. On the left is a graphic and well-preserved depiction of the story of Dives and Lazarus, the rich man and the poor man, together with some rather worn but still frightening scenes of devils tormenting sinners; and on the right are the Annunciation, the Nativity, the Flight into Egypt and the Presentation in the Temple.

There are more depictions of the torments undergone by the damned on some of the column capitals. So Moissac had moral edification for the pilgrims, and its lessons were enhanced by the vivid quality of the carving.

Within the porch is the narthex where the pilgrims would have gathered before going into the church. This is chiefly plain, but there is a bold sweep to its powerful

South porch of Moissac: the prophet Jeremiah

South porch of Moissac: the Flight into Egypt

South porch of Moissac: infant Jesus presented in the temple

stone vaulting, and there are vividly carved capitals on the columns in the corners, including a man struggling with a lion, and other ferocious animals with birds or smaller animals in their jaws.

Above the narthex – and nowadays reached from the cloister – is another plain, but most impressive room, tall and vaulted, in which half a dozen arches converge to form an oculus at the centre, open to the sky. This construction, too, is thought to show the influence of Islamic architects with their vaulting skills. The capitals here are more stylized.

Moissac had been a religious centre long before pilgrims started to wend their way to Santiago. Just when it became Christian is uncertain but it could have been in Roman times, when there was already a town there. The foundation of the abbey, according to legend, was the doing of Clovis, king of the Franks, who had swept across northern Gaul in the fifth century and who defeated the Visigoths, another Germanic tribe which had until then controlled the south, near Poitiers in 507.

The story goes that Clovis hurled his sword from the nearby hills and that when it landed in the marshland near the Tarn, that was declared the site of the new abbey. It was called the 'Abbey of the Thousand Monks' in memory of the 1,000 men lost by Clovis and the Franks in the battle against the Visigoths.

More prosaically, historians have placed the abbey's foundation in the seventh century, perhaps by St Didier, Bishop of Cahors; and it was certainly there when the Arab armies poured across the Pyrenees from Spain in the following century and ravaged it twice.

This was only the first of a series of disasters undergone by what is now such a peaceful town. In the ninth century the abbey recovered its prosperity thanks to support from Charlemagne and his Carolingian successors, but it was then pillaged by Vikings, who had sailed up the Garonne on their way to Toulouse, and a few years later by the Magyars.

In the thirteenth century it was badly damaged after the siege and capture of Moissac by the northern French armies during the Albigensian War; and in the fourteenth and fifteenth centuries it suffered again during the Hundred Years War between England and France. There was more devastation when it was stormed by a mob during the French Revolution at the end of the eighteenth century.

Much has survived, however, from the eleventh and twelfth centuries, when the abbey of St-Pierre was a power in the religious life of the time. This position was largely due to its link with the abbey of Cluny (see page 61), established in the middle of the eleventh century. Moissac was a leading member of the Cluniac community, in which its abbot ranked second only to the abbot of Cluny itself.

Earlier, the abbey had been under the protection of the counts of Toulouse, who had emerged as the great lords of the Languedoc region after the disintegration of the Carolingian empire. But the counts had handed the abbey over to lesser nobles, and it had become a pawn in the local power struggles and fallen into ruin.

The incorporation of the abbey into the Cluniac system was carried out at the request of the counts of Toulouse and other regional powers, both religious and secular, and arranged with St Odilo, one of the great abbots of Cluny. St Durand de Bredon was the first abbot to be appointed by Cluny. He began the process of reform, and for some years combined his position at Moissac with being Bishop of Toulouse.

It was Durand and a number of distinguished successors over a period of years who rebuilt the abbey. The new abbey church was consecrated in 1063, and in 1097 Urban II, the Cluniac Pope who two years before had launched the First Crusade, came to Moissac to consecrate the high altar. It is believed that the church was then domed.

The cloister was completed by the end of the eleventh century – although the pointed arches that now link the columns are the result of restoration in the thirteenth century after the damage done during the Albigensian War – and the porch in the following decades.

There is little else left of the abbey itself. But the old abbot's palace, a charming building, originally in red brick, is now the museum of local history and, while it has been much changed over the centuries, it still has two of the original chapels, one of which dates from the eleventh century.

Up above it is a battlemented tower from which there are good views of the church, the tiled roofs of the town and the surrounding countryside – as well as of some gaunt-looking surviving buildings that were cut off from the rest of the abbey when the railway was driven through the surviving buildings in the nineteenth century (it was only just possible to save the cloister).

At its zenith, however, the abbey occupied a sizeable part of the town of Moissac, and was itself surrounded by walls and watchtowers. There were libraries and residential buildings, refectories and stables, gardens and cemeteries. The abbey was equipped not just for the spiritual life of its monks but to house and feed the poor – and especially the pilgrims who poured into Moissac on their way to Santiago de Compostela.

Along with the porch, it is the cloister, the oldest in France so well preserved, that most certainly evokes those distant times. It is a wonderfully tranquil place, shaded by a huge cedar, with marble columns of different tones (almost certainly taken from earlier buildings), and there too there is an exotic richness in the

Cloister of Moissac: capital with masks

carvings on their capitals, damaged though many of them are. They range from biblical scenes and incidents from the lives of saints to legendary monsters and lovingly worked abstract designs.

Complementing them are the ten full-length figures, mainly representing the Apostles but also including an engaging portrait of St Durand de Bredon, which are carved in low relief on the bases of ancient sarcophagi. They have a formal, almost Byzantine quality, but each figure is different, with his own individuality.

It is worth spending time in the cloister, and taking a close look, not just at the main body of each capital, but at the upper part, or abacus, where there are immaculately carved strips running round the edge: formal flower patterns, eagles, lions, monsters and much else.

Altogether there are no less than seventy-six capitals, with three main types of subject-matter. More than half of them are historiated, with stories from the Bible and the lives of saints. The others have figurative designs, in which animals, birds, snakes and even human figures are presented in formal, and often dramatic, poses; or else they are purely ornamental, with largely floral designs whose origins can be traced as far afield as Persia, Coptic Egypt and Muslim Spain.

Taken together they make a sumptuous mix. The biblical scenes and the lives of the saints are often simply carved, with a touching naivety, and, as is to be expected, they convey a strong religious feeling. They include such subjects as the Annunciation to the Shepherds, the Baptism of Christ, the Miraculous Draught of Fish, and the Wedding at Cana; while St Martin is seen cutting his cloak in two to give half to the beggar, and St Saturninus, the first Bishop of Toulouse, is shown being dragged to his death by a bull (see page 276).

But there is also a marvellous vigour in the strange, medieval beasts that complement these narrative scenes; and the purely ornamental capitals, with their formal designs, have a jewel-like quality which is one of the outstanding features of the cloister.

They illustrate the many different influences there are on Romanesque art, and the important place Moissac has in it.

Souillac

The Benedictine monastery of Souillac, on the north bank of the river Dordogne, lay midway between two of the main pilgrim routes to Santiago de Compostela (see page 249), and only a short distance from each. It was itself a stopping point on one of the minor routes, which began at Clermont in Auvergne, and the church that the pilgrims visited remains one of the glories of the ancient region of Quercy.

Built in the first half of the twelfth century, it is among the most successful of the domed churches of south-western France, with a line of three domes dominating the nave and the transept crossing, and a wonderful *chevet*.

It also has some of the best sculpture of the Romanesque period. This originally formed part of a porch like those of Moissac (see page 262), Cahors (see page 254) and Beaulieu-sur-Dordogne (see page 250), but the porch was dismantled and its parts installed inside the church in the seventeenth century, when the damage caused during the Wars of Religion in the previous century was being repaired.

Souillac is on a main road and, until the recent opening of a new motorway, it was often jammed with slow-moving traffic. But the old part of the town is full of charm, and there is a fine view of the *chevet* from across the open space to the east of the church.

The broad semi-circular apse, the five polygonal chapels and, above them, the dome over the crossing and its tiny turret make this a masterly variation on the theme of the pilgrimage church, with a contrast between rounded and angular forms. There is a touch of austerity, not least in the two arms of the transept, since the bare stone walls are punctuated only by small windows set in round arches. But the overall effect is grand and imposing.

Priory church of Souillac: the 'chevet'

At the western end of the church is a simple tower which is thought to date from the tenth century, and to have formed the narthex of an earlier church, built in Carolingian times. While the top level of the tower was added much later to hold the bells, there is still a line of the original corbels, including human and animal heads, high up on its walls.

Inside, Souillac has a sense of spaciousness that is characteristic of the domed churches of the region, with its three cupolas and a rounded apse. Large pointed arches span the nave supporting the cupolas, which rest on pendentives, and there is a shapely choir in which the broad pointed arches over the openings to the chapels alternate with narrower round ones. There are no side-aisles, so that light comes in evenly through the small windows of the nave, the transept and the apse.

Unlike the cathedral in Cahors, another domed church which was completed a few years earlier and is thought to have been a model for it, Souillac was not added to or rebuilt in later architectural styles. It is also better proportioned, with smaller cupolas than Cahors, and so it displays at their best the pure lines of this particular type of Romanesque church.

Most of the walls are plain, with deep-set, rounded windows, but there are some simple capitals in the transept and the choir, some of formalized plants and birds,

Souillac: the prophet Isaiah

some of biblical scenes, including a charming Annunciation, that add a decorative touch.

Above all, there is the sculpture from the vanished porch, erected on the wall at the western end of the church. Here is the magnificent figure of Isaiah, all lightness and movement, with swirling robes richly decorated at the collar and the hem, as he throws one long leg over the other in a scissor-like pose; and opposite him Hosea, stationary and overshadowed by the bravura of his fellow-prophet, but still a finely carved figure.

Equally arresting, if in a quite different way, are a *trumeau*, which was originally the central pier of a double doorway, and a sculpture that appears to have been part of another *trumeau*. The two of them have some of the most singular – almost surrealistic – scenes in Romanesque sculpture, in which savage-looking monsters stand in pairs, one male and one female, with their necks twisted round, and devour whatever is nearest to them, whether animal, bird or human being.

The main *trumeau* has four pairs of these monsters, one above the other, on its main face, and, tumbling down between them, a man, a dove, a dog and a deer, all being torn to bits.

By contrast, there is a vivid and moving scene of Abraham about to sacrifice Isaac to one side of the *trumeau*, with an angel rushing down from the clouds to put a ram in Isaac's place; and on the other, another mysterious scene in which three human couples, one above the other, stand and embrace.

Only the scene of Abraham and Isaac is clear and unambiguous. Various explanations have been put forward for the other two: that the one with the three couples represents sin, for instance, and the main scene its consequences. On that interpretation, Abraham's willingness to sacrifice Isaac and the intervention of the angel represent redemption.

However that may be, from a purely visual point of view the *trumeau* is quite exceptional. And the same is true of the smaller work in which there are just two monsters, meticulously carved with their tails entwined, that are tearing apart a ram.

There are many similarities to the sculpture of Moissac, not least in the pairs of monsters, with their bodies forming an X, which are like the lions and lionesses on the Moissac *trumeau*. And the figure of Isaiah, with his crossed legs, has a close resemblance to that of Jeremiah on the same *trumeau*. They appear to be the work of sculptors from the same school.

The remaining sculpture at Souillac may well have come from the side-wall of the original porch, and has another dramatic, if involved, story to tell. In between magisterial figures of St Benedict and St Peter, sitting enthroned with entwined monsters under their feet, is being played out the drama of Theophilus, a church functionary of Adana in Cilicia.

According to legend, Theophilus had been stripped of his position by a new bishop, and out of pique made a deal with the devil, who had him reinstated. Theophilus then repented of what he had done, and prayed to the Virgin Mary to help him, which she did. She snatched back the document which recorded Theophilus's deal with the devil and returned it to Theophilus, who died soon afterwards, restored to his former sanctity.

The sculpture shows this in three small scenes, set closely together: first, Theophilus and a suitably gruesome devil making the deal, and then Theophilus formally submitting to the devil, who looks clearly triumphant. The climax is in the upper part of the frame, where Mary, accompanied by angels, reaches out of the clouds to hand the document back to Theophilus, who is lying asleep near the church.

The beginnings of Souillac are lost in the distant past. It stands near the point at which the river Borrèze joins the Dordogne, and its name comes, it seems, from an ancient word, *souilh*, meaning a marshy area. According to tradition, it was founded in the seventh century by St Eloi, adviser to the Frankish King Dagobert I at a time when many such monasteries were being created.

By the ninth century Souillac had come under the authority of the abbot of Aurillac, and from then on it grew steadily in importance and wealth, with a link to the abbey of Cluny (see page 61). In the fourteenth century it had more than eighty churches and priories dependent on it. It was not, however, until the sixteenth century that Souillac was granted the title of abbey by papal bull.

Toulouse: St-Sernin

The basilica of St-Sernin in Toulouse is one of the few surviving examples of the early group of churches built specifically to accommodate large numbers of pilgrims (see page 12). And it is a most inspiring one, a large and stately church that has majesty and style in its proportions and, in addition, some outstanding sculpture.

The church's tall nave and transept, each covered by a barrel vault and round transverse arches, have a harmony that is distinctively Romanesque; while on the outside the two porches on the south side, the Porte Miègeville and the Porte des Comtes, have some of the best sculpture of the period. There is more sculpture

Pilgrimage church of St-Sernin, Toulouse: the 'chevet'

inside the church, in the ambulatory, as well as an array of carved column capitals, and there are even a few mural paintings.

Toulouse had been a prominent city since Roman times, and even before that, but it was particularly influential in the Romanesque period when the counts of Toulouse were the dominant power in south-western France. Their court and the wealth of the city attracted troubadours, artists of various kinds, and increasing numbers of pilgrims.

In early days, the pilgrims were attracted by the tomb of St Saturninus or Saturnin, whose name became Sernin in the local dialect. He had been the first Bishop of Toulouse, and was said to have been martyred in 250 by being dragged across the city tied to a maddened bull. A church was erected over his tomb, but by the end of the fourth century a new and bigger one was needed on the site, which was outside the walls that then surrounded the city; and that is where the present church still stands.

Later, as pilgrims began to make their way to Santiago de Compostela, Toulouse also became one of their main stopping-points (see page 39), lying as it did on the southern route that began in Arles (see page 282). Over the years it accumulated the relics of numerous other saints, in addition to those of St Saturninus, and these added to its appeal. After leaving Toulouse, the pilgrims headed for Auch and then the Somport pass across the Pyrenees.

It was to provide room for these pilgrims and to give them the opportunity to venerate the various relics, while leaving space for the church's college of canons to continue their normal liturgy, that St-Sernin was built, between 1080 and 1120, to the distinctive design used also in the four other leading pilgrimage centres: Tours, Limoges, Conques (see page 174) and Santiago de Compostela itself.

Like Conques and the great cathedral at Santiago, St-Sernin has a tall, majestic nave topped by barrel vaulting, side-aisles which are covered by galleries that open through pairs of small, decorative arches onto the nave, and an ambulatory round the back of the choir with small chapels radiating off it. There are also side-aisles in both arms of the transept, and this arrangement enabled the pilgrims to circulate in the nave, the aisles and the ambulatory. They could stop at the shrines in the ambulatory while the liturgy was being performed in the centre of the church, and especially in the choir, where the high altar was placed.

St-Sernin is a rarity in being constructed partly in brick, like many other buildings in Toulouse, which gives it a pink tinge. It is also the only one of the three pilgrimage churches that has two aisles on each side of the nave, which gives the church greater width and makes for some arresting views across it, through the columns. The nave is indirectly and subtly lit, as in many Romanesque churches, by the windows in the gallery and smaller ones in the aisles.

The effect is satisfying, as it is in Conques and Santiago, because of the proportions, the decorative ensemble formed along the two sides of the nave by the round arches, columns and capitals, and the use of space and light. That also applies to the two arms of the transept which have the same height as the nave and the same design, and which, because of their scale, create the impression of a second church, cutting across the main one at right angles.

In the middle is an octagonal cupola over the crossing, borne on squinches and given a star-like appearance by the ribs radiating out from the central oculus; and at the east end the characteristically Romanesque semi-circle of columns and arches, topped by an apse, which encloses the choir.

A jarring note is struck by the four massive, and intrusive, columns at the corners of the crossing. They were erected to support the cupola and the bell-tower above it when the upper levels of the tower and the spire were added in the Gothic period, and greater strength was needed. And the choir has heavy baroque decoration these days, including the high altar, while the choir stalls used by the canons extend into the nave.

But the visitor can catch a glimpse through the ironwork railings of the ancient high altar, consecrated by Pope Urban II in 1096 and signed by Bernardus Gilduinus, or Bernard Gilduin, one of the few artists known by name from those days, who is thought to be responsible for other sculpture in St-Sernin. The altar is carved with great delicacy, with angels and birds in foliage along its edges.

There are well-carved capitals, mainly of vegetation, high up in the nave, and more in the transept, where there are a number of historiated ones, with figures of angels, humans and animals. And the north arm of the transept also has some mural paintings, only rediscovered during restoration work in recent decades. They include a scene of Christ with Mary Magdalene after the Resurrection, and a large composition in which Christ is surrounded by the Virgin Mary and St John the Baptist, as well as Old Testament prophets and the Three Holy Women at the empty tomb.

Entrance to the ambulatory and its chapels, and to the crypt beneath the choir, is from the north arm of the transept. This was the route followed by pilgrims for many centuries, and much of the work to be seen there today is from long after the Romanesque period. But the architectural style that is so marked in the rest of St-Sernin is visible in the ambulatory too, in the groin-vaulted ceiling and the chapels, and it provides a grandly Romanesque setting for the works of later centuries.

One exceptional, Romanesque feature is the set of seven large relief carvings set

St-Sernin: Christ in Majesty, in ambulatory

into the inner wall of the ambulatory, depicting Christ in Majesty and individual angels and Apostles. They are relatively early works, from the late eleventh century, and still have a certain stiffness about them; but the central figure of Christ, surrounded by the symbols of the four evangelists (see page 263), is a powerful image, poised and serene; and the others are individual and engaging.

Down below, in the little chapels under the arches of the crypt, are reliquaries containing the many remains of saints and other holy relics acquired over the years by the basilica. They include a delicate reliquary in Limoges enamel, dating from the twelfth century, said to contain a piece of the True Cross, and another in silver gilt from the early thirteenth century, containing the relics of St Saturninus himself, with a scene showing his martyrdom on the outside.

There is much to be seen on the outside of St-Sernin, too. The west end was never completed and the two towers that were planned were never built, so that apart from a formal arched doorway it is now largely plain. But the east end is a supreme example of a Romanesque *chevet*, in which the tiled roofs of the apse, the ambulatory and the radiating chapels appear to cascade down over decorative cornices with bands of tiny corbels, and tall windows are topped by linked arches.

The soaring spire above is, of course, Gothic, and so are the two upper levels of the tower, with the angled tops to their windows. But the three lower levels have round arches, and it is possible to imagine the majestic octagonal tower in Romanesque style that was planned.

Finally, there is the sculpture on the two porches on the south side of the church. That on the elegant Porte des Comtes, which is reminiscent – with its two arches – of a Roman triumphal arch, is the older: a set of vivid historiated capitals showing the torments inflicted on the wicked, and above all the wicked rich, by devils and monsters; and also a happier scene of the soul of Lazarus, the beggar, being carried up to heaven by angels.

These capitals date from the end of the eleventh century, and still display an engaging naivety. They are thought to have come from the same workshop as some of those inside the church, in the transept and the ambulatory.

The Porte Miègeville is smaller, but it was built later, in the early twelfth century, and underneath a decorated cornice it has an inspired range of sculpture which makes it one of the high points of the Romanesque period. These works are altogether more ambitious than those on the Port des Comtes, with larger figures and greater plasticity and expressiveness.

At the centre is a sculptured tympanum depicting the Ascension of Christ. It has a formal composition that lacks the imaginative quality of some other Romanesque tympana, but the individual figures in the scene have a poise, and a sense of movement in their upraised arms and flowing robes, that put them among the finest achievements of the period.

Christ is being borne up from the Earth by two angels who twist round to give him their support, while four others, two on each side, hail the event. Down below, under a frieze of grapes and grape-leaves, the Twelve Apostles are shown in a state of jubilation, together with two bonneted figures, one on each side, representing the 'men in white apparel' described in the *Acts of the Apostles*.

On either side of the single arch stand large, hieratical figures of St James and St Peter, each raising a hand in blessing, together with some allegorical groups. On St James's side there are two men entwined in foliage above his head and a man flanked by two women riding on the backs of lions beneath his feet; on St Peter's, two angels above his head which are a later addition, though from the same period, and beneath his feet Simon Magus flanked by two devils.

There are other historiated capitals on the columns that frame the door, and they have been identified as the work of Bernard Gilduin, who was responsible for the high altar of St-Sernin. They, too, are graphic works which depict the Massacre of the Innocents, the Annunciation and Visitation, Adam and Eve in the Garden of Eden, and an allegorical scene of lions caught in foliage. Further in, immediately below the tympanum, there are two carved stone brackets showing David with his lyre and two women holding lions on their laps.

All in all, there is a richness and beauty of composition in the sculpture of St-Sernin which complements the lines of its architecture. And there is more to be seen in the Musée des Augustins, also in Toulouse, which has a masterly collection of Romanesque sculpture, some of it originally from St-Sernin, some from the cathedral of Toulouse, and some from the demolished monastery of Notre-Dame-de-la-Daurade.

There are many good pieces there, well displayed, among them a haunting capital from the cathedral that shows the beheading of St John the Baptist. The little scene in which Herod looks lasciviously at Salome, while holding her chin, is a masterpiece.

Provence

Provence is the part of France which was most thoroughly Romanized. It is also a region that suffered badly over the centuries through the invasions and disruption that followed the collapse of the Western Roman Empire, and it did not recover any stability until after the last of the invaders, the Saracens, had been dislodged from their strongholds there towards the end of the tenth century.

As a result, there are only a few early Romanesque churches to be found in Provence. But the churches of the twelfth century, when prosperity had returned, show technical mastery, including beautifully cut stonework, and most noticeably, strong influence from the classical world of Greece and Rome.

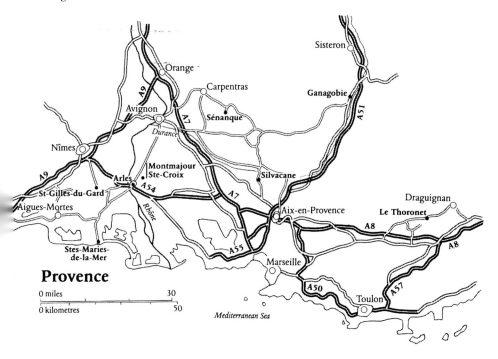

The former cathedral of St-Trophime in Arles has a monumental west front which is a combination of classical and medieval, and there is an even more splendid one at St-Gilles-du-Gard which, being on the far side of the Rhône, is not strictly in Provence, but came under the same influences.

Mosaics were also a heritage of the classical world, and there is a superb array of them in the abbey church of Ganagobie, on a hilltop above the valley of the Durance.

Both Arles and St-Gilles-du-Gard were pilgrimage centres, and the same was true of the abbey of Montmajour, an ancient religious centre which stands on a hilltop just outside Arles. Montmajour has a towering abbey church built in the twelfth century, but it also has one of the few early Romanesque churches in Provence, a charming little eleventh-century structure built into the rock and, a short distance away, a pretty twelfth-century chapel built for pilgrims.

Like St-Trophime, the abbey church of Montmajour is skilfully constructed, with a tall, pointed barrel vault, and is quite austere, with little decoration inside. On the other hand, both churches have delightful carved capitals in their cloisters.

One of the most unusual churches of the Romanesque period stands in the small town of Saintes-Maries-de-la-Mer, on the outer edge of the vast marshland of the Camargue, south of Arles. It is a fortified church that was designed to provide protection against attacks from the sea, and it has a Romanesque interior including some carved capitals.

A significant presence in Provence is that of the Cistercians. The Order established itself in the region in the twelfth century, and there are three remarkable Cistercian abbeys there, known as the 'Three Sisters' – Sénanque, Silvacane and Le Thoronet. All are in country settings – not least Sénanque which is in the bottom of a valley surrounded by lavender fields – and they have the simplicity and style which were the mark of early Cistercian architecture.

The three abbeys have similar architecture, but each has its distinctive features, and they are all worth visiting.

Arles

Arles, which was the starting point for the southernmost of the four main pilgrim routes across France to Santiago de Compostela (see page 39), has perhaps the finest of the Romanesque churches of Provence, St-Trophime. This is a former cathedral, largely built in the twelfth century, whose nave and aisles are in the austere Provençal style, but which also has two splendidly decorated features,

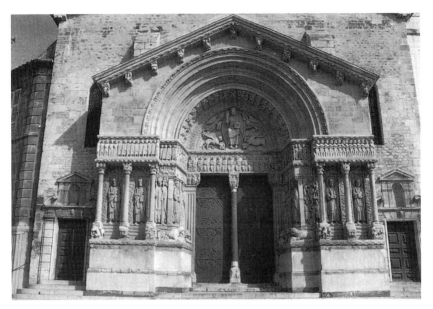

Former cathedral of St-Trophime, Arles: the west porch

both mostly constructed towards the end of the century: the west porch and the cloister.

The west porch, recently cleaned, dominates one corner of a handsome square, the Place de la République, and like the porch at St-Gilles-du Gard (see page 295), not far away and built at around the same time, is strongly influenced by the region's Roman heritage. The cloister, although only two of its four galleries are Romanesque, has column capitals of great power and charm, and also clusters of full-length statues of Apostles and saints which stand alongside panels carved with biblical scenes.

Arles itself has a long and distinguished history. In late Roman times, when it was known as Arelas or Arelate, it was one of the most prominent cities in the empire, standing in a strategic position on the banks of the Rhône, near the mouth of the river. In about 400 it was made the administrative centre for the whole of Gaul, taking the place of beleaguered Trier, on the German frontier. In 417 it became the seat of the ecclesiastical Primate of Gaul.

Like the rest of Provence, Arles suffered badly during the long centuries of confusion that followed the collapse of the western Roman Empire, and the city was sacked several times in the ninth century by both Saracens and Vikings. But it remained Provence's leading city, and recovery finally began after 972, when

William, the Count of Arles, succeeded in dislodging the Saracens from their base at Fraxinetum in the nearby Massif des Maures.

William, known as 'the Liberator', proclaimed himself Marquis of Provence, and in due course Arles gave its name to the kingdom of Arles, also known as the kingdom of Burgundy, of which it became the capital. The kingdom was part of the German Empire for a time, and in 1178, with a fanfare, the Emperor Frederick Barbarossa came to Provence to be crowned King of Arles in St-Trophime, then the cathedral.

Provence including Arles only became properly part of France in the fifteenth century. Arles remained an archiepiscopal see until the French Revolution.

This enchanting old town has long lost its past eminence, but it still has the Rhône and the Mediterranean sunlight and with them some outstanding survivals from both the Roman and the Romanesque periods. From the first there are the Roman arena, the theatre and several other archaeological sites, including the Alyscamps cemetery, which continued to be used in medieval times. From the second are St-Trophime, named after the Greek missionary who is believed to have brought Christianity to Provence, and the little church of St-Honorat in the Alyscamps.

St-Trophime is mainly Romanesque today, although its choir is Gothic and so is part of the cloister, and its west porch shows the continuing awareness in Provence of Roman architecture and motifs. A deep central arch, like those on a Roman triumphal arch, is set into a high, angular pediment, and rests on a sculptured frieze. Below that is a line of marble columns, some of them topped by acanthus-leaf capitals.

But as at St-Gilles, the twelfth-century sculptors have taken the Roman framework and Roman decorative motifs and adapted them to their own purposes. The result is an ornate and complex design, with a mixture of classical decoration and Christian themes, and a wealth of detail from both traditions, lovingly carved.

The tympanum, for instance, shows Christ in Majesty, surrounded by the four symbolic figures representing the evangelists – the lion, the bull, the eagle and the winged man, all of them quite stylized (see page 263) – and inside the arch, instead of a Roman-style pattern, an engaging phalanx of angels soars upwards on either side, with three of them cavorting in mid-air at the top while triumphantly blowing long horns.

The main frieze is another classical feature, but it has a strongly Christian and moral message that is presented in a formal but compelling way. To the left is a long line of the blessed, male and female, waiting to be presented by an angel to Abraham, Isaac and Jacob, who then seat them on their laps. To the right a corresponding line of the damned, stripped and chained together, with flames licking at their legs, are advancing towards a devil with a pitchfork. In the middle, under the tympanum, is a row of Apostles sitting serenely and in style.

If all this is deliberately formal, there are also some tellingly emotional scenes. To the right of the Apostles a haloed figure sits squarely on top of a man on all fours, presumably a sinner, and to the right of him there is a dramatic scene in which an angel closes the door of Paradise on a group of sinners who clasp their foreheads in dismay.

The story begins on the far left of the porch with an engaging depiction of Adam, Eve and the serpent in the Garden of Eden and, down below, St Michael weighing souls of his scales (see page 51); and it ends on the far right with a horrific figure of Satan, who has two naked sinners under his arms and a naked female figure, sitting on a giant lizard, between his legs.

One of the porch's main features is a line of full-length statues of Apostles and saints that flank the doorway on both sides, below the frieze. These are generally rather wooden in style but they include a powerful St Trophime, who has a fixed, visionary expression, and one of the niches is filled more vividly with the stoning of St Stephen, whose soul in the form of a young child is being taken up to Heaven by two angels.

There are other lively scenes in a smaller frieze above their heads which has a series of biblical stories. These include the Annunciation, the Nativity, the dream of Joseph, who is being admonished by an angel, and several scenes relating to the three Magi – they are shown tucked up together in bed before being woken by an angel, being received by Herod, and presenting their

St-Trophime, Arles: detail of west porch

gifts to the new-born Jesus. Two of the most moving scenes are the Flight into Egypt and the Massacre of the Innocents.

And there are even carvings on the bases of the columns. On one, Daniel sits looking contemplative between two lions. On another, Samson is shown fighting a lion and then, while being seduced by Delilah, having his head shorn.

The interior of the church is a contrast. St-Trophime has a tall, soaring nave which was built earlier in the twelfth century. It has a pointed barrel vault, flanked by two narrow side-aisles, each with round arches beneath a half-barrel vault. The effect is inspiring, but decidedly austere. The angular piers that divide the nave from the two side-aisles have strong, pure lines, and a clerestory of small rounded windows lights the vault from high up on both sides. But though the stonework is immaculate, the carved decoration is minimal: just acanthus leaves and some small fluted columns high up on either side under the vault.

Such decoration as there is is provided by three paintings by Finsonius, the seventeenth-century Flemish painter, and by some late Roman sarcophagi, strongly carved with Christian themes. One, depicting Christ's miracles, serves as a font. Two others, one showing the Israelites crossing the Red Sea and the other Geminus, a Roman official, appearing before Christ, are used as altars.

The cloister, on the other hand, is full of carved decoration, and the two Romanesque galleries date from the late twelfth century when the canons of St-Trophime, after centuries of a relatively relaxed régime that had allowed them to live their own lives away from the cathedral, were put under the Rule of St Augustine. This was altogether more rigorous, and required them to live a communal life in the cathedral precincts. But it did not preclude visual beauty.

To reach the cloister, you have to go round the side of the church and across an open courtyard, originally part of the archbishop's palace, from which there is a good view of the tall and shapely bell-tower. This, like the nave, was built in the earlier part of the twelfth century, and it can be seen from many parts of Arles. It has a robust and well-found simplicity. The two lower levels are decorated with Lombard bands, the strips of blind arches often found in early Romanesque (see page 18), and the one above has Corinthian pilasters. At the top is a row of tiny rectangular windows covered with a cornice.

The first impression of the cloister is of its sheer beauty – particularly the two Romanesque galleries, with their pairs of slender columns divided by round arches and, at intervals, more solid pilasters in classical style, with acanthus-leaf capitals. In the middle are pink-flowered oleander bushes, and up above is the bell-tower of the church. The two Gothic galleries, erected in the fourteenth century, are plainer, but do not mar the harmonious effect.

The Romanesque capitals have some moving biblical scenes, and it is worth spending time studying them. However, it is the clusters of full-length statues of Apostles and saints, all of them expressively carved, that are the dominant feature.

They are accomplished works which show how far Romanesque sculpture had evolved by the end of the twelfth century.

The two most complex clusters stand at the north-western and north-eastern corners of the cloister. The first has a moving portrait of St Trophime in the centre, flanked by St Peter and St John, with scenes of the Resurrection and of the Three Holy Women preparing to visit Christ's tomb on the panels in between. The second has St Stephen in the centre, St Paul and St Andrew on either side, and scenes of the stoning of St Stephen and the Ascension.

Elsewhere there are clusters of just three statues including, in the north gallery, Christ displaying his stigmata between doubting Thomas and St James, and Christ as a pilgrim between the two disciples from Emmaus.

A noticeable characteristic of the sculpture in the cloister is the continuing influence of Roman art. Several of the figures wear Roman-style togas and sandals, and as in the west porch many of the decorative features – such as palm-leaves and entwined foliage – are derived from Roman architecture.

The endearing little capitals on the other hand, are wholly medieval and Romanesque, with the charm and often the poignancy that go with that. The subject-matter is mostly familiar: the Nativity, for instance, the three Magi being woken by an angel, the Massacre of the Innocents, and Christ riding into Jerusalem on Palm Sunday. But each subject is treated in a distinctive style that makes this series of capitals one of the high points of St-Trophime.

Another of the high points of Arles, the Alyscamps cemetery, was originally outside the walls of the Roman city, and it remains some way from the centre. 'Alyscamps' is the Provençal form of 'Champs Elysées' or 'Elysian Fields', and it is an evocative place, which appealed to both Gauguin and Van Gogh, each of whom painted it.

The cemetery was used for centuries, from Roman times until the later Middle Ages. It was said to have been consecrated by St Trophime in the presence of Christ himself, who descended from the sky for the occasion, and it came to attract large numbers of pilgrims. St Trophime was said to have been buried there, although his remains were later taken to the cathedral, and so were other saints.

The Alyscamps is essentially a long shaded avenue flanked by the occasional chapel and, most strikingly, a line of stone sarcophagi selected from the hundreds that have been found there during excavations. At the far end is St-Honorat, a small Romanesque church with a well-shaped bell-tower. Together with a few surviving buildings, and a clump of trees, it makes a most picturesque group.

Ganagobie

The priory of Ganagobie, which was affiliated for many years to the abbey of Cluny (see page 61), is one that should be better known. Its site is a glorious one on a steep hilltop high above the valley of the river Durance, and it has a set of twelfth-century mosaics that are among the best that have been preserved from the Romanesque period, and certainly the best in France.

They are in three main colours, red, black and white, and are spread like a carpet across the main transept of the monastery's church, and onto the floors of the sanctuary and the two side-chapels. There are snarling lions and strange mythical beasts, a centaur and two elephants, and a wealth of convoluted patterns. In one scene a knight in full armour and brandishing a long lance charges a hydra-headed dragon. Elsewhere another knight triumphantly transfixes another dragon.

Not all the mosaics can be clearly seen, and some of the best are completely invisible because Ganagobie is a functioning monastery; and visitors may not approach too close to the main altar, which has mosaics all round it. Besides, the mosaics have to be protected from the damage that could be caused by people walking over them. But most of them can be seen, and the sheer panache of their design, together with their colouring, makes a visit to Ganagobie an unforgettable experience.

Priory church of Ganagobie: mosaic floor

Their survival is itself an absorbing story. The monastery buildings, including the church, were sold off, like many others, in the French Revolution, and in 1794 the eastern parts of the church were deliberately destroyed on the orders of local officials. The mosaics were covered by the rubble, and their existence was forgotten.

It was only a century later, in the 1890s, when a community of Benedictine monks had recovered possession of the monastery buildings, that the mosaics were rediscovered. But even then they could only be photographed, and covered over with earth to protect them, and it was not until 1975 that restoration began as part of the process of restoring the whole church.

The hill on which Ganagobie stands, some 2,300 feet high, has been settled since prehistoric times, and the ancient sarcophagi that have been found on the site – one of which is in the nave of the church – show that there was a cemetery there. The monastery was founded in the middle of the tenth century by the Bishop of Sisteron at a time when the Saracens were still a threat in Provence, and in about 960-5 it was donated to Cluny, itself only about fifty years old. Like other monasteries, it received valuable gifts, often of land, from aristocratic patrons over the years.

The present church was built in the course of the first half of the twelfth century – with the mosaics dated about 1125 – and it has the austere lines, and the accomplished stonework, that are typical of Provençal churches of the period. The nave is tall and narrow, with a pointed barrel vault and transverse arches, and no sculptural decoration. There are high blind arches along its sides, with small windows on the south to let in the strong light, but no side-aisles.

At the east end there is a double transept, and beyond it the sanctuary, with a design that is also typical of Provence, in which the apse is divided into segments by four ribs, with a ring of round arches below. Two small chapels, each with an apse, flank the sanctuary.

These eastern parts of the church have had to be extensively rebuilt in recent years since less than ten feet of the walls was left standing after the destruction at the end of the eighteenth century. But great trouble has been taken to restore them as far as possible as they were in the twelfth century, including the use of many of the original materials. The main features that have not been rebuilt are the cupola that covered the main transept and the bell-tower above it.

The monks of Cluny, unlike the Cistercians, believed in embellishing their churches, and the austerity of the architecture would of course have been balanced by the fantasy and verve of the mosaics. Something of the same was true of the outside of the church. The *chevet*, for instance, is massive and almost fortress-like, with little decoration on the three apses, well-proportioned though they are, and only a blank, angular wall behind them.

But the west front has a feature that was added towards the end of the twelfth century: an ornate west door with several archivolts and a carved tympanum. In the tympanum Christ sits in a mandorla surrounded by the four figures representing the evangelists – the lion for St Mark, the bull for St Luke, the eagle for St John and the winged man for St Matthew (see page 263) – and by two other angels, while on the lintel below twelve small figures represent the Apostles.

The carving is simple rustic work that does not compare with the major Romanesque tympana in other parts of France, nor with the mosaics inside the church. It does, however, have a curiosity value and a naive charm because of the lobed stonework round the door and on two of the archivolts.

This was apparently a later addition for which the builders used stones that had been carved to lie flat on top of each other and make up engaged columns. They turned the stones on their sides and inserted them into the existing stonework to create the lobed effect. They also – in order to continue the lobes across the top of the doorway – cut away some of the lower part of the lintel, with the result that some of the Apostles lost their feet.

The church is open to visitors but only at certain limited times, and ordinary visitors may not visit other parts of the monastery. This means that the cloister, which is built in a style that is similar in style to others in Provence and simply decorated, is closed to them, and can only be glimpsed through windows that open onto it from inside the church.

The use of mosaics at Ganagobie was a sign of the continuing influence of Rome in Provence. Ganagobie is close to the old Via Domitia, first established by the Romans in the second century BC after their conquest of that part of Gaul. It followed the Durance valley and for centuries linked northern Italy with Spain.

But the techniques employed to lay the mosaics in the twelfth century were different from those used in Roman times. The tesserae, for instance, are not rectangular but pyramid-shaped, with a flat surface and a point that enabled them to be fitted into place. And the subjects are of course very different, too.

The mosaics at Ganagobie show the range of influences that is to be seen in Romanesque art as a whole. The intricately entwined patterns can be linked to the Celtic world, and the vigorously posed lions to that of the Persians. The charging knight has been identified with the Greek legendary hero Bellerophon, and the knight who transfixes a dragon with his lance, less surprisingly, with St George.

A Latin inscription round the mosaic in the sanctuary gives the names both of the prior who ordered the mosaics – Bertrand – and of the craftsman-monk who was responsible for them – Pierre Trutbert.

In so far as there is a dominant theme, it is the struggle against evil and sin, which are represented by the dragons and other monsters. But as so frequently in Romanesque art, there is much that is purely decorative, or visually striking, and the mosaicists seem to have been influenced by the embroideries and carpets brought back from the Near East by the Crusaders, with their fantastic beasts and elaborate patterns.

There is a great deal to enjoy in the detail. It is noticeable that the two elephants have ox-like bodies, apart from their trunks, and carry small turret-like structures like those used by rulers in the East. The lion and lioness, which are snarling at each other, have the tips of their tails twisted into formal patterns. A satyr is prancing in front of the charging knight, and a fox is peering out from between the dragon's claws. The centaur, too, has a bovine body. And a harpy is riding on the elongated neck of a bird, while surrounded by a snake. Such is the power of the Romanesque imagination.

Montmajour

The former abbey of Montmajour has a dominant position on a hilltop a short way from Arles (see page 282), from where it is clearly visible, and the towering cluster of buildings that survives is a sight for miles around.

The buildings date from several different periods, including the eighteenth century. At their heart is a tall Romanesque church erected in Provençal style in the second half of the twelfth century, together with a cloister from the same period and a slightly earlier crypt.

Both the church itself and the crypt draw on Roman models in the region for their construction techniques, and they have the immaculate stonework that is characteristic of twelfth-century

Abbey church of Montmajour: the 'chevet'

Provence. The crypt alone is a masterpiece of engineering, constructed on the sloping rock and still in perfect condition today. The cloister is on a smaller scale with an intimacy that contrasts with the grandeur of the other buildings, as well as some excellent capitals.

There are also two other smaller buildings at Montmajour, both of them linked to the abbey and both of great interest. There is a tiny eleventh-century church dedicated to St Peter, a simple, atmospheric place that was built into the rock on the south side of the hill long before the main church; while a few hundred yards down the hill is the enchanting chapel of Ste-Croix, dating from the twelfth century, that has a Greek-style central plan.

In its day, Montmajour was one of the richest and most powerful abbeys in Provence. Its hilltop site was an ancient one that had been settled since prehistoric times, and it is strange to think that even in medieval times it was still an island surrounded by marshes and only accessible by boat. It had long been used as a cemetery, and the abbey buildings are surrounded by empty tombs that were dug into the bare rock – and gave rise to the legend that they held the bodies of soldiers of Charlemagne killed fighting the Saracens.

It seems that the island was also used as a refuge by Christian hermits, especially during unstable times in the ninth and tenth centuries. In the middle of the tenth century a regular monastic community was set up there by a local benefactress known only as Teucinde, and it was patronized by other leading figures of the region, including for a time the Counts of Provence. The abbey became increasingly prosperous, partly because of that, and partly because, at a time when pilgrimages were popular, it claimed possession of a piece of the True Cross.

The little church of St-Pierre is the oldest building, and can be reached by a stone staircase down the outside edge of the rock. The church has a nave of three bays, with a simply built round barrel vault, leading to a choir and apse; while along its north side, beyond some sturdy pillars, is an aisle that is built into the rock, and has bare stone for its vault as well as its floor. Light comes in through a few small windows on the south side of the nave.

A point of special interest is that in between the main apse and the chapel at the east end of the aisle a narrow passage leads to what was once a primitive hermitage – a few basic chambers hollowed out of the rock. According to legend, this was the refuge of St Trophime (see page 284), the missionary who introduced Christianity to Provence, probably in the third century; but in any case it was evidently used by hermits before the abbey was founded.

The church was probably completed towards the end of the first half of the eleventh century. It has a handful of column capitals that are remarkable for their

formal patterns, based on floral designs,
and there is a singular carved pillar near
the passage to the hermitage, also with
floral patterns.

Up above, the interior of the main
church of Montmajour, built well over
a century later at the height of the
abbey's prosperity, is the product of a
different world. The nave was never
completed, and is missing three western
bays that it should have had. But even
so it is a fine structure, tall and wide
with a pointed barrel vault – and
although like other churches built in
Provençal style it has minimal decoration, the stonework is beautifully cut.

The transept crossing was rebuilt
later in Gothic style, but the two arms
of the transept have the round barrel

Montmajour: transept crossing and apse

vaults of the Romanesque period, and so do the little chapels on their east side.
There is also a wide apse in Romanesque style with the design that is common in
Provence, where flat stone ribs divide it into segments.

The upper church has no ambulatory but the crypt has one. To reach it, you
walk down over the bare rock which makes up much of its floor. The crypt, too,
was never completed, but it is vast and cavernous, with round barrel vaulting over
the nave, the two arms of the transept and the ambulatory, and with every piece of
stone perfectly cut and fitted. The inspiration for these powerful structures came
from the Roman amphitheatres still to be seen in Provence.

To provide for the many pilgrims, each arm of the crypt's transept had a chapel
on its eastern side; and five more chapels radiate out from the ambulatory. At the
centre of the ambulatory is a rotunda, with the altar in the middle and windows
through which the pilgrims could look in.

The abbey's cloister, alongside the upper church, was constructed over a long
period, and is dominated by a tall, crenellated tower, known as the Pons de l'Orme
tower, which was put up in the fourteenth century. But work began on the cloister
at the same time as the main abbey church, and its basic form dates from the second half of the twelfth century.

It is a harmonious design, in which broad relieving arches, divided by solid buttresses that are sometimes fluted, enclose rows of smaller arches, each decorated with column capitals. There is a well on the south side, and this, together with the oleanders which have been planted in recent years, makes the cloister a picturesque and peaceful place.

One feature is the series of corbels placed under the transverse arches that support the vaults inside each of the galleries. They include monsters devouring humans, heads of animals and a range of vigorous designs.

Only the eastern gallery has capitals dating from the twelfth century. They are similar to those in the cloister of St-Trophime in Arles (see page 282), and have the same charm, although they are less ambitious. They consist mainly of formal floral designs, sometimes including human masks; but one has the scene of the Temptation of Christ together with a malevolent-looking devil, and on the far side a small human figure struggling in a circle of tendrils.

Overall, Montmajour is an imposing, and even massive, place, and this applies in particular to the *chevet* seen from outside. Unlike Romanesque *chevets* in other parts of France, where there is a complex pyramidal structure related to the various component parts of the building, that at Montmajour, as elsewhere in Provence, is tall and relatively plain. Its walls of well-cut stonework have only a few decorative windows and, at their base, the ring formed by the chapels radiating off the ambulatory in the crypt.

There is nothing massive, on the other hand, about the chapel of Ste-Croix, built for pilgrims who had come to Montmajour to venerate the True Cross, or rather that part of it held by

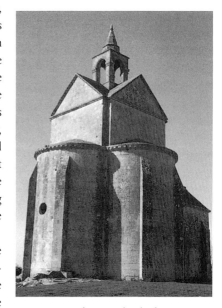

Montmajour: pilgrimage church of Ste-Croix

the abbey. Unfortunately, visitors may not go inside it, but they can see this simple, beautifully proportioned building from the outside, and peer through the grille in the doorway.

Ste-Croix too stands in the middle of an ancient cemetery, and is surrounded by tombs cut into the rock. It has a flower-like pattern formed by four small apses, each built onto one side of a high central square. Above them are four triangular pediments, and at the top is a tiny open belfry with a turret. A rectangular vestibule to the east, with a round arch over the doorway, provides the entry to the chapel.

As elsewhere at Montmajour, the masterly stonework is one of the most telling features of the chapel. But there is also some delicate decoration when you look closer: skilful carving under the cornices of the four apses, with formal patterns based on floral and other motifs.

St-Gilles-du-Gard

St-Gilles-du-Gard is a pleasant little town with the atmosphere of the past in its older streets, and all of it bathed in the clear sunlight of the Mediterranean – the sea is only a few miles away across the Camargue. In Romanesque times it was a far more important, bustling place since it was both an international trading port and one of the great pilgrimage centres, and the grandeur of its past is reflected in the remains of its abbey church.

The west façade is largely intact, though badly damaged, and is one of the most inspired of the Romanesque period, partly for its overall design, and partly for its range of sculpture. It is noticeably different from, say, the façade of Notre-Dame-

Abbey church of St-Gilles-du-Gard: the west front

la-Grande in Poitiers (see page 223), because the influence of Roman architecture is so strong; but both the subject-matter and its treatment are of the twelfth century, making it a combination of the classical and the medieval.

The classical influence comes, as frequently in the south of France, from the strong Roman presence in the region, which lasted for several centuries. It shows in the deep rounded arches over the three portals, reminiscent of a Roman triumphal arch, in the use of free-standing columns, topped by capitals made up of acanthus leaves, and in much of the detailed decoration – egg-and-dart friezes, rosettes, meander patterns.

Some of the scenes on the big frieze that runs the whole length of the façade, such as Jesus's triumphant ride into Jerusalem followed by the crowd of Apostles, or the long line of participants sitting behind the table at the Last Supper, show an even earlier influence, that of Athens of the fifth century BC, and the Parthenon in particular.

But the subject-matter in St-Gilles is, of course, Christian and medieval, and so is the emotion with which the sculptured figures are charged. There is an intensity of feeling in the sculpture that is purely Romanesque – in the Adoration of the Magi, for instance, in Jesus's washing of Peter's feet, and the kiss of Judas – and that is also true of the expressions and attitudes of the full-length statues of Apostles and saints that flank the main portal.

Romanesque, too, is the wealth of animal and plant life that makes up much of the detail on the façade – not just the acanthus leaves, but carefully worked floral and leaf patterns and, running below parts of the main frieze, small processions of lions, bulls and other animals, including a snake and even some human faces. The whole work has been interpreted as, among other things, a hymn to the Tree of Eternal Life.

The tragedy is that so much of it has been disfigured, chiefly the human faces – something that was clearly done deliberately. The three tympana, in particular, have been badly damaged, but one can imagine the power they must have had when they were intact.

Much or all of the central tympanum is in fact a seventeenth-century replacement, made necessary by the damage caused during the Wars of Religion in the previous century. It is often described as showing Christ in Majesty, surrounded by the symbols of the four evangelists (see page 263). But it has also been suggested that it represents a vision in the book of Daniel, in which the Ancient of Days is seen sitting on a throne surrounded by flames.

The left-hand tympanum is the best preserved of the three, and is full of grace and movement. The Virgin Mary sits in the middle with the infant Jesus on her knee, while on one side the three Magi offer their gifts – one of them pointing to the star in the sky – and on the other an angel swoops down to admonish Joseph in his dream.

The right-hand tympanum has the Crucifixion, and the interpretation of part of that, too, is disputed. Mary and John stand on either side of the cross, and to the left are the remains of a group in which two people, possibly the centurion and another soldier, gesture towards the crucified Christ. To the right is a vivid scene in which a female figure is toppled over, pushed by an angel, and a formal crown is falling from her head. The figure has often been interpreted as representing the Jewish synagogue, but it is also argued that she is a symbol of outside powers in general.

The frieze that runs under and between the tympana is, on the whole, in better condition, and has some of the liveliest scenes, vigorously modelled. They include Christ riding into Jerusalem and driving the merchants out of the temple, his prediction to Peter of the latter's denial of him, the Last Supper, the Flagellation, Mary Magdalene prostrate before Christ, and the Three Holy Women first buying spices and then taking them to the empty tomb.

Below are the statues of the Apostles and saints, with St Peter and St John on one side of the central door, and St James the Greater and St Paul on the other, all

West front of St-Gilles-du-Gard: the kiss of Judas

standing on lions that are devouring
human figures. And under them are
more carvings, some symbolic – a
dromedary with two chained monkeys,
for example – and some biblical.

An especially engaging scene, full of
movement, shows Cain and Abel making their offerings to Jehovah, followed
by another of Cain's murder of Abel.
Others have David being summoned by
an angel from the fields, where he is
playing his lyre while watching over his
sheep, and, later, his beheading of the
huge prostrate Goliath.

Altogether there is a great variety of
subjects and, in spite of the damage
done to them, they show how far Romanesque sculpture had advanced by
the second half of the twelfth century

West front of St-Gilles-du-Gard: an Apostle

when the façade is thought to have been completed.

St-Gilles took its name, and its appeal, from Aegidius, or Gilles, a healer and
miracle-worker who was born in Greece in the seventh century and came to live in
the south of Gaul. Almost everything that is known about him is legendary. The
story goes that at one time he was living as a hermit in a cave with a doe as his only
companion. The king of the country, a Visigoth, was out hunting one day, and one
of his huntsmen shot an arrow at the doe but hit Gilles by mistake and wounded
him.

The king realized what had happened and, by way of compensation, founded
an abbey in the area of which Gilles became the abbot. There Gilles worked his
miracles, and the miracles continued after his death around 720 when he was
buried in the abbey church. His tomb became a pilgrimage centre.

The abbey suffered during the turmoil of the succeeding centuries, not least the
outbreaks of fighting caused by dynastic rivalries in the region, now known as
Languedoc. But it survived, and it seems that it came into its own after 1066 when
like many others it was affiliated to the abbey of Cluny (see page 61), which reformed it along Benedictine lines. The link was brought about by Raymond IV,
Count of Toulouse, who had St-Gilles within his sphere of influence, and who
transferred his rights there to St Hugh, one of the great abbots of Cluny.

The Cluniacs set about building a new church, and its altar was consecrated in 1096 by Pope Urban II, in the same year as another pilgrimage church, also part of the Cluniac system, St-Eutrope in Saintes (see page 232). But building continued in St-Gilles well into the next century, and the west front was one of the last parts to be completed, probably in the late twelfth century.

The twelfth century was the heyday of St-Gilles, both the town and the abbey. The town is near the little Rhône and the network of canals connected to it, and it was an important port in those days, linked to the Mediterranean. It became a flourishing commercial centre, with an international fair that was frequented by traders from around Europe and the Mediterranean. It is known, for instance, to have had more than a hundred money-changers, who formed their own corporation.

For pilgrims, there were other attractions, and the town was one of the busiest pilgrimage centres in France. There was the tomb of St Gilles. There was the possibility of taking a ship to Rome or Jerusalem, the two principal shrines of those days. Last but not least, St-Gilles lay on one of the main pilgrim routes to Santiago de Compostela (see page 39), which began in Arles and, after St-Gilles, went on to Toulouse and the Pyrenees.

This affluence did not last long. Like other southern towns, St-Gilles was devastated during the Albigensian war of the thirteenth century when armies from the north of France stormed across the whole region, and the port then lost its trade to the new town of Aigues Mortes, founded on the coast by Louis IX. The numbers of pilgrims also dropped drastically.

There was further damage to the abbey, and to its church in particular, during the Wars of Religion of the sixteenth and seventeenth centuries. Most of the Romanesque church was destroyed, and it was replaced in the middle of the seventeenth century by a much smaller Gothic building of no particular distinction that still survives.

But the Romanesque west façade is also more or less as it was, and so is the crypt, which dates back to the late eleventh and early twelfth century. There are also substantial remains to the east of the existing church that show how much larger and more sumptuous the original church was.

The crypt is one of those moving survivals – like the crypt of St-Eutrope in Saintes – that convey the aura of medieval devotion. It is inevitably dark, but this adds to the atmosphere; and it has the tomb of St Gilles, which the pilgrims came to see. The crypt is in fact a substantial lower church in its own right, with its own nave and side-aisles, all covered by low and powerful vaulting, borne on massive columns.

There is even rib vaulting, with a zigzag pattern on the ribs and a small head of

Christ in the centre, over one of the bays of the nave. The area of the tomb has groin vaulting, while to the south of it is probably the oldest part of the crypt, with barrel vaulting. There, carefully preserved, is another tomb of historical interest: that of Pierre de Castelnau, a legate of Pope Innocent III whose murder in 1208 not far from St-Gilles was one of the incidents that led to the outbreak of the Albigensian war.

Up above, the remains of the church's original east end are also atmospheric, but in a different way. They have been excavated, and now lie in an open space to the east of the later building, with a cluster of trees. They show the stone bases of the choir, the ambulatory and the chapels that radiated off it, as well as some sarcophagi that were uncovered during the excavations.

The dominant sight is a towering section of the old church that has the beginnings of some decorative arches, some attractive carved capitals, and part of a circular window or oculus. It is best known for containing a spiral staircase, known as the 'Vis de Saint-Gilles', which originally provided access to the upper parts of the church. It is a most ingenious structure that has been studied by budding architects ever since for the way in which its stone steps were carved and fitted.

Not far away is a poignant relic of the past: the carving of a tiny human figure whose foot is caught under the base of a column. It is presumably a tribute to a workman killed in an accident centuries ago while the church was being built.

Saintes-Maries-de-la-Mer

The Romanesque church built in Saintes-Maries-de-la-Mer in the second half of the twelfth century was a simple one by the standards of the times. But few churches were so heavily fortified; and Saintes-Maries is an inviting little town which is interesting both for its setting, by the sea on the outer edge of the vast Camargue waterland, and for the fact that it is a pilgrimage centre for the Roma people.

Like many others, the church was from the beginning required to fulfil both a religious and a defensive function, and that accounts for its castle-like appearance. Saintes-Maries was once further from the sea than it is now but it was still exposed to attacks by pirates, including Saracens in the ninth and tenth centuries, and the church was the central rallying point where the inhabitants took refuge when attacks were made.

The fortifications round the upper part of the church, which are the most

Fortified church of Stes-Maries-de-la-Mer: the 'chevet'

prominent feature, date mainly from
the fourteenth century. But the solid
walls built in the twelfth century, of
pink and ochre stone which glows in
the Mediterranean sunlight, and with
only a handful of tiny windows, still
stand. So, significantly, is the well from
which the besieged townspeople could
draw water – in the nave.

In spite of this military role, however, and the lack of light, the church
has a stylish interior in Provençal style,
with a pointed barrel vault with transverse arches over the nave, leading to
a short choir and an apse. And it has
one feature that stands out: a ring of
blind arches below the apse whose
marble columns have eight meticulously
worked capitals.

Stes-Maries-de-la-Mer: the south side

Most of the capitals have formalized foliage with human masks or busts in the
middle, similar to those in the cloister of St-Trophime in Arles (see page 282). But
two are historiated, one depicting the events surrounding the Incarnation, including the Annunciation and the Visitation, and the other Abraham's proposed
sacrifice of Isaac.

On the outside the *chevet* has Lombard bands, the decorative arrangement
of blind arches that was common in early Romanesque (see page 18), and a
single window, pleasingly framed by a round arch and two marble columns. A
blocked-up doorway on the south side is flanked by two very worn statues of
lions.

Perhaps because of its position, Saintes-Maries-de-la-Mer is enveloped by
legends, and one in particular has persisted. According to this the two Maries, one
the mother of John and James the Greater and the other of James the Less, were
cast ashore nearby, together with Sarah, their servant, and other Christians. They
had all been put out to sea aboard a boat without sails or oars by the Jews of
Jerusalem, and were brought to the Provençal coast by divine guidance.

The two Maries and Sarah remained in Saintes-Maries, according to the legend,
and in due course were buried there. At some point their relics were hidden under
the choir to protect them from raiders. Then in 1448, in the presence of King René,

Count of Provence, the floor of the choir was excavated, and the relics were discovered.

René ordered the building of the crypt, in which the relics of St Sarah are now
displayed, and the lengthening of the nave by the addition of two extra bays at the
western end. The relics of the two Maries were put into the chapel high above the
choir, which was once the guardroom.

This enlarged the original Romanesque church, and since then the church has
been a pilgrimage centre, particularly for the Roma, as I have said, who regard
St Sarah as their patron, and there are Roma ceremonies in May and October.

Cistercian abbeys in Provence:
Sénanque, Silvacane and Le Thoronet

They are known as the Three Sisters, and they certainly have a strong family
resemblance: Sénanque, Silvacane and Le Thoronet, three well-preserved and fascinating Cistercian abbeys in Provence. All three were mainly built in the second
half of the twelfth century, very likely to plans by the same master builder or architect, and all three have the pure lines and immaculate stonework that were the
mark of Provençal building of the time.

They also have the distinctive architectural style found in many twelfth-century
Cistercian abbeys – most noticeably in their broad naves covered by slightly
pointed barrel vaulting – and, above all, their Cistercian austerity (see page 33).
The order banned the use of decorative features such as figured capitals, sculptured
tympana, paintings or mosaics, in its monasteries, and so the three Provençal abbeys, like those elsewhere, relied on the beauty of their lines to make their impact.

A few concessions were made – mainly formalized plant patterns on column
capitals – and these are to be found, in different places, in the three abbeys. But the
outstanding features of all three are the forms and proportions of these plain
unadorned churches, as well as of the other monastic buildings such as the chapterhouses and dormitories, while their cloisters have a simple intimacy.

All three abbeys are also in pleasantly rural settings. The Cistercians deliberately
sought out remote spots for their monasteries, as we have seen, insisting only on
a good supply of water so that they could clear and work the surrounding fields.
Sénanque is in a particularly dramatic position on the floor of a steep-sided valley,
watered by the little river Sénancole, where it is now surrounded by fields of
lavender – and it can be seen from above from the road that descends one side of
the valley.

Cistercian abbey of Sénanque, from the north-east

Silvacane is in a more accessible spot near the river Durance, but was once surrounded by marshes, as is indicated by its name, which means 'forest of reeds'. Le Thoronet, more typically, is still encircled by woods near a stream that flows into the river Argens.

The three churches are of similar dimensions. Their naves are flanked by side-aisles, and they all have transepts, also with pointed barrel vaulting. At both Sénanque and Le Thoronet, where building began at the same time in about 1160, there is an apse over the sanctuary, and two small chapels, also with apses, on either side. Sénanque has a rare decorative feature at the transept crossing: an octagonal cupola resting on squinches which are patterned, with a small fluted pilaster set into the stonework below.

Another untypical feature of Sénanque is that, presumably because of the lie of the land in the Sénancole valley, the nave runs from south to north, rather than from west to east as was normal in medieval times, so that the sanctuary is in the north end of the church, not the east.

Silvacane was built some years later than Sénanque and Le Thoronet, between 1170 and 1230, and the interior of its church is in some ways the most beautiful of the three. It has no apse at the east end: just a flat wall with a pleasing arrangement of windows, and flat walls in the side-chapels, too. But the proportions of the nave and its carefully planned articulation, with engaged columns embedded in pilasters and resting on brackets ten feet above the level of the floor, give it a special appeal.

The relatively late date of the church is shown by the fact that the transept crossing has rib vaulting – the technique that was first developed by Romanesque builders but later became one of the distinctive features of Gothic (see page 10).

Silvacane also has a west front that is more developed than the corresponding façades of the other two, a harmonious arrangement of windows and doorways, topped by a gable, which makes a stately sight as one walks up the gentle slope on which it stands.

Cistercian abbey of Silvacane: the nave

By way of contrast, it is the *chevets* of Sénanque and Le Thoronet, in the north and east respectively, which have the greater impact. At Sénanque the apse and, above it, the cupola and a small square bell-tower, all of them covered by slates made of local stone, are a sight to remember when seen across the lavender field, with the wooded side of the valley high above them.

At Le Thoronet there is no cupola but there is a taller, more sharply pointed bell-tower, and the apse is covered by the rounded clay pantiles of Provence. That too makes an inspiring picture when seen against the light green leaves and the red earth of an olive-grove.

All three abbeys have a range of monastic buildings that are set out according to a broadly similar plan. The three chapterhouses are vaulted in near-Gothic style, with the arches springing from two central pillars – on which there are capitals with formal, engagingly naive designs. Sénanque has a warming-room with a fireplace and a stout central column with a decorated capital where the monks used to work at copying manuscripts.

Some of the grandest rooms are the three great dormitories, which are long and high, with barrel vaulting. Each of them originally had a staircase down to the cloister, and another that led down into the church.

The cloister was the focal point of any abbey where the monks read and

Cistercian abbey of Le Thoronet, from the south-east

meditated, and all three Provençal cloisters are peaceful places today, with formal gardens at their centre and glimpses of the rural surroundings beyond the walls. The Cistercian view, put forcibly by St Bernard of Clairvaux (see page 33), was that monks should not be distracted by 'ridiculous monsters', 'unclean apes', 'fierce lions', 'monstrous centaurs' and so on, and so there are none of the wilder flights of fancy of Romanesque sculptors.

At Sénanque, however, there are some shapely capitals based on floral and plant designs, and they make a contrast to the austerity of the church. In Provençal style, the cloister has broad relieving arches that spring from solid pillars on each of its four sides, and within each of those arches a set of three smaller arches, supported by pairs of columns.

There is also a diabolical head, with horns and bared teeth, that has been carved on the inside of one of the walkways of the cloister, opposite the entrance to the chapterhouse, and this must have been placed there deliberately as a reminder to the monks to remain on their guard.

The cloister at Silvacane is plainer and less well preserved, with some larger arches more or less intact, but little left of the smaller arches that filled the space within them. But it has great charm, and has the remains of a Gothic-style fountain and a handful of floral carvings.

Sénanque: the cloister

Because of the sloping ground, the cloisters at both Silvacane and Le Thoronet had to be built on different levels, with steps leading from one to the other. Le Thoronet's also has an irregular shape for the same reason. There too the cloister is mostly plain, but it has been much restored and in the process has been given some floral capitals that are similar to those elsewhere in the abbey. They sit on stocky columns which each support an oculus and twin arches within a range of broader arches.

This cloister, too, has great appeal. A distinctive feature is the well-preserved little building, covered by a Moorish-style rib vault, which was used by the monks for their ablutions. It has a still functional fountain from which water pours down into two large circular stone bowls, one above the other.

Roussillon and Languedoc

Roussillon is a notably spectacular region since it has the eastern Pyrenees as a backdrop. It and the nearby parts of Languedoc have some of the earliest Romanesque churches in France, often in beautiful settings, and Roussillon also has some exceptional sculpture, much of it carved in the marble that is found in the foothills of the Pyrenees.

One Roussillon church, at the former abbey of St-Michel-de-Cuxa, is even regarded as pre-Romanesque because it was built towards the end of the tenth century and has exotic-seeming horseshoe arches that date from that period.

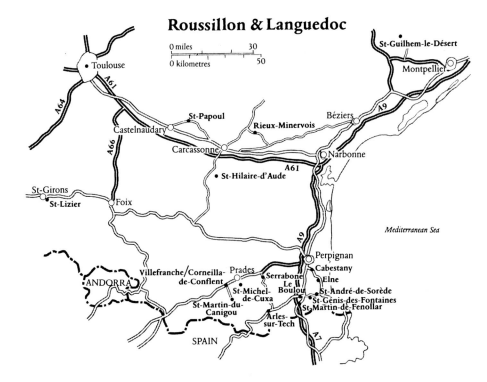

Roussillon & Languedoc

Cuxa's cloister is incomplete but like other churches in the region it still has excellent capitals, carved in marble, that date from the twelfth century.

The Romanesque period was a relatively prosperous time for Roussillon, when it had close links to what is now Spanish Catalonia, and that accounts for the presence of numerous churches in the First Romanesque style on both sides of the Pyrenees (see page 17). Roussillon only became French in 1659 under the terms of the Treaty of the Pyrenees.

St-Martin-du-Canigou, which is tucked away in a remote mountain setting, has an early stone vault over its nave, as well as many other features of the First Romanesque: three apses in its *chevet*, the 'Lombard bands' of shallow blind arches, and a square bell-tower with tiers of round arches. The cathedral in Elne, though modified over the years, was originally in the same style; and both churches have some marvellous capitals of the twelfth century.

The First Romanesque is also found further north, in Languedoc. In the gorges of the river Hérault there is another church in a distant mountain area, St-Guilhem-le-Désert, which was a pilgrimage centre in its own right, and was also on the pilgrim route to Santiago de Compostela that began in Arles (see page 39). It has a mostly eleventh-century church, with a superb *chevet*.

Painting must once have been an important feature of the region's churches, as it was elsewhere, but very little of it has survived. There are, however, some moving frescoes in the little chapel of St-Martin-de-Fenollar that date from the first half of the twelfth century, and they give an indication of what has been lost.

Sculpture, on the other hand, has survived, and it had early beginnings in Roussillon due, no doubt, to the availability of marble. St-Génis-des-Fontaines, south of Perpignan, has a naive but vivid lintel firmly dated to 1019-1020, and there are similar works at St-André-de-Sorède, a few miles away, and at Arles-sur-Tech.

From the middle of the twelfth century there are also the moving and distinctive works of a sculptor known as the Master of Cabestany. He has been given this name because his best-known work is a marble tympanum in Cabestany, outside Perpignan. But several other works in Roussillon and Languedoc have been attributed to him.

Some of the region's most striking sculpture is in an original style that was developed in the twelfth century and that used a marble with pink colouring which is mined in the Conflent area, in the upper reaches of the river Tet. This is the style, and the marble, that is found at St-Michel-de-Cuxa and St-Martin-du-Canigou, and also in some exquisite capitals in the churches of Corneilla-de-Conflent and Villefranche-de-Conflent.

Perhaps the most thrilling of them all is the remote little church of Serrabone, which seems quite simple outside, but has an amazing array of carving inside, on a marble tribune that stretches across the nave, as well as in an open gallery on its south side.

There are to be seen lions and eagles, centaurs and griffins, saints and angels, all skilfully posed in the middle of various formal patterns – and creating one of the most fascinating ensembles of the Romanesque period.

The Master of Cabestany: Cabestany, St-Hilaire-d'Aude, St-Papoul, Rieux-Minervois, Le Boulou

The tympanum of the mysterious Master of Cabestany is a powerful and original work which has a place of its own in the history of Romanesque church sculpture. It is preserved in a pleasant little church, mainly of a later date, in the small town of Cabestany. It has three scenes relating to the Virgin Mary: at the centre, her glorification by Christ, beside whom she stands; on one side, her resurrection from the tomb; on the other, her Assumption, when she is taken up to Heaven.

The tympanum would have been intended for the space above a church door, but may or may not have originally been carved for Cabestany. Until the early twentieth century it was embedded in an outer wall of the nave, but it was removed from there and is now free-standing inside the church.

It is a moving and, for the period, unconventional work, and it is one of a number in a similar style, some found as far afield as Italy and Spain, that are attributed to the Master of Cabestany. Nothing is recorded about him. However, the style of the various works is so marked that they are generally thought to have been carved by a single man, or at least by a team working with him, probably in the middle of the twelfth century.

In the Cabestany tympanum, Christ, a forceful, rather grim figure, dominates the scene, with an adoring Mary on one side and a defiant St Thomas on the other. The three figures form a compelling group, and demonstrate some of the features of the Master of Cabestany's style: expressive faces in which the eyes are emphasized by two holes drilled one on either side of the eyeball; carefully carved, flowing drapery; and, for Christ and Mary, exceptionally large hands.

The presence of Thomas is uncommon, but he is holding a belt or sash, and that is a clear reference to the story, current at the time, that he had doubted Mary's

Cabestany: Assumption of Virgin Mary, by Master of Cabestany

resurrection, as he had earlier doubted that of Christ himself, and had received her sash from the sky by way of proof.

The scenes on either side are equally moving and characteristic. On the left, Christ raises Mary solicitously from her tomb, watched by the heads of six angels and, at the bottom, St Peter and St John. On the right, Mary is wafted up to heaven, with her eyes closed, inside a mandorla carried by angels, two of whom sprinkle incense over her.

The calm and beauty of Mary in her mandorla, her long hands spread out over her robe, contrast with the boyish vigour of the angels who, in addition to their accentuated eyes, have the low foreheads and high ears favoured by the Master of Cabestany. The whole tympanum seems almost modern in the bold, expressive manner in which traditional themes are presented.

Most of the works attributed to the Master of Cabestany are found in a region including Languedoc, Roussillon and, across the Pyrenees, Catalonia, all of which were politically and culturally linked in the Middle Ages. So although he has sometimes been thought to have been of Italian origin, it seems just as likely that he came from that region, and was influenced by the sculptors of Toulouse and Roussillon, as well as by surviving works in classical style from late Roman times.

He must have travelled to both Italy and Spain, possibly following the pilgrim routes to Rome and Santiago de Compostela. There is sculpture that is attributed to him in the abbey church of Sant' Antimo, near Siena, and in the museum of San Casciano, Val di Pesa, outside Florence; and a tympanum and lintel from Errondo, near Pamplona, which are now in The Cloisters museum in New York, are also thought to be his.

One of his most arresting works, which demonstrates how he drew on classical models, can be seen not far from Cabestany. It is a marble altar, designed in the form of a sarcophagus – like many to be found in cemeteries dating back to the Roman period – which is in the church of the abbey of **St-Hilaire-d'Aude**, south of Carcassonne.

It is a powerful piece of carving, which illustrates the martyrdom of St Saturninus, or St Sernin as he was known in the local dialect of Toulouse (see page 276). St Sernin was the first Bishop of Toulouse, who was put to death in the third century by being tethered to the hooves of a bull and dragged across the city, as we have seen.

The event is graphically presented in two scenes on the front of the altar. On the right, the bishop is arrested by a group of tough-looking men, while people's heads peer out from what is presumably the Capitol, the seat of government in Roman Toulouse. On the left, the bull, maddened by a lance being driven into its

St-Hilaire-d'Aude: arrest of St Sernin, by Master of Cabestany

St-Hilaire-d'Aude: martyrdom of St Sernin, by Master of Cabestany

hide, leaps across the scene, nostrils flared, and pulls St Sernin, who is noticeably calm and raises his hand to bless two watching women, behind it.

There are two other scenes on the short sides of the altar, though they are less easy to see. On the right is a formal group: St Sernin flanked by two disciples, St Papoul and St Honest, who succeeded him as Bishop of Toulouse. On the left is another poignant scene, in which the body of St Sernin is being placed in a tomb, while a woman caresses his head and a small human figure, representing his soul, is carried up to heaven by an angel.

There is much else in this very original altar: angels sprinkling incense on St Sernin's tomb as he is buried, women bringing perfumes and, on the front, a strange array of human and animal heads peering out from under the main actors. It is full of movement and demonstrates the skill of the Master of Cabestany in creating dramatic scenes filled with a wealth of detail.

There are two more places in the Carcassonne area where he worked, both peaceful villages: St-Papoul to the north-west and Rieux-Minervois to the northeast. The abbey church of **St-Papoul** has a Romanesque bell-tower and *chevet*, and the Master of Cabestany is thought to have carved two elaborate capitals on the outside of the apse, as well as several of the singular corbels supporting the cornice that have animal and human heads on them.

The two capitals are small, but they are carved with the same graphic vigour as the sculptor's larger works. One shows Daniel in the lions' den surrounded by snarling beasts and gratefully seizing the food brought to him by Habakkuk. The other has more ferocious lions who are devouring several people, and is thought to represent the punishment later meted out to the Babylonians for what they had done.

The church in **Rieux-Minervois** is itself a rarity because in its initial Romanesque form it was circular, or rather polygonal, with fourteen short sides and an inner ring of seven round arches topped by a cupola. This original part of the church survives, although chapels were added later that radiate outwards, and it is a very satisfying design that gives a foretaste of the Renaissance. The church still has in its outer ring fourteen capitals thought to have been carved by the Master of Cabestany, or at least by masons working under his direction.

The outstanding one, which must have been his own work, is another representation of the Assumption of the Virgin Mary. She is a slight, girlish figure, with folding drapery and elongated hands; and she is again within a mandorla, which is being raised by vigorous young angels, with her eyes closed. Above her head is an ornate abacus, with intertwined tendrils emerging from the mouths of two monsters.

Corbel on 'chevet' of St-Papoul: Daniel in the lions' den, by Master of Cabestany

Several of the other capitals in the
outer ring take the theme of the
Corinthian capital, with the acanthus as
its main feature, and develop it; and
they have a rare beauty. But there is also
one that has two pairs of posed lions,
all with well-cut manes, and with each
pair sharing a snarling muzzle at the
corner of the capital.

The main entrance to the Romanesque church of Rieux-Minervois was
by a doorway on the west side. This
was subsequently enclosed by a vaulted
chamber, now used for the organ, but
there are still some fascinating Romanesque capitals, thought to be possibly
by the Master of Cabestany, on either
side of the doorway. On one side they
have Corinthian-style designs, on the

*Rieux-Minervois: Assumption of Virgin Mary,
by Master of Cabestany*

Rieux-Minervois: capital by Master of
Cabestany

Rieux-Minervois: capital by Master of
Cabestany

other three distinctive subjects, all treated with the expressiveness and imagination of the Master.

One has two amiable-looking lions standing against a background of vegetation; another a more savage lion devouring an animal; and the third, in the centre, a peculiar subject found elsewhere in work attributed to the Master of Cabestany: three creatures whose arms apparently emerge from their heads are each blowing two long horns.

One of the most prominent capitals at Rieux-Minervois is a large one that is apart from the others, high up on one of the columns that form the church's central ring. Here again there are lions, formally posed with each pair sharing a muzzle, but on three of the sides there is a man standing forcefully between them and holding them apart – possibly Daniel or a 'master of animals'.

Down towards the Pyrenees there is another work attributed to the Master of Cabestany which is one of his most appealing, but which, because it is small and high up, is very hard to see. This is a frieze that runs above the doorway of the church of **Le Boulou**, a few miles south of Perpignan, and presents an engaging sequence of scenes from the events surrounding the birth of Christ.

The sequence begins on the right with the angel's announcement to the shep-

Rieux-Minervois: Daniel, or the 'master of animals', by Master of Cabestany

herds, their flock behind them, and continues with a Nativity scene. Then come the bathing of the infant Christ, the Adoration of the Magi, the Flight into Egypt and, finally, the Virgin and Child resting during the journey.

Binoculars are needed to see the frieze properly, or perhaps a ladder. But it is clear from photographs taken from close up that the subject-matter is treated with the emotional power of the Master of Cabestany, and also a sense of intimacy. The sculptor gives prominence, for instance, to the bathing of Christ, which is carried out by two kneeling women while Joseph sits nearby and holds the robe in which the infant will be dressed.

Similarly in the final scene Mary lies with the infant on her breast, and another woman, probably the servant seen elsewhere, lies beside her. Three people, including Joseph, watch over the sleepers.

The Nativity, the Adoration of the Magi and the Flight into Egypt are all compelling images. In the first, Mary seems overwhelmed by events as she lies cocooned in her robes, her eyes wide open and staring, while the infant Jesus, also cocooned, lies at an angle to her, the star above his head, and the ox and the ass look on. An angel can be seen under her bed blowing a horn.

Later, Mary sits on an ornate throne, with the servant behind her, as the Magi approach, and she holds out the child towards the first of them. The first of the Magi kneels wide-eyed, and an unknown person engages the other two in conversation. The three horses wait behind.

The Flight into Egypt is treated quite formally. In another realistic touch, Joseph is having to pull the donkey, but Mary is sitting side-saddle in the traditional pose of the Virgin in Majesty, with the child in her arms. A female onlooker stands behind in a position of prayer, and the servant brings up the rear, holding a spoon in one hand and a bowl in the other.

It is a good example of the ability of the Master of Cabestany to convey strong feeling and drama in his treatment of religious themes, with a touch of realism.

Corneilla-de-Conflent and Villefranche-de-Conflent

The mountainous region of Conflent, which surrounds the upper reaches of the river Tet in Roussillon, produced some of the best carving of the Romanesque period in the course of the twelfth century, most of it done in the local marble, with its pink colouring. As well as St-Michel-de-Cuxa (see page 338), Serrabone (see page 343) and St-Martin-du-Canigou (see page 335), there are good examples of it at two churches that are not far apart: Corneilla-de-Conflent and Villefranche-de-Conflent.

Corneilla-de-Conflent is an ancient town in a mountain setting where the counts of Cerdanya had a palace – part of which still stands. Its church has a majestic bell-tower, erected in the eleventh century in the First Romanesque style (see page 17). It also has a pretty *chevet* and a fine west front, both of which were added in the following century, and both have marble carving.

In those days the whole region was part of Catalonia, and the counts of neighbouring Cerdanya controlled Conflent. In 1025 they took over the jurisdiction of the church from the Bishop of Elne (see page 321), and some years later Guillaume-Raimond I, Count of Cerdanya from 1067 to 1095, gave instructions just before his death to his son, Guillaume-Jorda, to establish a college of

Corneilla-de-Conflent: capitals on west doorway

Augustinian canons that would be attached to the church. The canons arrived in 1097.

The bell-tower, therefore, dates from before the arrival of the college of canons, and it is similar to others elsewhere in Roussillon, constructed with small stones, neatly trimmed, with good examples of Lombard bands – the panels of tiny blind arches used as decoration.

The west front and the *chevet*, on the other hand, which were built many years later by the canons, are more ambitious, with large, regular blocks of granite into which the marble of the western doorway, the window above it, and the three windows of the *chevet* is set.

In the *chevet*, only the central apse extends beyond the eastern wall of the transept, but its decoration, which dates to 1150-75, is especially ornate. It has a ring of blind arches under the cornice, and ornamental archivolts with a variety of designs frame each of the windows. There are pairs of columns with capitals on either side of the windows, presenting a mixture of plant designs and fantastic animals, and the occasional human mask.

The capitals on the western doorway date from a few years later, the late twelfth century, and are complex and full of movement. Winged lions prance in pairs on their hind legs, sharing a head at the corners. So do rams. Meanwhile the faces of humans, and of monsters, peer out sardonically from the midst of it all. The carving is masterly – and one of the final achievements of the Romanesque marble workers of Roussillon.

As in other churches where they worked, few of the capitals have overtly religious themes. But there is also a rare feature at Corneilla-de-Conflent: a tympanum over the west doorway on which the Virgin Mary sits in the middle of a mandorla with the Infant Jesus on her lap, and a crouching angel swings a censer on either side.

The interior of the church is spacious, with harmonious proportions. A slightly pointed barrel vault covers the nave. Round arches, with some sturdy pillars between them, divide it from the aisles, which have half-barrel vaulting.

The nave dates mainly from the end of the eleventh century, when the canons rebuilt it. They added the transept, which has two small apsidal chapels on each of its arms, in the twelfth century, and also an attractive new sanctuary, with a central apse and three windows in the semi-circle below it. Each of the windows is enclosed in a pair of round arches, and has carved marble capitals over the columns.

Also in the sanctuary are three wooden statues of the Virgin and Child, all of them carved and painted in the Romanesque style, although at different periods. The most notable is the one on the left, known as the Virgin of Corneilla, which

was carved for the church in the second half of the twelfth century. It is a touching work, with sensitive handling of both mother and child.

Villefranche-de-Conflent is also linked to Count Guillaume-Raimond I, since
it was founded by him as a 'free town', like others of the same name elsewhere in
France, and granted a monopoly as a market for the surrounding area. It stands in
a strategic position on the bank of the Tet, and became the capital of Conflent.
Later, in the sixteenth century, it had walls built round it.

Those walls still stand, and Villefranche today has a charm of its own, with narrow streets that have views of the surrounding mountains at their end. Its church,
like its other medieval buildings, has been much changed over the centuries; but it
has two marble doorways, both now on its north side, that date back to the twelfth
century and that have some of the outstanding carved capitals made then.

Both doorways have the pinkish Conflent marble. As elsewhere in Conflent,
their capitals are a lively and complex mix of plant and animal motifs, with a few
human faces in the middle. There are lions, winged and otherwise, prancing and
snarling, and there is the ornamental vegetation that derives ultimately from the
acanthus of the Greeks and the Romans.

One of the most vivid images is of lions with their bodies bent in a bow shape
as they strain to gnaw at some prey lying on the ground. It is a motif that is also

Villefranche-de-Conflent: capitals on doorway on north side

found at St-Michel-de-Cuxa and Serrabone, and is characteristic of the marble-workers of Roussillon.

Elne

Elne was once the most important city in Roussillon, a fortified hilltop in a tumultuous region, and its cathedral dominates the surrounding area, its two bell-towers visible for miles around. It is a delightful old town with some colourful streets, and the cathedral, built in the eleventh century, is an interesting example of early Romanesque style, with some especially good twelfth-century capitals in the cloister.

Elne's name derives from St Helena, the mother of the Roman Emperor Constantine. It was originally a Celtic hill-town called Illiberis; but in the confusion of the sixth century, when the invading Visigoths had themselves been defeated by the Franks, but held onto that part of southern Gaul, it was given both a bishopric and a new name, Castrum Helenae. It lost the bishopric to Perpignan in the seventeenth century but kept the name.

Both the cathedral and the cloister have a family likeness to other Romanesque

Cloister of Elne cathedral: decorative capitals

buildings in Roussillon – and across the Pyrenees in Catalonia. Elne's two towers stand at either end of a mostly plain western façade, and while the smaller of them is a more recent addition, built in brick, the tall southern tower, mainly constructed in the eleventh century and in stone, is a handsome structure similar to those of St-Michel-de-Cuxa (see page 338) and St-Martin-du-Canigou (see page 335).

Like the others, it has tiers of arches one above the other on each of its four sides, some of them open and some blind, and all of them rounded. The tower was constructed over a period of time, and it is noticeable that the stone of the upper tiers, which were added some time later, is more finely cut.

The nave, too, was several years in the building, with changes of plan along the way. There are indications that when work began in the first half of the eleventh century, the intention was to have a timber roof and windows, but it was eventually given a barrel vault supported by transverse arches, together with half-barrels over the side-aisles, which it has today. The nave vault is rounded for the greater part of its length but pointed at the west end, which was built later. The aisles still have the arches that supported their original vaulting.

The change to a vault over the nave meant doing away with the windows, and as a result the body of the cathedral is dark. But its height and its proportions, and the articulation of its pillars, engaged columns and arches, create a balanced and stylish ensemble.

There are also some early capitals that date from the middle of the eleventh century, high up on the engaged columns at the eastern end of the cathedral. One has a tiny human figure with his arms raised; but mainly they are made up of formalized plant designs and patterns. And there is a carved Romanesque altarpiece, similar to others in south-western France, at the approach to the sanctuary.

There is no transept but a semi-circular apse over the sanctuary, whose windows were enlarged in the nineteenth century, and small chapels, each with an apse, on either side.

The cloister at Elne seems like a different world, and not just because it is bathed in light, compared with the dark inside the cathedral, and uses marble for its columns and capitals rather than stone. It was in fact built much later, beginning in the twelfth century, and only the capitals of the south gallery, which runs alongside the cathedral and was put up first, are properly Romanesque.

The other galleries came later, and all four galleries have Gothic vaulting inside them. But interestingly, the outer faces of the later ones are in a similar style to that of the south gallery, with sets of three round arches supported on columns and, between them, more substantial pillars; and many of their capitals are copies of those in the south gallery, though not of the same quality. So the cloister as a whole makes a pleasantly homogeneous impression, with the two towers standing over it.

The capitals in the south gallery have been dated to the final third of the twelfth century, and so were some of the last to be carved in Romanesque style by the marble workers of Roussillon, who created so many masterpieces, in Serrabone (see page 343), St-Michel-de-Cuxa, St-Martin-du-Canigou and elsewhere.

Some of the most interesting of them are the extensive scenes carved on the pillars, where there was more space than on a column capital. They show, for instance, the *Quo Vadis?* scene, in which St Peter meets Christ while fleeing from Rome and decides to return, and the conversion of St Paul on the road to Damascus; and in the panels above there are hideous snakes or dragons with long twisted tails. One of the pillars has beasts and birds standing in almost heraldic poses inside circular tendrils.

The columns are grouped in pairs, and have meticulously carved capitals with similar subjects to those elsewhere in Roussillon: lions either single or in pairs, sirens with double tails, a pair of rams, all set in the midst of decorative designs. Many of the capitals have plants and leaves in formal patterns. One has biblical scenes: the creation of Adam and Eve, and their act of disobedience in the Garden of Eden. The carving is vigorous, and they make an exhilarating array in a beautiful setting.

Elne cathedral: capital in cloister showing soldiers accompanying Saul, later St Paul, on road to Damascus

It is also worth stopping to look at two immaculate funerary marbles set into the wall at either end of the gallery, in each of which a recumbent figure, his arms crossed across his chest, is ministered to by angels. Both represent religious dignitaries, one of them a Bishop of Elne, and they have been attributed to the same artist, Raimond de Bianya, who worked in Romanesque style at the beginning of the thirteenth century.

There is one last point of interest in Elne. In the fourteenth century there was an ambitious plan to pull down the Romanesque *chevet* of the cathedral and replace it with a much larger Gothic structure. It was never completed, but the lower part of the new *chevet* was built, and can be seen on the outside of the cathedral, surrounding, but not replacing, the three Romanesque apses of the eleventh century.

St-Génis-des-Fontaines, St-André-de-Sorède and Arles-sur-Tech

The ancient village of **St-Génis-des-Fontaines**, not far from Perpignan, has a good view of the Pyrenees to the south. It also has one of the earliest works of Romanesque sculpture in France: a carved marble lintel over the west door of the church which shows Christ in Glory, flanked by angels and six of his Apostles, and has an inscription that, as I said earlier, is uncommon in that it gives a firm date – 1019-20.

It is a naive work but full of power and charm. The central figure of Christ is both vigorous and benign, seeming to lean forward from his seat with his right hand raised in blessing and his left holding the Bible, his eyes wide open and looking fixedly ahead. On either side of him is a kneeling angel with wings extended who strains to hold the mandorla in which Christ sits, while further along each of the Apostles has his own niche in a row of tiny arches.

Sculpture often played an important role in Romanesque architecture, being treated as an integral part of the design of a building, whether on the inside or the outside. This was true of the style in Roussillon as well, but with a difference, as the lintel in St-Génis shows.

I have mentioned that Roussillon had some of the earliest Romanesque architecture, in First Romanesque style, which was based on skilful stonework and the use of form and volume. But it also had marble and some talented workers in it, and they formed a separate group from the workers in stone, the masons. So it was the marblers who did the carving for a church like St-Génis rather than the masons, as was most common elsewhere.

Lintel of St-Génis-des-Fontaines: Christ in Glory

There is a similar lintel in the village of St-André-de-Sorède, only a few miles away, and another early work, in the form of a cross, in the old town of Arles-sur-Tech up in the foothills of the Pyrenees. Both these works are in marble.

The St-Génis lintel was clearly influenced by manuscript paintings, and is in very low relief, with only the beginnings of three-dimensionality. The features of the various figures, and their clothing, are outlined on a more or less flat surface, without conveying volume. But it is a beautifully balanced composition with a strong sense of movement at its centre, not just in the figure of Christ but in the two angels, who lean outwards, flexing their stylishly carved wings.

There is also a pretty border with a design of tendrils and leaf patterns.

The mandorla in which Christ sits is an irregular shape made up of two incomplete circles, both decorated with tiny pearl-like shapes and joined at the level of Christ's seat. According to the theology of the time, the upper, larger circle represents the supernatural sphere, and the lower one that of the earthly globe. Christ has the letters alpha and omega on either side of him; and the design is thought to make references both to the Ascension and to the promise of the Second Coming.

Interestingly, the arches under which the six Apostles stand are all horseshoe-shaped and provide a close-fitting frame for their haloes, just as the columns supporting the arches, each topped with a decorative capital, frame their bodies.

Horseshoe arches are also found elsewhere in Roussillon, at St-Michel-de-Cuxa (see page 338) and St-Martin-de-Fenollar (see page 333), and their use is thought to date back to the Visigoths.

The tiny figures each carry a book, presumably the Bible, and are engagingly naive, with formal robes, all of them carved differently. It appears that the first one to the right of Christ, with a fringe of hair and a beard, is St Peter, and that the bald figure in the centre of the three on his left is St Paul.

St-Génis had been the site of a monastery since the ninth century. The lintel must have been made for an earlier church which stood there in the early eleventh century, and have been moved to its present position on a new west façade when the church was rebuilt around 1153.

The inscription that dates it is written in Latin, and runs along the top of the lintel. It says that the lintel was made on the orders of William, Abbot of the monastery, in the twenty-fourth year of the reign of King Robert. That is taken as a reference to the Capetian King Robert II of France who reigned from October 996 to 1031, and was the nominal ruler of Roussillon, although he had little real power in the region.

The nave, with its pointed barrel vault supported by round transverse arches, dates from the twelfth-century rebuilding, while the plan of the east end, with its narrow transept and three apses, survives from the tenth-century church. The cloister was originally built in the thirteenth century, but it was dismantled in the early twentieth century and has been recently reconstituted, using columns and capitals that had been sold and were recovered.

St-André-de-Sorède is another village with a long history, and the lintel there also has Christ sitting at the centre surrounded by a mandorla. The mandorla is held by two angels as at St-Génis, and there, too, there are three arches on either side, each with a tiny figure inside it – though unlike the lintel at St-Génis the arches are round, and only the four outer ones have Apostles in them, the two innermost ones being filled by a seraph and a cherub, each of whom has three pairs of wings.

The presence of the seraph and cherub suggests that at St-André the lintel is referring to the Last Judgment rather than the Ascension.

This lintel is in some ways less compelling than the one in St-Génis. Here also Christ raises his right hand in blessing while holding the Bible in his left, but there is not the same vigour in the central group of Christ and the two angels. Also the columns supporting the arches on either side seem quite short and stunted, which has the effect of constricting the space given to the four Apostles presented in them.

Lintel of St-André-de-Sorède: Apostles

But the lintel is endearing in its own way, and is the more technically advanced of the two. The sculptor or sculptors have begun to create a three-dimensional effect, so that the figures have depth and a degree of movement. Each of the four Apostles has an individuality that was not achieved on the St-Génis lintel; and the one on the far left, in particular, who is sitting with his head in his hand, is masterly.

The figure of Christ is calmer and less urgent than in St-Génis, and both his right hand and his feet seem disproportionately large. Much of the earlier naivety has gone. He is both more serene and better modelled, with his clothes elegantly draped around a bodily form. His figure illustrates the evolution of the Roussillon marble-workers at the dawn of the Romanesque period.

Up above the lintel is a window which also has marble carving round it. The sill has a row of four medallions with seraph wings between them. Two enclose symbolic representations of evangelists (see page 263) – the lion of St Mark and the bull of St Luke – and two have the heads of angels blowing horns. The symbols of the other two evangelists, the eagle of St John and the winged man of St Matthew, are up by the two upper corners of the window.

St-André, too, had been the site of an abbey since the ninth century. The church was built in stages between the tenth and twelfth centuries, as can be seen from the different styles of masonry on the outside walls, but in its present form it is a harmonious example of Romanesque style. It has a tall and elegant nave topped by a round barrel vault with transverse arches, a transept, and three apses. There is a good view of the *chevet* from outside.

And it has one further attraction: a marble altar table beautifully carved in the style of the tenth and eleventh centuries.

Arles-sur-Tech is a larger town, built on the slopes above the river Tech, and it, too, has good views of the Pyrenees. It had an ancient monastery as well, founded in the eighth century, and the narrow streets of the old town are dominated by the tall and handsome bell-tower of the former abbey church – one of several such towers in Roussillon, with ascending tiers of rows of round arches and battlements on top.

The church has a mostly plain entrance façade, and the cross-shaped marble carving provides a focal point on it. Here, too, Christ sits in a mandorla in the centre, and raises his right hand in blessing while holding the Bible in his left. And he is also surrounded by the four figures that represent the evangelists, one in each arm of the cross.

The carving is thought to date from about 1046, when a new church, still in the process of being built, was consecrated. It is small, and may have been inspired by similar carvings in ivory.

The figure of Christ is still rather flat, but he is powerfully serene and the details of his clothing, and even of the throne on which he sits, have been carefully picked out by the sculptor. The

West front of Arles-sur-Tech: Christ surrounded by evangelists

symbols of the evangelists, each enclosed in a circle attached to the mandorla, are naively shaped but have an engaging vigour.

A simple semi-circular frieze, decorated with formal leaf patterns, frames the cross, with a carving of a lion on either side. Above is a decorated window, similar in style to the one at St-André, although it is in limestone, not marble.

The monastery of Arles-sur-Tech was a prosperous community which was absorbed into the system of Cluny (see page 61) in 1078. The church was extensively rebuilt once again in the middle of the twelfth century, and it is now substantial. It has a tall nave topped by a pointed barrel vault, wide side-aisles, and three apses at the altar end, which is, for once, in the west.

The cloister was built in Gothic style in the thirteenth century.

St-Guilhem-le-Désert

St-Guilhem-le-Désert is an atmospheric old village that is hidden away in wild mountain scenery north-west of Montpellier, and that in Romanesque times was a stop on the pilgrim route from Arles to Santiago de Compostela (see page 39). Its church is an early one, which was mainly built in the eleventh century, and its nave is a good example of the First Romanesque style (see page 17). It has simple, pure lines and little in the way of sculptural decoration.

The church also has a magnificent *chevet* which was built a few years later than the nave, towards the end of the eleventh century. This has a broad central apse which is girdled by a colonnade of small, rounded arches, a decorative gable up above that, and two smaller apses. Together they make an eye-catching sight, with

Abbey church of St-Guilhem-le-Désert, from the south-east

their ochre stone set against the bare grey rock of the surrounding mountains, as you make your way up through the village streets.

Beyond it is a cloister in which, though much of it has long been dismantled, the peace and beauty of the mountain setting have been preserved.

St-Guilhem has a history which goes back to Carolingian times. Guilhem was a grandson of Charles Martel, and first cousin, therefore, of the Emperor Charlemagne. As Count of Toulouse he played an active role in the campaigns of Charlemagne's reign against the Saracen rulers of Spain. He fought them when they burst across the Pyrenees in 793, for instance, and he took part in the capture of Barcelona by the Franks ten years later.

But like Charlemagne's son and successor, Louis the Pious, Guilhem was a childhood friend of Witiza, a Goth who took the name of Benedict and became an influential religious reformer – the future St Benedict of Aniane. Benedict had founded an abbey at Aniane, near Montpellier, at which he had instituted the Rule drawn up by the original St Benedict, the Italian abbot of the sixth century.

So in about 800 Guilhem founded a monastery himself at Gellone, a desolate site not far from Aniane, and made it subordinate to Aniane. He donated extensive property to it in 804, and in 806 became a monk in Gellone himself. He died and was buried there in 812. After his death he was sanctified, and the monastery of Gellone, renamed St-Guilhem, became a centre of pilgrimage.

The story of Guilhem, the redoubtable warrior who became a monk, was such a romantic and appealing one that it later formed the basis for one of the best-known song cycles of the twelfth and thirteenth centuries, *La Geste de Guillaume d'Orange*, which centred on the legendary exploits of William of Orange, as Guilhem was known, and his family. These songs added to the attraction of the monastery at St-Guilhem-le-Désert, which soon declared itself an abbey in its own right, and independent of Aniane. It became rich and powerful, with property not only in France but also in Spain and Portugal.

There is little left of St Benedict's abbey in Aniane. But the church of St-Guilhem is still there, and the road to it from Aniane crosses a dramatically situated bridge, known as the Pont du Diable, or Devil's Bridge, which was built across the river Hérault in the early eleventh century to link the two monasteries. According to legend, Guilhem threw the devil into the river at this point.

It is an edifying tale. Even without it this is a spectacular place. The bridge is one of the best-preserved civil works of the Romanesque period, with two broad arches and two smaller ones built onto the rock, and it stands at the lower end of the Hérault gorge, with its jumble of stone and scrub, and the still green water far below.

St-Guilhem is further up the gorge, at a point where a smaller river, the Verdus, flows into the Hérault, and there are towering crags all round, one of them topped by the ruins of a castle. The village itself has not changed much over the centuries, and has winding, narrow streets leading up to the church, as well as a number of old stone houses that go back to medieval times.

The church's *chevet* is imposing from a distance, and also worth a close look from the road that passes close by it on the north side. From there you can see the beautiful, and exotic, carved capitals that top the marble columns on either side of the windows of the large central apse. They have entwined vegetation in a style that derives from Arab models brought from Muslim Spain by the Christian Mozarabs.

With its bold dimensions and its dramatic colonnade of arches, the central apse also shows the influence of Lombardy, birthplace of the First Romanesque style. It is clearly similar, for instance, to the apse of Sant' Ambrogio in Milan. Of the two smaller apses, the southern one was built a few years earlier than the northern one, and the stylistic evolution from a simple to a more complex design, with a lesser colonnade of arches, can be seen.

The entrance to the church is in a little square shaded by an gigantic plane-tree. The entrance porch is a relatively plain one in early Romanesque style, with archivolts framing the doorway and a handful of carved capitals. It was constucted later than the rest of the church, in the twelfth century, and has an even later tower, put up for defensive purposes in the fifteenth century, above it. It leads into a bare, vaulted narthex, also of the twelfth century.

The nave, by contrast, makes an immediate impression: tall and narrow, quite austere and, in the way of so many early Romanesque churches, very moving. Broad arches divide it from the aisles, and above them rounded windows throw light onto the barrel vault, which is supported by transverse arches. At the east end the church broadens out, and the transept and the three semi-circular apses give it a new, spacious dimension.

The east end was added on later than the nave, after 1076, and recent excavations, carried out in the 1960s, have shed light on the intentions of the monks of that time. They uncovered an unadorned crypt, dating back to the Carolingian period, which would originally have had the remains of St Guilhem, and which the monks wanted to leave intact. So they built the big central apse to go round the edge of it.

The stonework of the apses is plain, but there is a baroque altar under the central one, and under the southern one is the exquisite 'Altar of St Guilhem', which dates from the twelfth century. This is made of carved marble, with inlaid coloured

St-Guilhem-le-Désert: 'Altar of St Guilhem'

glass. It has been damaged over the centuries, but the two main scenes on the altar front can be clearly made out – Christ in Majesty and the Crucifixion – surrounded by a border of entwined vegetation.

In the first scene, Christ is surrounded by a lion, a bull, an eagle and a winged man, representing the four evangelists (see page 263); and in the second, by the Virgin Mary and St John, with the sun and moon above and small figures of people rising from the dead below.

The church's cloister is a shadow of what it once was. The upper story that it once had has completely gone, for instance, and much of its sculptural decoration is now in the museum of The Cloisters in New York. But the surviving sections, with their twin arches, have been carefully restored, and it retains a beauty of its own.

There is a good view of the outer wall of the nave with its decoration of Lombard bands (see page 18), the tiny blind arches divided by pilasters that are characteristic of the First Romanesque style, and beyond that of the mountains. In the foreground is a carp pool, and beside it an array of trees and shrubs, laid out in the centre of the cloister.

It is not the way the cloister would have been in the eleventh and twelfth centuries, but its spirit has been preserved, or rather re-created. And in the restored refectory, an airy Gothic building running along the west side, there is a small museum in which the surviving pieces of sculpture are displayed. It is a most interesting collection which ranges from the Carolingian to the Gothic period.

St-Martin-de-Fenollar

The little chapel of St-Martin-de-Fenollar, which stands in open country some miles south of Perpignan, not far from the Spanish frontier, is one of those jewels that one sometimes comes across in unfrequented parts of the French countryside. The building itself is a simple one which dates back to pre-Romanesque times, but it has a stunning array of frescoes from the first half of the twelfth century.

The best of them are on the walls of the tiny sanctuary, and one sees them through a horseshoe arch as one approaches from the nave, which is wider and now largely plain.

The artist or artists have drawn some lively and attractive figures, and they have used a wide range of colours: red and yellow ochre, brown, white and blue. A Christ in Majesty looks down from the vault, flanked by the four winged figures representing the evangelists, and he is surrounded not just by the Virgin Mary on the east wall in her own diamond-shaped mandorla but by a delightful parade of the Elders of the Apocalypse, lined up on three sides.

Lower down, on the side-walls, is the sequence of events surrounding the Nativity, from the Annunciation to the Adoration of the Magi.

Little is known of the history of St-Martin except that there was a church on the site in 844 which belonged to the influential abbey of Arles-sur-Tech (see page 328), not far away, and the present building may date from then, or perhaps the following century. The vaulting was added later, as were the frescoes. The frescoes have suffered over the years, not least when the building was used for agricultural purposes and a door was driven through its east wall, obliterating many of them. But we must be grateful that a great number have survived.

The early date of the chapel itself is shown by the horseshoe arch, a relic of Visigothic style, and the rectangular shape of the sanctuary, which has no apse. So it is interesting that the Romanesque artists of the early twelfth century made a deliberate attempt to create the impression of greater depth in the sanctuary, and even to make it look as though there was a round apse rather than a flat wall at the east end.

There are decorative strips, for instance, which run above the line of the Elders on either side of the sanctuary, and it can be seen that they descend gradually as they approach the east wall, creating an effect of depth through perspective. They continue on the east wall, where they drop more sharply and form a shallow V-shape when they join. The effect is to make the painting of Mary, which is above the V, seem to be on a rounded apse.

As in much Romanesque art, the painting combines the devout and the homely. Christ, the central figure, is austere and mysterious, enthroned within an oval-shaped mandorla, while the evangelist-figures swirl around him, their bodies contorted to fit into the framework of the design. Mary, on the east wall, is an alluring young woman who has her hands raised in prayer and is flanked by two more winged figures who gaze ardently at her.

The Elders of the Apocalypse, on the other hand, are a long line of old men, each sitting on a throne, who are treated with sympathy and a touch of humour, in rather the same way as those on the great tympanum at Moissac. Once again, each of them holds a stringed instrument and raises a cup holding perfumes.

The biblical scenes begin on the left wall with the Annunciation, and that is followed immediately by an extended version of the Nativity itself, in which Mary lies on a sumptuous bed, Joseph sits beside her deep in thought, and the infant Jesus, looking unusually adult, lies on another ornate bed, watched over by the ox and the ass. At the end a tall angel makes his announcement to the shepherds.

The stretch of wall is a well-balanced composition in which the various figures are fluently drawn, and are set in the midst of decorative detail. Mary is a more reserved and thoughtful person than the young woman in the mandorla on the east wall.

The shepherds must have been on the east wall where little is now left of the frescoes that were once there. But the story picks up again in the middle of the Adoration of the Magi, and it is just possible to see the arms and legs of the infant Jesus, presumably sitting on Mary's lap, as he reaches out to the first of them, with a formalized star in the background and an inscription explaining why the Magi came.

The Magi are also engaging figures, dressed in fine clothes and surprisingly young-looking and eager as they hold out their gifts. The right-hand wall is devoted to them, and the sequence ends with a scene of them riding their rather ungainly horses.

St-Martin-du-Canigou

Abbeys were often built in inaccessible places in the Romanesque period, but few were, or are, as hard to reach as St-Martin-du-Canigou in the Pyrenees in Roussillon. The church and a handful of other buildings are some 3,500 ft up on the thickly wooded slopes of Mont Canigou, the mountain that towers over the region.

Even today there is only a rough winding track for the last stretch of the way, and visitors have to leave their cars down below in the village of Casteil and walk up through the woods for half an hour or so.

It is well worth the effort, both for the magnificent plunging views on the way and for the enchanting old abbey church, which is itself in a wonderful setting surrounded by mountains. On the way up, you pass by St-Martin-le-Vieux, a pleasant little church which was used in the past for the burials of monks from the abbey, and has been rebuilt in Romanesque style in recent years.

The abbey church dates back to the very beginning of the eleventh century, and possibly even earlier, when Roussillon was still part of Catalonia. It is an outstanding example of the First Romanesque style (see page 17), a harmonious building on two levels, a main church and a crypt. Both are simply built in well-cut local stone, with the proportions and the intimate character that were the mark of Romanesque.

Alongside it is a bell-tower in the distinctive style of Roussillon, and down below, in a gallery which has sweeping views out over the mountainside, a colonnade with carved capitals that originally stood in the cloister.

The building of the church may have begun as early as 997, and was certainly under way by 1005, when Count Guifre of Cerdanya announced his intention of establishing a monastery there, and the observance in it of the Benedictine Rule. Guifre was the elder brother of Oliba, abbot of the influential abbey of St-Michel-de-Cuxa (see page 338), a few miles away, and he was a constant benefactor who in due course became a monk at St-Martin-du-Canigou himself.

The abbey was eventually dissolved in 1783, and its buildings lay abandoned for the whole of the nineteenth century. By the beginning of the twentieth century the site was no more than an evocative ruin. But most of the church still stood, including its bell-tower, and in 1902 the long process of restoration began under the leadership of the then Bishop of Perpignan, Mgr de Carsalade du Pont. St-Martin-du-Canigou returned to life.

The *chevet* is the first part of the church that you see when you reach the abbey, and it has the outline and proportions that were typical of the First Romanesque

Abbey church of St-Martin-du-Canigou: the bell-tower

style – a central apse and two smaller ones, with a triangular pediment above. Each of the apses is encircled by a Lombard band (see page 18), the string of shallow blind arches that was used to decorate the outside walls of churches. An extra chapel with its own apse was added to the south of them.

The bell-tower stands to the north of the church and, although it is attached to it, is structurally separate, as was often the way in Italy. It has the stylish design of other similar towers in Roussillon, with tiers of round-arched windows and more Lombard bands. It is less tall than some of them, and it has been suggested that it may originally have had an extra, higher tier but have lost it in the earthquake which is known to have damaged the tower in the fifteenth century.

Both levels of the church were principally built in the early years of the eleventh century. The upper church has a narrow nave and two side-aisles, all three with round barrel vaulting, and it is divided in two by a single transverse arch which runs up from floor level in the middle of the nave and supports the vault. There is no transept. The nave arch is tall and narrow, and has the effect of focusing the eye on the east end of the church, with its three apses, when you look from the west end.

Perhaps the most distinctive feature is the use of columns, with round arches between them, to divide the nave from the aisles. It was an archaic arrangement even in the early eleventh century, since it dated back to pre-Romanesque times when ceilings were made of timber and so were lighter. The effect is telling in St-Martin-du-Canigou, not least because of the naive and original carvings on the column capitals – mainly of formalized plant motifs, though there are also a lion and a wolf to be seen.

The nave has no windows and is indirectly lit by small windows in the south aisle. So, like many Romanesque churches, St-Martin is relatively dark, and like them, it has an atmospheric quality that is part of its appeal.

The same is true of the crypt, or lower church, which also has a nave and two side-aisles, all with low, rounded vaulting over them, and almost no direct light at all. The east end of the crypt is the oldest part, and the oldest part of the church as a whole. It has been suggested that it may date back as far as the eighth century when the Carolingian dynasty held power.

This is borne out by the probing that has been done of several of the square pillars that support the east end of the crypt, and the main church above. They have been found to enclose columns that are similar to those in the upper church but have crudely decorated capitals. The suggestion is that these were the columns of the original crypt which had to be strengthened when the upper church was built.

The cloister was always on a lower level than the upper church because of the steepness of the rock on which the abbey was built, and it had an irregular shape for the same reason. By the end of the Romanesque period it had two levels, the upper one built some time later than the lower. But most of it was demolished during the long years of neglect, and the capitals dispersed among the surrounding villages.

The site of the cloister has been turned into a garden which is rather different from what the cloister used to be, but is a charming sight, with arches around it. The south side of the cloister had almost entirely disappeared by the beginning of the twentieth century, and in the course of restoration a new gallery which faced outwards rather than inwards was built along that side. It is a beautiful place, both for its mountain views and for the columns and capitals that have been erected there.

The capitals were recovered from people who lived round and about, and are thought to have come from the upper level of the cloister, since the lower level was plain. Two of them, which are slightly taller than the others and have carvings of lions and birds, have been dated to the twelfth century; but the others were the work of thirteenth-century sculptors who continued to work in a Romanesque style.

There is a great variety of subject-matter, all of it treated with considerable verve: lions and winged monsters, monkeys and snakes, and at the centre of them a range of human masks, many of them quite stylized. One capital apparently shows a mitred abbot being sent to Hell for his sins. Another has a dancing woman naked to the waist, who symbolizes lust.

It is worth observing that at St-Martin-du-Canigou, as elsewhere in Roussillon, not many of the capitals are overtly religious, although several of them clearly conveyed a moral message. But there appears to have been an attempt to redress the balance because one of the best capitals, with fine carving on the abacus above it, shows an abbot celebrating Mass, together with a procession of monks, one of whom is carrying the cross.

St-Michel-de-Cuxa

The abbey church of St-Michel-de-Cuxa, or Cuixà in Catalan, is one of the grandest survivals from the Romanesque period – and from even earlier. It has been badly battered over the centuries. However, its magnificent bell-tower still dominates the mountain valley above Prades, in the foothills of the Pyrenees, and it has an exceptional range of structures from the tenth, eleventh and twelfth centuries.

St-Michel-de-Cuxa: the cloister

The church itself was built towards the end of the tenth century, and is a rare example of pre-Romanesque architecture, with massive stone walls and distinctive horseshoe arches. The bell-tower, built in the early eleventh century, is in First Romanesque style (see pages 17, 28), and so is the extensive crypt that lies under the slope leading up to the church's west end.

Finally, one of the glories of Cuxa is, or was, the great cloister to the north of the church, built in the first half of the twelfth century. This was completely dismantled in the course of the nineteenth and early twentieth centuries. But many of the columns and their superb capitals have been recovered and re-erected. So although it is incomplete, the cloister conveys much of the style and beauty of twelfth-century Cuxa.

The use of horseshoe arches in the church is one of the abbey's most distinctive, and arresting, features. Many of these arches were later done away with, to be replaced by the Romanesque round arch. Those that survive are an exotic sight.

It has been suggested in the past that they reflect the influence of Muslim Córdoba, conveyed by Mozarabs – the Christians who emigrated from Islamic Spain, often bringing architectural concepts with them. But it is now thought more likely that the arches are a late legacy of the Visigoths who ruled southern France as well as most of Spain before the Arab invasion in the eighth century, and used horseshoe arches in some of their buildings.

Cuxa is in Conflent, a mountainous region centring on the river Tet which, like the rest of Roussillon, was part of Catalonia in the Middle Ages. A monastic community was established there in 878 with the support of the counts of Cerdanya after its monks had been driven from an earlier site, higher up the Tet, by a catastrophic flood in which several of them died.

Cuxa proved much safer, and over the following century its abbots became a power on the European scene, with close links to the Vatican and a number of subordinate abbeys. One memorable incident took place in 978, when Abbot Warin visited Venice – and returned to Cuxa with the Doge, Pietro Orseolo, who gave up his office to become a monk. Orseolo remained at Cuxa until his death ten years later, and was subsequently canonized.

The present church was mostly built in those early days, and was consecrated in 975 in the presence of no less than seven bishops. The vaulting of the nave is a modern reconstruction, based on the roofing system that replaced the original timber ceiling in the fifteenth century, and the vaulting of the sanctuary is Gothic. But the solid, roughly constructed walls of the nave, aisles, transept and sanctuary are much as they were in the tenth century, if without the surface decoration they would have had. And the scale and proportions of the church are inspiring.

The nave is broad, with arched openings, some still horseshoe-shaped, to the aisles on either side. There are bigger arches, also horseshoe-shaped, leading to the two arms of the transept, which was originally longer than it is now, reflecting the influence of the Carolingian style. The transept once used to have two small apsidal chapels off each of its arms, but it lost its extremities and now has only one on each side. The sanctuary was, and still is, rectangular, raised a few steps above the level of the nave.

There are few windows in the church, and they are small. The nave originally had some horseshoe-shaped openings high up on its south wall, most of which were modified in subsequent times, and some small windows were opened in the side-aisles in the Romanesque period. This means that much of the church is barely lit by natural light, which makes it cavernous and atmospheric.

The next period of substantial building at Cuxa took place during the first half of the eleventh century when the First Romanesque style had been created, and was largely the doing of Abbot Oliba, the son of a count of Cerdanya, who held office from 1008 to 1046. Oliba was an active man who was Abbot of Ripoll in Catalonia as well as Cuxa, became Bishop of Vic, also in Catalonia, at the same time, and played a big role in Church affairs. He also carried out extensive building work in all three places.

At Cuxa he was responsible for the bell-tower, built over the south end of the transept – and for a second, similar one over the north end, that stood until 1839, when it collapsed in a storm. It was the building of these two towers that had the effect of shortening the transept. Oliba also built the crypt to the west of the church, and an ambulatory which led round the rectangular sanctuary and included three tiny apsidal chapels at the east end.

The bell-tower is similar to other such towers built at that time in Roussillon, and is one of the best examples of the style. It is beautifully proportioned, with tiers of arches one above the other and the distinctive Lombard bands, the shallow panels of tiny blind arches which were a decorative feature of the First Romanesque. The tower had to be shored up in the fourteenth century, as can be seen, but the greater part of it stands free.

Of the chapels built by Oliba at the east end of the church only the northern one survives, although the southern one has been reconstituted in modern times. Of the crypt beyond the western end, on the other hand, the greater part remains and, although it is dark and the walls and the vaulting are rough and undecorated, it is another moving area of the old abbey.

At its heart is the circular Chapel of the Virgin of the Crib, which has a massive column in the middle that holds up the barrel vaulting. On either side of it are two other chapels, both long and narrow, which are dedicated to St Gabriel and St Raphael, and beyond them a large rectangular area with three aisles running in parallel across it, all vaulted and divided by arches.

There was once a church dedicated to the Trinity immediately above the Chapel of the Virgin, which was also built by Oliba, but there are only a few traces left of that.

The great cloister of Cuxa was constructed many years later, probably in 1120-30, at the time of Abbot Gregory, who later became Bishop of Tarragona. It is tragic that it did not survive the French Revolution and its aftermath, when most of France's monastic buildings were sold off, because it had elaborate column capitals which were one of the great achievements of the Romanesque marble sculptors of Roussillon in the twelfth century.

Many of the capitals are now on display in the museum of The Cloisters in New York, a separate part of the Metropolitan Museum. They had been dispersed around southern France when the cloister was dismantled, and were bought from a number of owners by George Grey Barnard, an American collector, in the early twentieth century. Barnard took them back to New York, where they were eventually bought by the Metropolitan Museum with funds from John D. Rockefeller Jr.

In Cuxa, however, the cloister has been partly rebuilt in recent years, using the columns and capitals that could be recovered in France, and it makes a splendid sight, with the church and its bell-tower in the background and the mountains all round. The arcading is in newly-cut Conflent marble, with its strong pinkish tints, as it was in the original cloister, and the re-erected columns and capitals are carved in the same marble.

No one knows exactly where each of the columns originally stood, and some did not come from the cloister. But it was possible to establish the cloister's out-lines, and there are enough of the columns and their capitals to give an impression of how it would have looked: a complete set of columns along the south side, shorter stretches on the adjacent parts of the eastern and western sides, and a few at the north-eastern corner.

They are astonishing. The designs of the capitals are complex and sophisticated, with lively combinations of beasts, plants, human masks and the occasional human figure. They are unforgettable, not just for their imaginative power, but for the vigour of the carving.

Huge lion heads appear to be devouring their prey, surrounded by foliage and tiny human masks. Mysterious human figures stand in forceful poses between grimacing monsters with complacent expressions on their faces. Intricate leaf pat-terns, exquisitely combined, occupy the whole of several capitals. Lions in various poses occupy many of the others.

St-Michel-de-Cuxa: capital in cloister

It can be seen that there is hardly a single overtly religious theme on the capitals that were originally in the cloister – although there are a few on the capitals that come from other parts of the abbey, and that have been erected in the northeastern corner. It is hard to interpret the cloister capitals as representing anything more specific than a general struggle between Good and Evil.

But what a visual feast they provide! It seems that, like others in Roussillon, the sculptors took visual motifs from embroideries, manuscripts and other such materials, often from the Near East and, in particular, from Persia, and used them for decorative purposes.

There is one other feature of the abbey that has been partly reconstituted in the cloister: the marble tribune that used to stand in the church. The surviving piece consists of a single arch, beautifully carved in low relief, which has been set over one of the doorways into the church.

The original tribune must have been much larger, and similar in style to the complete one that still stands in the former priory church of Serrabone (see below), a few miles away. The two were probably the work of the same artisan. The Cuxa tribune has lively little carvings of the lion of St Mark and the bull of St Luke, and of two seraphs, and a frieze of various animals caught in a long, winding tendril.

Down below are two of the pillars of the tribune, with low relief carvings of St Peter and St Paul and, on the sides, more animals and an owl, also in decorative settings. Like much that has been lost or destroyed at Cuxa, the tribune must have been superb.

Serrabone

Serrabone, or Serrabona in Catalan, means 'good mountain'. It is an admirable way to describe an out of the way former priory, built beside a stream in the foothills of the Pyrenees, which has one of the outstanding works of the Romanesque marble sculptors of Roussillon in the twelfth century.

The site is surrounded by thick woods, and the church itself, seen from the outside as one makes one's way up towards it along a mountain track, seems to be no more than a simple, rustic example of Romanesque architecture. It is built of blocks of locally-quarried schist which form a rough surface, and its nave, transept, apse and bell-tower give it the proportions and the balance of the style.

Inside, however, the church has an ornate marble tribune stretching across the nave, with its round arches resting on a small forest of columns, and a profusion of

Priory of Serrabone: the marble tribune

carving – across its west front, inside the arches and, above all, on the column capitals. And there are more carved capitals in the open gallery running along the south side of the church, which looks out over the mountainside, and served as a cloister for the canons.

The marble is that other locally-quarried stone – Conflent marble with its strong pinkish colouring – and it gives a special tint to the capitals which range from a dramatic St Michael, transfixing a Satanic serpent at his feet, to vigorously carved lions and eagles and an array of expressive human masks.

The tribune is clearly a purely medieval work. But with its classical proportions, reminiscent of a Roman triumphal arch, and the harmonious arrangement of its arches and columns, it looks ahead, like so many other Romanesque works, to the Renaissance.

It is fascinating that a work of such sophistication should have been created for this inhospitable site, 2,000 ft up in the mountainous area around Mont Canigou. People living in the surroundings were unable to do much more than scratch a bare living from the soil, and the area was known as Aspre, meaning 'harsh'. It has been speculated that if Serrabone was called a 'good mountain', it was only because it received direct sunshine and was sheltered from the wind, unlike other even less favoured spots.

Aspre, like the rest of Roussillon, was part of Catalonia during the Middle Ages. It is known that there was a church there in the eleventh century, which was taken over in 1082, when various local aristocrats, headed by Raimond Bernard, Viscount of Cerdanya, decided to install a priory alongside it made up of Augustinian canons.

There seem never to have been more than a handful of canons at Serrabone, which had an unsettled history in later years. But they clearly had influential backing from the start, and in the twelfth century the priory came to own and control a number of churches on both sides of the Pyrenees.

Not least, the canons were able to reconstruct and extend the church, which was formally re-consecrated in 1151 in the presence of an awe-inspiring gathering of bishops and abbots. They kept the nave of the eleventh-century church, a simple structure with a pointed barrel vault, but added on a new east end, with a transept, a broad central apse and two smaller ones. They also added the side-aisle to the north of the nave, the outer gallery on the south side, and the bell-tower which stands at the north-west corner of the church.

The tribune is thought to date from the second half of the twelfth century, and was used by the canons as a raised choir. It is similar to one that used to stand in the abbey church of St-Michel-de-Cuxa (see page 343), a few miles away, of which only fragments survive, and it may have been designed by the same master sculptor.

It has intricate carving in low relief across its west front, including formalized floral designs, animals trapped in thickets and, in a central position, the Lamb of God surrounded by the four figures symbolizing the evangelists – the lion, the eagle, the winged man and the bull (see page 263). A tiny head of an angel blows a horn at the left-hand end, and two larger angels stand above with their wings crossed.

The east front also has a carved doorway, though it is otherwise plain, and the ribbed vaulting on the underside of the tribune, where six bays are supported on the pink-tinted columns, is a masterly use of the space.

The glory of the tribune, however, is the column capitals, and it is interesting that as elsewhere in Roussillon, they have barely any overtly religious scenes. Instead, there are winged griffins, lions devouring their prey, a centaur armed with a bow and arrow who is confronting an antlered stag, a diabolical simian figure squatting on some wretched human's head, and other products of the sculptor's imagination.

They show the plastic skill of the Roussillon sculptors of the time and their ability to make the most of the small space available on a capital.

Serrabone: detail of tribune

Serrabone: detail of tribune

Serrabone: detail of tribune

Much of the subject-matter again appears to have been influenced by manuscript illustrations, and by embroideries and other materials brought from the Near
East, including Persia. Pairs of lions or eagles stand in formal poses, for example,
and share a head at the corners. However, there is an earthy undercurrent, as so
often in Romanesque art. In one of those engaging examples of medieval humour,
a human face that peers out over a pair of posed eagles is twisted in a peasant's
grimace.

The subjects on the column capitals of the south gallery, or cloister, are similar:
lions snarling, lions devouring their prey, griffins and eagles, as well as tiny human
faces, or masks, and some formalized foliage. They too are both ornate and lively,
and they add an extra dimension to what is in any case an enchanting place, which
has views out over the little stream and the wooded mountainside beyond, and is
lit by the sun.

There are four pairs of columns, and it is clear that different sculptors were
responsible for the inner and outer capitals of each pair. The four inner capitals
have the vigour and plastic quality of the capitals of the tribune, with ferocious-
looking beasts and expressive human masks. The outer ones are stiffer and more
archaic in style. But they too are part of the enchantment of Serrabone.

Central Pyrenees

The foothills of the central Pyrenees have a number of interesting Romanesque churches, some in small villages, others in ancient towns that in days gone by were more important than they are now.

St-Lizier, which stands on a hilltop above the larger town of St-Girons, has a former cathedral with Romanesque murals and a charming twelfth-century cloister. Lescar, on the outskirts of Pau, is also on a hilltop, and its church, which was also a cathedral in the past, has a harmonious Romanesque interior with carved capitals and some outstanding mosaics.

Between the two is St-Bertrand-de-Comminges, which was founded by the Romans and has a stunning setting on a sheer outcrop of rock, with mountains in

Central Pyrenees

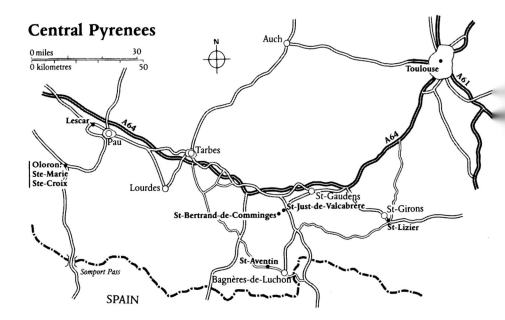

the background. Its cathedral is now largely Gothic but it still has a twelfth-century cloister; and down below, barely a mile away, is the Romanesque church of St-Just-de-Valcabrère.

Pilgrims heading for Santiago de Compostela had, of course, to cross the Pyrenees, and Lescar was on one of the main routes (see page 39), which began in Arles, passed through Toulouse, and climbed up to the Somport pass.

Oloron-Ste-Marie was one of the main stopping points for the pilgrims as they struggled up the slopes to the pass after leaving Lescar, and it still has two churches that date back to Romanesque times. The older of the two is Ste-Croix, which stands on the highest point of the town and is predominantly Romanesque, with carved capitals and a ribbed cupola over the crossing that shows Islamic influence from Spain.

In the lower part of the town is Ste-Marie, which was formerly a cathedral and, though now largely Gothic, has a magnificent Romanesque portal.

One of the inviting Romanesque churches you come upon in the Pyrenees is in the village of St-Aventin, a few miles to the west of the resort of Bagnères-de-Luchon. It dates back to the First Romanesque style but also has twelfth-century sculpture on its south doorway.

Lescar

Lescar, a small hilltop town just outside Pau, has a former cathedral which at first sight is rather unprepossessing, with a plain barn-like shape and a pseudo-Romanesque western doorway. But this impression is misleading because the church also has an elegant *chevet* which can be seen from the cemetery, and a magnificent interior, with a tall barrel-vaulted nave, a wealth of capitals and a rare feature: two mosaic floors in the sanctuary.

It was built in the course of the twelfth century when Lescar was a stopping point on one of the main pilgrim routes to Santiago de Compostela, known as the *via Tolosana*. After Lescar the pilgrims went on to Oloron-Ste-Marie (see page 353), and then crossed the Pyrenees by the Somport pass.

The church has been badly damaged over the centuries, and much restored. But the interior remains an outstanding example of Romanesque, with the balance and harmony of the style, and the great majority of its many capitals are lively and varied twelfth-century work. So are the mosaics, which have a vigour of their own.

Like Pau, Lescar is a town that looks out over the Pyrenees to the south, and has good views of them. It is, however, much the older of the two. In Roman times it

Former cathedral of Lescar: mosaic floor

was known as Beneharnum, and it was the principal city of the region that later became known as Béarn. It was devastated by the Vikings in the middle of the ninth century, and only began to recover two hundred years or so later. By then it had a new name, Lescarris, and the first cathedral was built – to be superseded by the present church in the twelfth century.

As was often the case, it was the eastern parts of the church that were built first: the *chevet* with its three apses and the transept. Work on them began about 1120 under an activist Bishop, Gui de Lons, and was completed by the time of his death in 1141. The nave and the aisles were finished later in the century.

The church suffered badly during the Religious Wars of the sixteenth century, and was for some years taken over by the Protestants. Like other churches, it was abandoned during the French Revolution at the end of the eighteenth century, and became badly dilapidated. The process of restoration began in the nineteenth century.

Lescar is an evocative town which has the remains of its medieval ramparts, a fourteenth-century town gate, and houses from many different periods. The church stands in a pleasant square, with trees to provide shade, and the *chevet* is surrounded by a walled cemetery.

The mosaics, which were only rediscovered in the nineteenth century, are one of the most interesting and delightful features of the church, partly because mosaics are so rare, but also because of their vigorous style. One of the floors has a hunter lunging with his lance at a huge boar, which looks balefully at him while a dog tears at his neck and a bird standing on the ground watches with interest.

Behind the hunter's back is a separate scene in which a huge lion seizes a gazelle by the neck, and a second appears poised to attack it from behind, while more birds stand or flutter about.

The other floor is more enigmatic. It also shows a hunter, but this one is a small, nimble, dark-skinned man with a bow and arrow, apparently Moorish, who has an artificial leg. Following him is a large mule, and behind the mule, attached to its tail by a halter, is an animal which could be a fox or a wolf, and which is plainly being dragged along unwillingly because it is pulling against the halter and has its tongue out.

Just what this may have meant is a mystery. Hunting scenes were a familiar theme in the art of the time, and the hunter who is lunging at the boar is not unprecedented. Nor are the lions that are attacking the gazelle behind his back; they show Persian influence. But the other scene, picturesque though it is, is hard to interpret. Artificial legs are depicted elsewhere, and there were still Moors in Spain, but one can only speculate on what, if anything, the artist wanted to convey.

What can be said is that the mosaics are full of life and highly decorative, with a range of colours, and that certainly seems to have been an important part of their function, whatever message may have been intended. An inscription clearly attributes them to Gui de Lons, who was Bishop from 1115 to 1141.

On the outside of the church, the *chevet* is notable for its proportions, and for the carved corbels which ring the apses. The apses are built in sandstone, which gives them a yellowish tinge, and the main apse has a stylish arrangement of round-topped windows and, between them, pairs of tall, narrow columns set into the buttresses.

The corbels have an engaging array of devils, animals, birds, monsters and humans, all intricately carved. In one, a man paddles a tiny boat, in another a devil lovingly fondles a snake, which he holds on his knees. In others, lions, owls or monsters stare menacingly down at the passers-by.

The interior of the church is especially inspiring when you stand at the west door and look up the length of the nave towards the central apse at the far end. The long barrel vault is supported by round transverse arches that rest on engaged columns set into rectangular pilasters, and there are more round arches, also resting on engaged columns, that divide the nave from the aisles.

It is a complex and well-balanced arrangement, also in yellowish sandstone, and it leads the eye towards the east end of the church. By way of contrast, the aisles do not have continuous vaulting, but each of their bays has a round barrel vault which runs north-south across the line of the nave. The pillars that stand between the bays are complex clusters like huge formalized tree-trunks, and are decorated with capitals at different levels.

The capitals draw attention in their own right, while also helping to articulate the structure of the church. Wherever you look, they provide a focal point, marking the springing of one of the many arches. They are also very varied, their themes ranging from biblical scenes to lions, monsters and decorative foliage, and art historians have spotted the influence of the sculptors of Toulouse.

There are scenes of Christ in Majesty, Christ with the Apostles and Abraham about to sacrifice Isaac, all graphically carved. But there are also monstrous heads swallowing human bodies, elongated monkeys on all fours, and a strange, very striking capital in which two men with large bulbous faces are crouched over their ankles, which are fettered together.

Some of the best capitals are in the arches that lead from the two side-chapels into the sanctuary. They show Adam and Eve in the Garden of Eden, and Cain and Abel making their offerings, but there are also formalized plant designs, pairs of eagles and, most dramatically, human figures being devoured by lions and by winged monsters with coiled serpentine bodies.

Some capitals have been restored, or even completely carved in more recent centuries. But, like the church as a whole, most show the achievements of the twelfth century.

Oloron-Ste-Marie

By the time they reached Oloron-Ste-Marie, another ancient hill-town south-west of Pau, medieval pilgrims had begun the long and arduous, if scenic, climb up to the Somport pass over the Pyrenees. Two of the churches that they would have seen there are still standing, and Oloron is a good place to stop. It stands at the junction of two mountain streams, with lovely views of the peaks to the south.

The Romanesque portal of Ste-Marie was constructed in the twelfth century and is an unforgettable sight, covered as it is with both religious and secular scenes. The church of Ste-Croix may be a few years older but it, too, dates mainly from the twelfth century, and it has an elegant Romanesque interior, with its Moorish-style cupola over the transept crossing.

Ste-Croix has the added attraction of standing on the hilltop that is the oldest part of Oloron – known as Iluro in Roman times – and having the narrow streets and timbered houses of the old town alongside it.

On the outside, it is a solid, chunky building which has been much restored, but even so it has the balance and proportions of a great Romanesque church, with a nave and two aisles, a short transept with the cupola over the crossing, and three apses in the *chevet*. It has a plain bell-tower that was used for defensive purposes, but its grim exterior is lightened by arched windows with columns in the main apse and at each end of the transept; and there is a decorative Romanesque doorway with a few damaged capitals on the north side.

Inside, it has a barrel vault with transverse arches over the nave, and partial barrel vaulting over the aisles. There are few windows so that the church is dark, but the proportions are well-judged, and the effect is similar to that in the former cathedral in Lescar (see page 349), with a harmonious sequence of round arches extending the length of the church to the sanctuary. There are simple but effective capitals, largely of formalized plant and fruit designs, that mark the springing of the arches in the nave and aisles.

The exceptional feature of Ste-Croix is its cupola. This is a complex structure in which eight different arches, springing from eight points on the octagonal base, criss-cross over each other to form a star-shaped pattern in the dome. Like a similar one in Hôpital-St-Blaise, a few miles from Oloron, it was clearly inspired by

Former cathedral of Ste-Marie, Oloron-Ste-Marie: Elders of the Apocalypse on west portal

Ste-Croix, Oloron-Ste-Marie: Moorish-style cupola

Moorish architecture, and in particular by the great mosque in Córdoba, whose principles would have been brought north by Mozarabs – the Christians who migrated from Islamic Spain.

The cupola rests on four squinches filled by large painted shells that were added later.

East of the cupola, in the three apses, there is also much later painting; but there are also some very original twelfth-century capitals, many of them with biblical scenes, on which restorers have attempted to repaint the original colours. The capitals are in flat relief, and have a naivety to them that adds to their power. They are good examples of carving of the middle of the twelfth century.

In the ring of arches beneath the central apse, for instance, there is a capital showing Adam and Eve in the Garden of Eden, with the serpent whispering seductively in Eve's ear; and on another the story of Cain and Abel, including Cain's killing of Abel. Elsewhere there are Noah's Ark, the story of John the Baptist – including his Baptism of Christ, Salome's dance before Herod, and his beheading – the Adoration of the Magi and the Temptation of Christ, all vividly presented.

One of the most compelling capitals, in the arch leading into the south apse, has a head made up of three different faces that emerge from foliage. It was once

Ste-Croix, Oloron-Ste-Marie: capital showing temptation of Eve

considered to represent the Trinity but is now thought to be more simply a personification of greed.

The great portal of Ste-Marie, across the river in the lower town, is monumental, even triumphal. Its principal theme is the victory of Christ and the Church, and there are clear references to the achievements of Gaston IV, Viscount of Béarn from 1090 to 1131, who was one of the leaders of the First Crusade, and who on his return found Saracens installed on his lands – whom he expelled.

One of the most eye-catching carvings is of a monster with staring eyes that emerges from an archivolt on the left side of the portal and is in the process of devouring a man in armour; the lower part of his body hangs from the monster's jaws. Under the man's feet is the head of another monster. Together the two represent evil, or the Devil.

But this apparition is balanced on the other side of the portal by a knight on horseback who is trampling a cowering human figure under the horse's hooves. The knight is the Emperor Constantine, who is triumphing, as in other similar Romanesque sculptures, over the Church's enemies; and the statue is an unmistakable allusion to Gaston of Béarn.

The message is made even clearer by the sculpture of the portal's *trumeau*, or central column, which shows two men who are obviously Saracen prisoners. They are chained together, back to back, and are straining to support the weight of the column on their shoulders.

The portal is the principal feature of an open arched porch that was built at the same time – although the forti- fied bell-tower above was added later. The porch protected the portal and that, together with the hardness of the Pyrenean marble of which it is made, has preserved it over the centuries. It is fascinating both for its vivid evocation of the events of the twelfth century and for the verve of its carving.

At its centre, over the doors into the church, is a triple tympanum, in which two smaller scenes are enclosed within a larger one. The smaller tympana, in which rampaging lions symbolize the tribulations of the Church, and then

Ste-Marie, Oloron-Ste-Marie: prisoners supporting central pillar of west portal

when pacified its triumph, are modern restorations; but the main central one is twelfth-century, and has a touching scene carved in low relief of the Deposition from the Cross.

In it, Joseph of Arimathea is supporting the body of Christ while Nicodemus removes the nails that fix one hand to the cross. A female figure takes the freed hand, while the Virgin Mary and St John stand on either side. At the top tiny faces represent the sun and the moon.

The tympanum is framed by two archivolts, and they have some of the most endearing sculpture. The outer one has the Twenty-four Elders of the Apocalypse, who are an engaging ring of old men, each of them different but all wearing crowns and each carrying a musical instrument and also, in most cases, a cup of perfume. The Elders were a common subject of Romanesque sculpture, as we have seen, and are depicted most notably in the great porch at Moissac (see page 263). Those at Oloron are a good example of the humorous way in which they were treated.

As interesting is the narrower archivolt inside that of the Elders. This shows peasants engaged in a range of typical activities, and it gives a vivid picture of rural life in the twelfth century. A boar is hunted, killed and prepared for the table, a huge salmon is caught, sliced up and cured, and a cooper makes a wine-barrel. Other peasants make cheese, or cut up ham. One interpretation is that the peasants are preparing a wedding feast. But there is no question that, like the ring of Elders, it shows the human touch of the Romanesque sculptors.

Like Romanesque art as a whole, the Oloron portal was religious first and foremost, but it also set out to be decorative and even entertaining. So at the head of the main archivolt, between two Elders, the Lamb of God stands in a central position, supported by two angels, with the head of another diabolical monster, also with staring eyes, immediately below. But the outer rim is filled with a carefully worked abstract pattern, and there is a ring of rosettes inside that of the busy peasants.

Higher up on the wall, standing on either side of the portal, are two large men who could be sentinels or servants. Just below them, at the springing of the tall, pointed arches which frame the sides of the porches, are two beautifully carved and perfectly grotesque capitals – one with two squatting human figures, naked and supporting huge faces in their hands, the other with hairy, toad-like creatures that grimace as they peer down from their perch.

And there is more vigorous carving on the capitals of the columns that stand on

Ste-Marie, Oloron-Ste-Marie: capital on west portal

Ste-Marie, Oloron-Ste-Marie: capital on west portal

either side of the door: birds, lions, entwined vegetation, and another grotesque human figure, female this time, who perhaps represents temptation.

The portal shows the astonishing range of twelfth-century sculpture, its power and its humanity. The pilgrims who struggled through Oloron on their way to Santiago de Compostela will not have easily forgotten it – any more than today's visitors can.

St-Aventin

As I have said before, one of the pleasures of the French countryside is suddenly coming upon a small Romanesque church, its characteristic features forming a harmonious whole, and towering over the village in which it was built in the eleventh or twelfth century. One such is St-Aventin, which has the added bonus of standing on the slopes of a wooded mountain valley, with the village of the same name just below.

St-Aventin was built in the eleventh century in the First Romanesque style (see page 17), and has the characteristic arrangement of its *chevet*: a large semi-circular apse, flanked by two smaller ones, all three ringed by Lombard bands, the panels made up of small blind arches. Beyond them is the nave, which has two square bell-towers rising from it, each decorated with tiers of round arches.

Its south doorway is slightly later than the main body of the church, and has several good sculptures, also of the twelfth century.

St Aventin was a local ninth-century hermit who was captured and beheaded by Saracens. According to legend, he stood up after his execution, picked up his head and carried it away. In due course he was properly buried by his followers; but the site of his tomb was forgotten, and it was only discovered nearly three centuries later by a bull which led local people to the spot, a short distance from the village.

These events are depicted in the sculptures of the south doorway. The tympanum over the door is a simple version of Christ in Majesty, the mandorla in which Christ sits being supported by four angels, each of whom carries a small head representing one of the evangelists – a lion's for St Mark, a bull's for St Luke, an eagle's for St John, and a man's for St Matthew (see page 263).

But there are pairs of double capitals on either side of the door, and one on the right shows scenes of the martyrdom of St Aventin: first his arrest, and then him carrying his head, with the executioner still wielding his sword.

Opposite are two more conventional scenes: Mary Magdalene anointing the feet of Jesus and the Massacre of the Innocents, in which a soldier snatches a baby from

St-Aventin, from the east

its mother, and a second one stands by
with his sword raised. The two outer
pairs of capitals each have an intricate
design of entwined ribbons, and the
right-hand one has tiny figures inside
the ribbons which, again, represent the
evangelists.

The bull's discovery of St Aventin's
tomb is carved on a separate, larger slab
of stone which is now embedded in the
wall of the church, but originally was
probably part of a second sculptural
group. The bull's expression as it turns
its head to look back at the angel pointing to the recumbent saint is one of
perfect astonishment.

There are several other larger pieces
also now embedded in the wall includ-   *St-Aventin: bull discovering the tomb of the saint*
ing some that were apparently taken
from tombs of the Roman period. There is a stately Virgin and Child from the later
part of the twelfth century which may have been the centrepiece of the vanished
group; and a musician who is playing a stringed instrument, and who might be
David, although he is not wearing a crown.

The inside of the church has the proportions and intimacy of Romanesque at its
simplest. There are no capitals but the nave and the two side-aisles are beautifully
shaped, with groin vaulting over all three, and there is a succession of tall, round
transverse arches, in both the nave and the side-aisles, which rise from the floor
between the bays.

These lead easily to the eastern end where the central apse, with three arched
windows and above them two round oculi, completes the nave, and a diminutive
apsidal chapel stands at the end of each aisle.

It is likely that most of St-Aventin would once have been painted. A few frescoes survive, mainly in the eastern parts of the church, which have been discovered
since 1877 under the plaster that covered them. They are only fragmentary but
they give a tantalizing idea of how the church was decorated.

In the apse, on either side of the central window, are portraits of St Aventin and
of St Sernin, the Bishop of Toulouse martyred in the third century (see page 276).
Above, in the hollow of the apse, is Christ in Majesty, and there are also complex

compositions in the vaulting of the two easternmost bays. One shows a bust of Christ in a medallion supported by six angels. The other also has a medallion in the centre surrounded by four angels and four seraphim, but the subject can no longer be identified.

St-Bertrand-de-Comminges and St-Just-de-Valcabrère

It would be worth visiting **St-Bertrand-de-Comminges**, an ancient town in the foothills of the Pyrenees, for its setting alone. It stands on a small steep outcrop of rock, with the wooded slopes of higher hills at its back; and the former cathedral that dominates the town is visible across the fields from miles away.

But St-Bertrand itself is well worth walking round, with its winding streets and old houses from the fifteenth and sixteenth centuries. And although the cathedral is mainly Gothic, with some carved wooden stalls from the sixteenth century that are well worth a detailed look, its western end is still largely Romanesque. So is its cloister, which has capitals from the twelfth century.

There is also, barely a mile away, the charming Romanesque church of St-Just-de-Valcabrère. The church has a tall bell-tower and an elaborate *chevet*, and it makes a harmonious sight – so characteristic of the Romanesque style – as it stands against the background of hills, with a cluster of cypresses around it.

The whole area is calm and peaceful today. That belies its dramatic past. St-Bertrand was originally a Celtic hill settlement where Pompey, the Roman general, is said to have founded the city of Lugdunum Convenarum in the first century BC. The city spread out over the flat land at the foot of the old settlement and eventually reached a population of some 60,000, with a forum, a temple, a theatre, baths and much else.

There is a well-established tradition that a few years after the crucifixion of Christ the Emperor Caligula exiled Herod and his wife, Herodias, to Lugdunum Convenarum – a long way from Galilee – and that Herod at least died there. What is certain is that in the fourth century the city became the see of one of the first bishoprics in Gaul, and the remains of a Christian basilica from that time have been found.

The Roman city did not survive the barbarian invasions. It was razed to the ground by the Vandals early in the fifth century. The remaining population took refuge in the old hilltop area, but even this was demolished by a Burgundian army in the sixth century.

It was only in about 1073 when Bertrand de l'Isle-Jourdain became the Bishop that the city began to revive. He had the ruins cleared away and a new cathedral built in the Romanesque style with a chapter of canons attached to it. After his death in 1123 he was canonized, and the city took his name – 'Comminges' deriving from 'Convenae', 'people who have come together'.

Not much of Bertrand's cathedral survives but the tall bell-tower at the western end was built in the Romanesque style later in the twelfth century, and it still towers over the small square at the high point of the town. The tall pointed arches and the ribbed vault that support it can be seen inside the cathedral.

The doorway at the foot of the tower has a carved tympanum and capitals that date from the middle of the twelfth century, and although they are damaged, they have style and movement. On the tympanum, the Three Wise Men approach the Virgin Mary and the Infant Jesus, both of whom have crowns on their heads, while three angels swing censers above their heads, and a fourth holds in place the star that the Wise Men had followed. Below is a line of Apostles standing beneath little arches.

Interestingly, the largest figure of all, who stands behind Mary with his bishop's crozier, is St Bertrand. He was given this prominence because of his importance to the cathedral, but he has no halo because he had not yet been formally canonized. That only happened in about 1218.

The capitals that top the columns on either side of the door have some vigorous scenes of the torments of Hell, including a miser who is being simultaneously devoured by serpents and tortured by devils as he sinks into the maw of a monster. Less gruesome and more picturesque are lions caught in tendrils, two of them with small figures mounted on their backs, and some crouching monsters.

The cloister of St-Bertrand is an enchanting place, with three of its sides lined by round arches and views from them out over the surrounding hills. The western side is the most interesting because it has capitals from the late twelfth century, towards the end of the Romanesque period. It also has a

Cathedral of St-Bertrand-de-Comminges: cloister, with column carved with statues of evangelists

central column that has, or had, full-length statues of the four evangelists, one on each of its sides, each of them carrying a tiny symbolic figure – lion, bull, eagle and man (see page 263). These figures are thought to have been modelled on ancient statuary, and although only three of them are at all well preserved, they are a powerful presence.

Sadly, the capitals are also badly preserved. However, it is possible to make out much of their designs. They include decorative plant patterns, dragons that are about to devour small humans while being attacked from behind by other humans, and also biblical scenes: Adam and Eve in the Garden of Eden and the death of Abel at the hands of Cain. Above the four evangelists are signs of the Zodiac and depictions of the labours appropriate to certain months.

One capital has animals and birds in various decorative poses, including a handsome owl with its prey gripped in its talons. Another has pairs of horses being led by a man and a woman, both of them with tall plants winding around them.

St-Just-de-Valcabrère is just a short distance away from St-Bertrand, and is a stately church with a well-judged balance between its various parts – the nave, the bell-tower and the *chevet*. It was built in the course of the eleventh and twelfth centuries on the site of what was clearly an ancient cemetery.

Many pieces of early tombs have been discovered there, some going back to

St-Just-de-Valcabrère, from the north-east

Early Christian times, and excavations have uncovered the foundations of an earlier church. The Romanesque builders used ancient columns, capitals, inscriptions and parts of sarcophagi, all of which they presumably found either on the site or among the ruins of the Roman city; and they can be seen set in the walls, both outside and in the church – occasionally upside down.

The age of the site is indicated by one inscription in particular that was found in the ground outside the apse in the nineteenth century and is now on the western wall of the nave, inside the church. It records the burial of two Christians, Valeria Severa and a priest, Patroclus, in 347. It includes the Chi-Rho symbol representing Christ which was still rare at that time.

A feature of St-Just that stands out is the *chevet*. Basically, it consists of a rectangle in which the central apse is enclosed and the rounded shapes of the two smaller ones. But there is a complex arrangement of semi-circular vaults that conceals this underlying form, and the effect is most satisfying, with arches and tiled roofs nestling beneath the bell-tower.

If the western end of the church is plain, there is an ornate doorway on the north side that dates from the late twelfth century. This has full-length statues of four saints, capitals that apparently depict incidents from their lives, and a tympanum of Christ in Majesty flanked by the four evangelists.

Three of the saints are martyrs: St Just and St Pastor, who were put to death in Spain in 304 and to whom the church is dedicated, and St Stephen, the first martyr. They are solemn, dignified figures, also probably based on classical statues, and the capitals above their heads have vivid scenes of their fates: St Pastor being arrested and scourged on the right, St Just being beheaded on the left, and behind him St Stephen being stoned.

The fourth saint is a woman who is crowned and is thought to be St Helena, the mother of the Emperor Constantine. But there is uncertainty about the significance of the scene on the capital above her head, which appears to show a man dressed as a pilgrim offering a ride on a horse to a woman, who is also dressed as a pilgrim.

The church was constructed in two main stages. Work on the nave, the aisles and the *chevet* began towards the end of the eleventh century, and was perhaps completed early in the twelfth century, with a timber ceiling. Later in the twelfth century vaulting replaced the timber ceiling, and the nave was given extra height, with a barrel vault supported by transverse arches and half-barrels over the aisles. There was no transept, and so the bell-tower was built over the easternmost bay of the nave.

The various features fit together easily inside the church, with the nave and the aisles being divided by tall, round arches, and the eye being led towards the three apses at the eastern end. The central apse is ringed by arches, and columns with simple archaic capitals. The smaller chapels on either side have horseshoe-shaped arches.

St-Lizier

The little hilltop town of St-Lizier, which has a scenic position overlooking the valley of the river Salat and the Pyrenees, also dates back to Roman times, when it was an important centre, and it has traces of its fifth-century ramparts. It has a former cathedral which, while it was added to over the years, was first built in the eleventh century in the Romanesque style, and a delightful cloister with Romanesque capitals from the second half of the twelfth century.

The cathedral was built outside and below the old ramparts, and has a pleasant square on its north side. Up above it is the seventeenth-century Palace of the Bishops, now partly a folk museum, which stands within the line of the ramparts and has another smaller cathedral attached to it, also originally Romanesque.

The outstanding feature of the larger church is the sanctuary, which was only completed in the course of the twelfth century, and has some Romanesque mural paintings from the first years of that century. The paintings were uncovered recently, many of them being quite fragmentary; but they are still in their original setting, a ring of tall round arches, complete with capitals, that run round the walls beneath the principal apse, and were also once painted.

The best of the paintings have some powerful and moving images, with their colours well preserved. They include portraits of the Apostles and other saints, biblical scenes, and a touching Visitation in which Mary and Elizabeth embrace.

The murals are thought to have been the work of a travelling artist whose paintings have survived in other churches in the Pyrenees, and particularly in Catalonia. Some of the faces have a Byzantine intensity. It has been suggested that the artist may have been from Italy, but influenced by Greek style.

The sanctuary as a whole is a stylish arrangement, with its apse and, preceding it, a single bay of barrel vaulting. The vault is supported by two large transverse arches, each of which has carved capitals. The hemisphere of the apse has a strong painting in the Gothic style of Christ in Majesty, also only partly preserved, and below it is the ring of round arches that frame the Romanesque frescoes, which extends as far as the crossing on either side.

The oldest part of the cathedral is the nave which dates back to the eleventh century, and originally had a timber roof – although it now has a rib vault prob-

Former cathedral of St-Lizier: capitals in the cloister

ably built in the fourteenth or fifteenth century. The transept and the *chevet* were added later, and the two small apses, whose walls are two metres thick, date from that rebuilding. The large central apse, which is polygonal on the outside, was not completed until well into the twelfth century.

The octagonal bell-tower over the crossing, which has angular arches over its windows like those of St-Sernin in Toulouse (see page 276), was later still. Its construction began about 1300.

It is the cloister that is the high point of a visit to St-Lizier. Like the cathedral itself, it is relatively small, but it has some vigorous capitals, particularly on its north side which runs along the outside wall of the nave.

In several of them, small human figures and animals are caught in picturesque but constricting tendrils, with large formalized leaves all round – some apparently fighting each other, others just struggling to escape. In others, there are simply intricate and exquisite compositions in which tendrils wind in and around each other in purely decorative patterns.

It is thought that the capitals on the north side were the first to be carved, in about 1150-80, and that most of the others were carved later over a long period. The artists then modelled themselves on the capitals of the north side but without being able to achieve the same mastery.

There are some exceptions. When the transept of the cathedral was enlarged at the end of the thirteenth century, its wall was extended into the cloister space and the whole of the eastern side of the cloister had to be dismantled and rebuilt; the northern and southern sides were both shortened. But some of the old capitals were reused – specifically on the two double columns on the eastern side. And like the others they show the talent of the artist or artists of the twelfth century.

Index